WHAT THE ODDS ARE

A-to-Z Odds on Everything You Hoped or Feared Could Happen

LES KRANTZ

 HarperPerennial

A Division of HarperCollins*Publishers*

Les Krantz

Editor-in-Chief

Sports Editor: **Mark Mravic** *Contributing Editors:* **Jordan Wankoff, Jim McCormick.**

Special Thanks: To my parents and the Frenzel and Glass family who provided photographs and to English wood engraver Thomas Bewick (1753-1828) whose illustrations I was privileged to bring to life again in the pages of this book.

HarperCollins books may be purchased for educational, business, or sales promotional use. For information, please call or write: Special Markets Department, HarperCollins Publishers, Inc., 10 East 53rd Street, New York, NY 10022. Telephone (212) 207-7528; Fax: (212) 207-7222.

FIRST HARPERPERENNIAL EDITION

LIBRARY OF CONGRESS CATALOG CARD NUMBER: 91-055386

ISBN: 0-06-271521-6

0-06-273060 (pbk.)

92 93 94 95 96 FTM 10 9 8 7 6 5 4 3 2 1

92 93 94 95 96 FTM 10 9 8 7 6 5 4 3 2 1

CONTENTS

Have you ever had to make a major decision or reach an important goal and wished you had an expert to assess your chances of success? *What the Odds Are* is about major decisions, goals and fears, too—founded and unfounded.

It is also about expert opinion, that is, how the most authoritative sources assess the chances. When sources are cited, they refer to the data used in our analysis and not our commentary. These sources are identified at the end of the alphabetical entries. In instances in which data was culled from more than three sources, the credit for the information is identified as "compiled research by editors," however, the sources are usually credited in the commentary.

To understand *What the Odds Are,* it helps to know what we mean by odds, and the various ways they are presented in this book.

Odds can be expressed many ways. Statisticians prefer traditional number-to-number expres-sions (i.e., 2 to 1). Most general reportage in the media use percentages to express the chances that something might happen.

There are also odds which don't necessarily reflect specific risk factors; rather, they reflect rates of occurrence. They are expressed as numbers of occurrences in a group, usually in the lowest common denominator (i.e., 3 in 5). These statistics, however, are generally regarded as the overall probability that an event will occur to the average person in that group.

Odds in the general population can be helpful in evaluating proability, if taken in the proper perspective. For example, it is correct to say that in a two-income household, 1 in 5 working women earns more than her husband. Odds for this circumstance, as a statistician would prefer to express them, would be exceedingly complicated and cumbersome for the general reader. In the case of a wife's versus a husband's income, for example, statistical probabilities depend on ages, educations, locations, economic conditions at the time and much more. Equations which take into account all of these critical factors are often referred to as "actuarial odds." By necessity, we did not present all of this very cumbersome data, because some of them would require enough pages to fill an entire book. Instead, we present material as it relates to an average person, or a broadly-based group such as men, women, age groups and many others.

Because *What the Odds Are* taps expert opinion, we have used various methods of expression which different experts generally use to express their equation to the general population. Some are statistically pure odds, which are expressed as number-to-number, but most are rates of occurrence among the general population. Some are expressed as per capita occurrences, which are culled from U.S. government data, authoritative publications, polls and many other sources.

To keep it simple, we often reported on how many occurrences take place in 100, or 1,000 and so on. Sometimes, we rounded off figures or expressed them with the lowest common denominators. Occasionally, we did not, especially in the many lists in this book. When odds in lists are very close to each other, we rounded off to the nearest one-tenth or one-hundredth.

Finally, odds are serious business, but we didn't want to lose our sense of humor. We therefore attempted to inject a bit of the whimsical. The hope is that this presentation will be as entertaining as it is informative.

A a

ABORTION

Definition: The removal or intentional killing of a fetus in the womb.

According to Stanley Henshaw of the Alan Guttmacher Institute, the most pressing need in the reduction of unintended pregnancy and abortion in Western developed countries is improved contraceptive use among young, unmarried women. In Eastern Europe, on the other hand, the greatest concern is providing contraceptive services and supplies to married women, and encouraging their use.

Eight of the ten countries with the highest rates of abortion are those that have either until very recently been under the cloak of communism or remain so. According to the most recent reliable data, Romania leads the world in induced abortions.

The Odds: In the U.S., odds that a pregnancy will end with an abortion are almost 1 in 3. In such Eastern European countries as Romania, the Soviet Union and Bulgaria, the odds are better than 1 in 2 that a pregnancy will end in an abortion. In developed countries, the lowest odds are found in the Netherlands where the odds are 1 in 11. The following list represents the countries with the highest odds that a pregnancy will end in an abortion.

Romania	56 in 100
Soviet Union	55 in 100
Bulgaria	50 in 100
Yugoslavia	49 in 100
Cuba	45 in 100
South Korea	43 in 100
Czechoslovakia	42 in 100
Hungary	40 in 100
Singapore	33 in 100
China	31 in 100

Source: Source: Stanley K. Henshaw, "Induced Abortion: A World Review, 1990," Family Planning Perspectives, 1990.

ABORTION

Out of State

Definition: The act of going to another state in order to remove a live fetus from the womb, usually because abortions are unavailable in your state.

Lack of available abortion services can prevent women who would otherwise choose to terminate a pregnancy from doing so. For instance, in Wyoming, which has the lowest abortion rate in the country, at 5.1 abortions per 1,000 women, more than half of all women who choose to obtain an abortion travel out of state to do so. In fact, of the ten states with the lowest abortion rate, eight of them are in the top ten in the percentage of their female residents who receive abortions out of state. It's not hard to figure out that for many women, especially those with low incomes, the costs, both economic and emotional, of traveling out of state for an abortion have an effect on the choices they make.

The Odds: The following list represents the states in which it is hardest to get an abortion, as measured by the ratio of residents who must travel outside the state to receive abortion services:

Wyoming	1 in 2
Kentucky	1 in 3
West Virginia	1 in 4
Mississippi	1 in 4
Maryland	1 in 4
Indiana	1 in 4
Arkansas	1 in 4
South Dakota	1 in 4
Missouri	1 in 5
Idaho	1 in 5

Source: Stanley K. Henshaw and Jennifer Van Vort, "Abortion Services in the United States," Family Planning Perspectives, May-June, 1990.

ABSTINENCE

All Kinds

Definition: The personal conviction that you will not have any fun.

The Odds: In America the proportions of people who abstain from various activities are as follows.

No Booze	1 in 3
No Movies	2 in 5
No Daily Papers	2 in 5
No Drugs	4 in 5
No Church	3 in 5
No Sex (Singles)	1 in 10
No Sex (Divorced)	1 in 11
No Sex (Divorced Twice)	1 in 33
No TV	1 in 50

What's the use! They might as well be dead.

Source: Data compiled by editors.

ABUSE BY FAMILY

Definition: The act of sexually exploiting, humiliating or otherwise harming an individual, usually one who is not able to defend himself, especially children and the elderly.

Abuse of family members has long been swept under the rug. Few children or elderly, the most commonly abused, would discuss such matters with family outsiders. Each year in America, over 2 million children are abused or neglected. Over 1,000 die from such treatment.

The Odds: In 1988, 1 in 28 children were abused or neglected; 1 in 1,877 died as a result. Abuse tends to run in families. Among children who have been abused, 3 in 5 boys will grow up to be abusers themselves; among women, 1 in 20.

Parents to Children (any kind)	1 in 20
Parents to Children (low income)	1 in 30
Prison Inmates (as children)	4 in 5
Elderly (any kind)	1 in 12
Elderly (by family)	1 in 13
Women (any kind)	1 in 33
Women (by estranged husband)	1 in 32

Source: Compiled research by editors.

Also See: Child Abuse.

ACCIDENTS

Fatality-prone Countries

Definition: An unexpected event which causes death ranging from an individual slipping in the bathtub to blowing everyone in town to kingdom come.

Accidents will happen wherever and whenever you go. There are, however, some spots where accidents seem to happen more often than in others. Whether such clumsiness is the result of excessive relaxation, outright carelessness or the will of God, one can never surely say.

The Odds: The following list represents the most troublesome spots for accidental deaths and the odds an average citizen will meet his maker during the course of a year.

Hungary	1 in 1,315
France	1 in 1,577
Austria	1 in 1,946
Switzerland	1 in 1,965
Poland	1 in 2,004
Ecuador	1 in 2,049
Portugal	1 in 2,075
New Zealand	1 in 2,212
Greece	1 in 2,304

Source: National Center for Health Statistics.

Also See: Accidental Death, Accidents, Fatal.

ACCIDENTAL DEATH

Definition: Meeting your maker quite unexpectedly and under the most unfavorable conditions.

Each day 5,937 people die from various natural and unnatural causes, ranging from infant mortality to inevitable accidents caused by the decreased physical ability of the elderly. The odds that you will go naturally are 22 in 23. The alternative way to pass on to the next world, in an accident, accounts for 4.3% of all deaths in America.

The Odds: Dying in an accident, as opposed to from natural causes, is a 1 in 23 shot. If you catch your lunch in a mishap, the odds are that it will be associated with the following fatal circumstances:

Automobile	
Accident	1 in 2
Fall	1 in 9
Drowning	1 in 17
Fires or Burns	1 in 20
Poisoning	1 in 23
Suffocation	1 in 26
Shooting	1 in 52
Gas or Vapor	
Inhalation	1 in 128

Source: National Safety Council.

Also See: Automobile Accidents, Bicycles, Buses, Falls, Farms, Fireworks, Friendly Fire, Job Injuries, Highway, Household, Machinery.

ACCIDENTS

In the Workplace

Definition: A hazardous occupational worker's constant concern, a widow's nightmare and a lawyer's dream come true.

Some of the most hazardous occupations according to *The Jobs Rated Almanac* are ranked as follows:

1. Firefighter
2. Race Car Driver
3. Astronaut
4. Football Player
5. Police Officer
6. Fisherman
7. Farm Worker
8. Lumberjack
9. Taxi Driver
10. Truck Driver

Each day 4,932 workers are injured. The most common causes and percentages of job related ailments are highway accidents (27 percent), heart attacks (12 percent), industrial equipment (11 percent), falls (11 percent) and electrocutions (10 percent).

The Odds: One in 61 workers will be injured on the job in an average year. Though the odds are highly in favor of returning home unscathed, at some jobs the odds are very poor. Most firemen and athletes report at least one minor or major injury each year. Following are the odds of being injured in any given year at some hazardous jobs. Odds

9

were computed with the latest available data from the National Safety Council and the Bureau of Labor Statistics.

Mining	1 in 23
Agriculture	1 in 19
Construction	1 in 27
Manufacturing	1 in 37

Source: Complied research by editors.

ADOPTION

Definition: To become legal parent or parents of someone else's child.

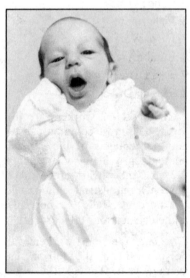

The Odds: A recent study published by the National Center for Health Statistics gives new hope to couples wishing to adopt. The study suggests that for couples wishing to adopt, the odds of getting a child are 1 in 3. Contrary to what many believe, the odds against infertile couples wanting to adopt are 4 to 1.

Improving the Odds: Couples willing to adopt black children, should consider siblings who cannot be separated and handicapped children. They are more available than most children for adoption.

The Cost: Adoption fees generally begin at $8,500, not including various legal costs and the costs of preparing the home for the child. Prospective parents may also have to put up with visits from child welfare agencies.

Source: Compiled research by editors.

AFFAIRS AND MONEY

Definition: The propensity of married people to spend their spare cash and spare time for outside sexual pursuits, rather than familial ones.

Marital infidelity is directly relational to employment status and income. More working wives slip between the sheets with someone other than their husbands than non-working wives. Among men, the more they earn, the more likely they are to be unfaithful.

The Odds: Estimates of marital infidelity are high, with a range as broad among couples as 1 in 8 to 1 in 2. Whatever it actually is, estimates are that between 1 in 6 and 7 in 10 married Americans who work will have an affair, the rate being somewhat determined by income. The higher it is, the more likely the wage earners are to be untrue to their spouses. According to a *Playboy* magazine poll, only 1 in 5 non-working women have affairs, verses 2 in 5 working women.

The following list represents the increase in the odds that married men will have affairs as their annual incomes increase, according to data in a study by *American Couples*:

Under $5,000	1 in 6
$5,000-10,000	1 in 4
$10,000-20,000	1 in 3
$20,000-30,000	9 in 20
$30,000-40,000	11 in 20
$40,000-50,000	2 in 3
$60,000 or more	7 in 10

Source: Compiled research by editors.

Also See: Marital Fidelity.

AFFLUENCE

Definition: 1) Abundance of money, property, wealth; 2) the state of being on hundreds of junk mailing lists.

Despite rumors to the contrary, the ranks of the affluent are growing and the odds of your household making $50,000 or more increased substantially during the 1980s.

The Odds: Among whites, 1 of every 4.5 households reach the $50,000 + category. Among blacks and Hispanics, the ranks of the affluent are substantial, but not nearly so substantial as among whites. One of 10 black households will reach the $50,000 + mark, while 11 of 100 Hispanic households will. The reason behind the growing odds of affluence is the growing phenomenon of the two-income household, a phenomenon, which along with improved income, brings costs in the form of day-care, transportation and that all important meal, lunch. In the future, odds are that affluent households will grow more conservative with their money as the economy slows and the baby boomers get older.

Source: Future Vision, The 189 Most Important Trends of the 1990s, Sourcebooks Trade, 1991.

AIDS

Definition: Acquired Immune Deficiency Syndrome, a disease preventing a body's immune system from being effective and eventually leading to death.

The Odds: The Federal Center for Disease Control estimates that 1 in 250 Americans (one million) have been infected with the HIV virus, but only about 1 in 5 HIV carriers (200,000) have AIDS symptoms, which represents 1 in 1,250 Americans.

Though relatively few Americans have AIDS, the national awareness of the danger is now profound. In 1989, 1 in 6 American's knew someone who then had AIDS, according to a poll by the American Association of Blood Banks. By 1991, the ratio grew to almost 1 in 4. Magic Johnson's courageous admission to being infected with HIV virus has brought the disease out of the closet even more.

According to medical experts, an uninfected individual can contract AIDS only by accepting into his or her body the bodily fluid (such as blood or semen) of an HIV-infected individual. Such transfers most commonly take place through sexual intercourse (with the receptive partner at greater risk) and the sharing of hypodermic needles among drug addicts. Anal sex is the most dangerous sexual practice, because the virus can easily make its way through the highly permeable walls of the lower intestine. Oral and vaginal sex are lower risk. Blood transfusions had been another common means of contracting AIDS, but screening procedures have greatly reduced the threat from contaminated plasma. Thus, for an AIDS-free monogamous heterosexual couple, who do not use intravenous drugs, the chances of becoming infected are miniscule.

Source: Compiled research by editors.

Also See: AIDS Among Children; AIDS and Condoms; AIDS from Blood Transfusions; AIDS, In the Cities; AIDS, By Race; HIV in Blood.

AIDS AND CONDOMS

Definition: The relative risks of contracting Acquired Immune Deficiency Syndrome when using a prophylactic device which is fitted to the male partner while performing a sex act.

The Odds: In low-risk groups, the odds of getting AIDS through sexual contact with a safe partner without using a condom are 1 in 5 million; the odds in the same case, but with a condom, decrease to 1 in 50 million. The risk in both cases is less than that of being killed in an automobile accident on the way to the sexual encounter *(see Automobile Accident).* In sexual contacts with members of high-risk groups (including prostitutes, hemophiliacs, homosexuals and intravenous drug abusers) the odds range from 1 in 10,000 to 1 in 100,000, even when using a condom. The greatest odds of becoming infected with AIDS arise from having sex without a condom with a partner who carries the AIDS antibody. The odds of getting AIDS over several years of regular, unprotected sexual activity with an infected partner are 2 in 3. With a condom, the risk is still a very dangerous 1 in 11.

ODDS IN HETEROSEXUAL INTERCOURSE

1 Encounter With Safe Partner

With Condom   1 in 50 Mill'n

Without Condom   1 in 5 Million

With Partner You Don't Know

With Condom   1 in 5,000 to

                 1 in 5 Million

Without Condom:

                 1 in 500,000

                 to 1 in 500

With Partner with AIDS

with condom   1 in 5,000

without condom: 1 in 500

Caution: Risk data regarding safe sex are often unreliable and are continually being revised

Readers are not advised to use the statistics in this volume to make decisions regarding sexual behavior.

Source: Compiled research by editors.

Also See: AIDS; AIDS Among Children; AIDS from Blood Transfusions; AIDS, In the Cities; AIDS, By Race.

AIDS, RISKIEST CITIES

Definition: Places at which the hot-to-trot would be well advised to take a cold shower.

Below are the cities which are hardest hit and rates of occurrence among the populace.

Newark   1 in 75

San Francisco   1 in 82

Miami   1 in 91

Atlanta   1 in 136

Washington, D.C   1 in 142

New York   1 in 286

Los Angeles   1 in 305

Houston   1 in 334

Philadelphia   1 in 522

Chicago   1 in 799

Source: HIV/AIDS Surveillance Report.

AIDS AMONG CHILDREN

Riskiest States

Definition: The occurrence of Acquired Immune Deficiency Syndrome among those under the age of 13.

AIDS, of course, is not limited to the gay community. In fact, reports now suggest that Acquired Immune Deficiency Syndrome is growing most rapidly not within the gay community, where awareness and education have brought about a change in behaviors that helped spread the disease, but among intravenous drug abusers, who may be less educated about the dangers of AIDS. Sadly, the legacy of this ignorance is a growing population of children infected with the virus — since a pregnant mother who is infected may be extremely likely to infect her fetus as well. Approximately 7 in 10 children born to AIDS-infected mothers will be born with the disease. Researchers are studying the uninfected children born to AIDS mothers, believing they may be a key in finding a preventative.

Below is a list of the states with the most incidences of AIDS among children:

New York	364
New Jersey	163
Florida	141
California	93
Texas	43
Connecticut	33
Illinois	28
Maryland	28
Massachusetts	26
Pennsylvania	26

Source: Centers for Disease Control.

AIDS BY AGE

Who's at Risk?

Definition: Acquired Immune Deficiency Syndrome and age groups most affected.

AIDS cuts across age barriers, jumps the generation gap, and stalks us all. Even fetuses are not immune — for they often pay mortally for the ignorance and excesses of their progenitors.

The Odds: Though teens are frequently regarded as the most at-risk age group, those most stricken are those in the age brackets from 25 to 44, which represents 3 in 4 of all known HIV infections. Only 1 in 17 of all AIDS cases strike those above the age of 55.

The following list represents the proportions of AIDS cases in

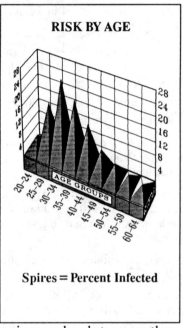

RISK BY AGE

Spires = Percent Infected

various age brackets among those with the disease:

30-34	1 in 4
35-39	1 in 5
25-29	1 in 6
40-44	1 in 7
45-49	1 in 13
50-54	1 in 20
20-24	1 in 25
55-59	1 in 33
60-64	1 in 50
65 +	1 in 100

Source: HIV/AIDS Surveillance Report.

AIDS FROM BLOOD TRANSFUSIONS

Definition: Contracting Acquired Immune Deficiency Syndrome through a blood transfusion.

Until recent years, getting a blood transfusion was considered a fairly safe procedure. But consequent with the arrival of AIDS in the U.S. population, the nation's blood supply became a thing to worry about. As overall blood supply levels began to drop in the late 1970s, the American Red Cross, fearing a shortage, stepped up its campaign to promote blood donations. At the same time, however, unknown even to doctors and medical researchers, AIDS starting making its deadly inroads into the life and welfare of America. Inevitably, unwitting AIDS carriers were among the large numbers who answered the Red Cross's call. The dreadful result was that transfusions with tainted blood became the primary cause of AIDS among heterosexuals who did not fall into any other risk group.

The Odds: Since the discovery that tainted blood was a major source of AIDS, hospitals began a rigid screening process for blood donors, and thus fewer AIDS carriers are now donating blood. In a 1989 Red Cross report, the odds of getting AIDS from a blood transfusion in 1987 were placed at 28,000 to 1. The study's authors reported that the odds were dropping by about 30 percent a year. Using these figures, it can be calculated that the odds of contracting AIDS through a blood transfusion in 1991 were about 81,000 to 1.

Unfortunately, for the unlucky few who receive a tainted transfusion, the odds of becoming infected are high. Ninety-five percent of those who receive bad plasma become infected with the disease; half of those people develop AIDS within seven years.

Source: American Red Cross; New England Journal of Medicine; New York Times, October 5, 1989.

AIDS CASES
By Race

Definition: The occurrence of Acquired Immune Deficiency Syndrome among the three principle racial and national groups in the United States: whites, blacks and Hispanics.

It is well known now that AIDS is a behavior-related disease. The HIV virus which causes the disease does not recognize color lines or national origins. Certain groups, however, do behave differently as a whole when it comes to sexual practices and intravenous drug use, the two principle factors related to the onslaught of AIDS.

The Odds: The list below represents the proportion of the population infected among racial and national groups in the U.S.:

Whites	1 in 1,873
Blacks	1 in 552
Hispanics	1 in 583

Kiss-and-tell lovers: Making matters worse, AIDS among the poorest American minorities is spreading faster than it is elsewhere in the population. As a response to contain the epidemic, the University of Southern California conducted a survey of lower socioeconomic homosexuals and bisexuals of Hispanic origin, and selected out those who were infected with AIDS. In the group which was studied, it was found that 45 percent of the Hispanics remained sexually active after finding they were AIDS victims. Better than 1 in 2 Hispanics (52 percent) failed to inform his or her sex partners.

Source: Compiled research by editors.

Also See: AIDS; AIDS Among Children; AIDS Cases By Race; AIDS Cities; HIV in Blood.

AIDS TRANSMISSION

Behavioral Risks

Definition: The ways Acquired Immune Deficiency Syndrome is transmitted from one person to another.

Sexual intercourse and the sharing of hypodermic needles are the most common means of transmission. Although homosexual contacts make up the majority of transmissions in the U.S, the epidemic is by no means confined to the gay community. In fact, as that community has become more educated and has begun taken more precautions to prevent transmission, the acceleration of spread of the virus has slightly quelled. Unfortunately, intravenous drug users often lack education about the dangers of shared needles, and attempts among AIDS activist groups to distribute needles free to drug users has met with intense opposition.

The Odds: Worldwide, 3 in 4 cases of AIDS are transmitted through heterosexual contact. The incidence of the disease is thought to be highest among women prostitutes, though no reliable statistics exist.

The following list represents the proportions of AIDS infections in the U.S. relative to those diagnosed with the disease:

Male Homosexual/ Bisexual Contact	6 in 10
Intravenous Drug Use	1 in 5
Male homo/bisexual/ contact & IV drug use	1 in 14
Heterosexual Contact	1 in 20

Other Undetermined
Factors   1 in 25
Transfusion of
   Infected Blood   1 in 50
Hemophilia/Coagul-
   ation Disorders   1 in 100

Source: HIV/AIDS Surveillance Report.

AIR CRASH

Definition: An airplane accident, an unintentional or unexpected happening in an aircraft, especially one resulting in injury, damage, harm or loss.

The Odds: In most cases, air safety is very good indeed. Less than 1 in 250,000 flights has even the most minor of accidents. Fatal accidents are even more rare. Of all scheduled flights, less than 1 in 1.6 million ends in deaths of passengers, crew or people on the ground.

On the unlikely chance that there is an accident, the odds are 1 in 5 the mishap will occur during takeoff, 1 in 6 it will be while the airplane is cruising, 1 in 7 it will be during approach and 1 in 9 it will be during landing. The odds are just better than 1 in 10 that it will be during the climb, less than 1 in 10 it will be during descent and 1 in 15 that it will happen while the plane is taxiing to or from the runway. It is sometimes difficult to point to just one cause of an airplane accident; however the chances are better than even that pilot error was a factor and slightly less than even that weather was a factor.

Source: National Transportation Safety Board Annual Review of Aircraft Accident Data; U.S. Air Carrier Operations Calendar Year 1987, 1991.

AIRLINE BUMPERS

Definition: Overbooked airlines which kick you off your flight, usually before the plane has left the ground.

Though there is no known case in which an airline crew threw a passenger out in mid-flight, today, anything is possible amidst the air war environment in the passenger transportation industry. Every year, nearly half a million airline passengers are "bumped" or "bounced" (denied the right to board) from flights for which they hold tickets or reservations). Airlines normally "overbook" (that is, sell more tickets than there are seats), especially during busy seasons, in the expectation of a certain number of cancellations or no-shows.

Continental Airlines: In the midst of its financial difficulties, the operators of the big birds, achieved the dubious distinction of bumping a record 1 in 645 passengers. The problems start when the number of overbooked seats exceeds the number of cancellations, a practice the airline has been said to do excessively in the past, but is doing less and less.

During this period when Continental gate agents wore the biggest boots on the concourse, a passenger was six times more likely to get bumped than on competitive carriers. Overall, however, a passenger was 50 percent less likely to get booted on Continental than on an "average" airline.

The Odds: Approximately 1 in 4,000 passengers are bumped when making an air trip on a major carrier. But where some see problems, others see opportunity. In overbooking situations, airline ticketing agents often offer domestic flight vouchers for free air travel. There are some cunning travelers who know how to exploit this system to perpetually fly free. The big three — American, United and Delta — have been the least bumpy airlines, in part because their wide-ranging flight schedules allow them to offer overbooked passengers quick rescheduling for a flight to their ultimate destinations. America West has had the most bootings.

The following list represents the proportion of passengers who were bumped on major carriers:

America West	1 in 1,148
Southwest	1 in 1,721
TWA	1 in 2,720
Pan Am	1 in 3,831
USAir	1 in 5,154
Continental	1 in 6,098
Northwest	1 in 10,000
Eastern	1 in 10,638
Delta	1 in 17,544
United	1 in 27,777
American	1 in 125,000

Source: Department of Transportation.

AIRLINE SCREWUPS

Most Common Complaints

Definition: A set of circumstances which occur, not during normal air travel, but when you are traveling to be the best-man or brides-maid at your best friend's wedding, or an important one-time business event.

Since the demise of People's Express, the airline industry has lacked an identifiable bad guy, but the generic infamies of the other carriers have proven more than sufficient to stir consumer ire. First among complaints of commercial travelers in 1988 was the frequency and duration of flight delays resulting from technical difficulties. Problems with baggage, though still vexingly frequent, took a distant second place in the complaint box.

When complaints against airlines occur, the following list represents the odds which can be expected for the following screwups:

Flight Difficulties	1 in 2
Baggage	1 in 5
Refunds	1 in 5

Ticketing Problems	1 in 13
Overbooking	1 in 14
Smoking	1 in 35
Fares	1 in 42
Advertising	1 in 134
Credit	1 in 420
Tour Problems	1 in 485

Source: U.S. Department of Transportation, Air Travel Consumer Report.

Also See: Airport Delays.

AIRPORT DELAYS

Definition: A circumstance which results in using all the available credit on your credit card at the cocktail lounge in the airport you hate the most.

The more crowded, overbuilt and under-thought an airport is, the more time you are likely to spend time there, on a trip-to-trip basis. Our biggest worries are of mid-air collisions in over-trafficked skies, but the perils in the hangar, at the gate and on the ticket line are also considerable. Following are the odds that you will be delayed at some of the nation's airports with the worst on-time records:

Philadelphia	76 in 100
Chicago-O'Hare	76 in 100
Denver	77 in 100
New York-Kennedy	77 in 100
Boston	78 in 100
Pittsburgh	79 in 100
Dallas–Fort-Worth	79 in 100
Atlanta	79 in 100
Newark	80 in 100
Seattle	80 in 100

Source: U.S. Department of Transportation

Also See: Airline Screwups.

ALCOHOLISM

Definition: A disease which affects the victim by convincing him that there is paradise at the bottom of a bottle.

While alcohol is often used as a social lubricant, its dangers also permeate many of society's worst problems. The odds are greater than 50 percent that alcohol had something to do with your neighbor's latest brawl, your friend's divorce or an accident in an automobile.

The Odds: According to an early 1980s poll conducted by the Gallup organization, the odds are 1 in 3 that an alcohol-related problem will occur in your home or your neighbor's. According to the lowest estimates, the odds are at least 1 in 20 that a young boy or girl will become an alcoholic. The odds are higher among Irish; Catholics and men and lower amongst Italians, Jews and women. Men are five times more likely to become alcoholics than women. Some sociologists think the odds of women becoming alcoholics will increase as they continue to enter the work force in greater numbers.

Source: Jones, Brian et al, *Social Problems*, McGraw-Hill Book Company.

ALCOHOLICS

Where To Find 'Em

Definition: Those plagued by addiction to alcoholic beverages.

Contrary to popular opinion, one does not find the highest incidences of alcoholism in the cold, bleak Rust Belt cities where one

imagines unemployed auto workers drowning their sorrows at the local tavern. On the contrary, the ten cities with the highest rates of alcohol abuse among their citizenry are located in temperate climes—California, Florida, North Carolina and, most of all, Nevada.

The Odds: In the two gambling capitals of Reno and Las Vegas, the odds are the greatest that you will encounter drunks. In these towns, where the wheels spin all day and all night, dreams of the big jackpot are fueled more often than not, by high-proof beverages. And although people are flocking to the Sun Belt with its promise of economic growth and moderate climate, the disruption such a move might have on the psyche could account for the high rates of alcoholism in those locales. A number of the cities with the lowest incidences of alcoholism are college towns—State College, Lawrence, Bloomington, Iowa City and Provo are all homes to large universities.

HIGHEST INCIDENCES RANKED

1. Reno, NV

2. Las Vegas, NV

3. Albuquerque, NM

4. Stockton, CA

5. Asheville, NC

6. Redding, CA

7. Winter Haven, FL

8. Fresno, CA

9. Pueblo, CO

10. Raleigh-Durham, NC

LOWEST INCIDENCES RANKED

1. State College, PA

2. Lawrence, KS

3. Bloomington, IN

4. Iowa City, IA

5. Bismarck, ND

6. Rochester, MN

7. Green Bay, WI

8. Provo/Orem, UT

9. Lancaster, PA

10. Sheboygen, WI

Source: The Best and Worst of Everything.

Also See: Alcoholism, Drinking Problems

ALCOHOLISM

Definition: A dependence on alcohol that reaches the morbid stage of physical and mental impairment and the inability to function socially or vocationally.

The Odds: With 2 in 3 Americans occasional or inveterate drinkers of alcoholic beverages, clearly the hard stuff has a lot going for it. Just as clearly, from the statistics on alcohol-related murders, accidental deaths, suicides, and drownings, a line must be drawn between social and occasional business drinking and becoming an alcoholic. The National Institute on Alcohol Abuse puts this line at two drinks a day before trouble begins, which would include brain damage (see senility), heart attack (see heart disease, high blood pressure), and cirrhosis of the liver, a disease that itself ranks among the 10 leading causes of death in the U.S. Four drinks a day becomes borderline alcoholism, studies show, at which time drinking begins to impair vision and sexual function and causes malnutrition, skin disorders, decreased resistance to infection, pancreatitis, and weakening of bones and muscles. Studies show that 1 in 6

drinkers consume more than four drinks a day. What are the odds of becoming an alcoholic? For men it is 1 in 62,000; for women, 1 in 210,000, with the odds for women dropping year by year, because, sociologists say, of the low self-esteem and the defeat they feel in their female roles. Finally, among abusers of alcohol, 1 in 5 will develop cirrhosis of the liver.

The following list represents the proportions of alcohol-related deaths in the U.S.:

Murder	1 in 2
Accidents	1 in 2
Drownings	1 in 3
Suicides	1 in 4

Source: The Merck Manual: Better Homes and Gardens, *Women's Health and Medical Guide;* The Columbia University College of Physicians and Surgeons, *Complete Home Medical Guide.*

ALZHEIMER'S DISEASE

Definition: An age-related disease which kills brain cells, robbing its victim of memory and ability to reason, eventually resulting in death.

The condition was first discovered in 1907 by a German physician, Alois Alzheimer. The doctor found after performing an autopsy on a 56-year-old demented woman that she had high concentrations of two microscopic objects on her brain: "tangles" or twisted nerve fibers and "plaques," dead or dying cells surrounding a substance called beta amyloid.

The Odds: Each year some 100,000 Americans are diagnosed with Alzheimer's disease. The probability that an average individual will be victimized is elusive, due to the fact that in generations past the life expectancy was shorter. Alzheimer's, being an age-related illness, will affect those who live long lives. Today, there are only 4 million cases reported, hence the overall odds average only 1 in 63. Among those who can expect long lives, such as baby boomers, the odds increase to 1 in 3, a frightening prospect.

As people age, the odds of being stricken with the disease are as follows:

At Age 65	1 in 13
At Age 75	1 in 4
At Age 85	1 in 2

Source: Parade Magazine, October 13, 1991

Also See: Longevity.

AMUSEMENT PARKS

Definition: An oasis of fun, fantasy and escapism for all ages.

America goes to Disneyland; America goes to Six Flags; America goes wherever the thrills come fast and the lines come long. Big fun is big business, and the customer is always right, so long as he spends, spends, spends.

The Odds: Ask a child where he most wants to go on the family vacation. Odds are it is Walt Disney World, the most visited acreage on the globe. Visits to movie-related theme parks account for 4 in 7 of those to major American amusement parks.

The following list represents the ratios of various amusement parks' annual attendances to the U.S. population:

Walt Disney World	1 in 9
Disneyland	1 in 19
Knott's Berry Farm	1 in 50
Universal Studios Hollywood	1 in 54
Sea World of Florida	1 in 66
Sea World of California	1 in 76
Kings Island	1 in 78
Six Flags Magic Mountain	1 in 81
Cedar Point	1 in 81
Busch Gardens, Dark Continent	1 in 83

Source: *Amusement Business* magazine.

ARCHITECTS

Definition: A licensed professional who designs or participates in the process of creating or altering buildings or structures.

Although the do-it-yourself spirit of middle-America is an indisputable national resource, one of the highest marks of a society's attainment is the concentration of architects and other professional design initiates, to lay the foundation for that civilization's expansion and perpetuation. Indeed, it is no surprise that our most populous and logistically involved settlements in California and New York afford the most opportunities for certified architects.

The Odds: There is at least one and often three or four architects for nearly every building in developed states, yet only about 1 in 3,000 citizens of those states is an architect. In lesser developed states such as Alaska, some building codes do not require the participation of an architect. In the total U.S., only 1 in 6,250 Americans makes his living in this profession. Only 1 in 4 architects design buildings. The remainder do everything from writing building codes for government to marketing their firm's services to prospective clients.

The following list represents the ratio of the population who are architects in the states with the highest and lowest concentrations:

HIGHEST CONCENTRATIONS

California	1 in 1,612
New York	1 in 1,960
Texas	1 in 2,040
Illinois	1 in 2,381
Pennsylvania	1 in 2,777
Ohio	1 in 2,941
Florida	1 in 3,448
Michigan	1 in 3,571
New Jersey	1 in 3,704
Massachusetts	1 in 4,000

LOWEST CONCENTRATIONS

Alaska	1 in 166,666
Oregon	1 in 125,000
Nevada	1 in 90,909
District of Col.	1 in 55,555
South Dakota	1 in 50,000
North Dakota	1 in 33,333
Delaware	1 in 33,333
Vermont	1 in 25,000
Wyoming	1 in 14,286
Arizona	1 in 9,999

Source: U.S. Bureau of Labor Statistics.

ARMS EXPORTS

The Arms Merchants

Definition: Guns, tanks, hand grenades, bombers, bayonets, land mines, flame throwers, assault rifles and other antipersonnel devices shipped around the world to make it a safer place in which to live.

One of the most graphic lessons of the showdown in the sands (Desert Storm), was that the wanton sales of leading-edge weapons to loose-cannon, Third World megalomaniacs must be checked. The problem, of course, is that the American government has kept the economy on a war footing for a half a century, and our defense industry relies implicitly on the ability to subsidize its over-priced wares by indiscriminate sales to Nervous-Nelly autocrats.

For all the chest-thumping about third-world hot spots, the top five arms exporters in the world are the nations that had, until very recently, been the main combatants in the Cold War. With the serious contraction of the former Soviets' once widespread empire, its loss of former client-states, and its dangerous internal turmoil, one expects that it will soon relinquish its top spot on the list of global arms exporters.

The Odds: The following list represents the proportion of the world's armaments supplied by the largest exporters of war materials:

Soviet Union	1 in 3
United States	1 in 3
France	1 in 10
Britain	1 in 20
Germany	1 in 25
China	1 in 34
Netherlands	1 in 71
Sweden	1 in 90
Brazil	1 in 90
Czechoslovakia	1 in 111

Source: International Peace Research Institute.

ARMS IMPORTERS
The Biggest Weapons Buyers

Definition: The leading nations which buy by the gun. . . and have leading heads of state who often *die* by the gun.

In 1990, Iraq's expenditures for articles of war accounted for 1 in 10 of every dollar on the open market for arms (not to mention that nation's gray- and black-market acquisitions). Iraq's frenzied weapons purchasing was surpassed only by Third World giant India, which has had the last two consecutive heads of state assassinated.

Is it just a coincidence that six of the top ten world importers of weapons were either direct or indirect participants in the Persian Gulf war? The sad fact is that since the official end of that conflict, Israel has signed a new arms-purchase agreement with the U.S., and China has made public its plans to sell missiles to Syria.

The Odds: The following list represents the proportion of the world's arms exports which are purchased by the top ten armaments importers:

India	1 in 7
Iraq	1 in 9
Egypt	1 in 16
Saudi Arabia	1 in 21

Israel	1 in 22
Japan	1 in 27
Syria	1 in 27
Turkey	1 in 29
Czechoslovakia	1 in 29
Angola	1 in 32

Source: International Peace Research Institute

Also See: Arms Exporters.

ARTHRITIS

Definition: Inflammation or degeneration of the joints.

The Odds: In the U.S., some 34.7 million persons, or about 14.6 percent of the non-institutionalized population, suffer from some form of arthritis, making the odds about 6 to 1 against any particular random person suffering. If one does suffer, the odds of the disease limiting one's activities are about another 5 to 1. In other words, most people who do suffer from arthritis don't suffer from it seriously enough to hinder such daily activities as working or housekeeping.

Arthritis will undoubtedly increase in prevalence as the baby boomers age. Whereas only 1 in 38 people overall are limited in their activity by arthritis, among those above the age of 75, the prevalence of the disability rises to 1 in 8. Thus, the odds of contracting a debilitating form of arthritis increase almost five-fold as one ages.

Arthritis strikes women more often than men. Odds against a woman having arthritis are slightly greater than 5.6 to 1, while for a man, the odds drop to 9 to 1 against the disease. The illness strikes whites and blacks in about equal proportion, but Asians and Latin Americans are about three times *less* likely to contract arthritis than the general population.

The following list represents the states with the highest and lowest arthritis rates and the proportions of the population in them which suffer from the disease:

HIGHEST STATES

Florida	18.1 in 100
Dist. of Columbia	16.8 in 100
Pennsylvania	16.3 in 100
Arkansas	15.8 in 100
New Jersey	15.7 in 100
Rhode Island	15.7 in 100
Connecticut	15.6 in 100
Kentucky	15.5 in 100
New York	15.5 in 100
Missouri	15.4 in 100

LOWEST STATES

Alaska	8.8 in 100
Utah	10.7 in 100
Hawaii	10.8 in 100
Wyoming	11.3 in 100
Colorado	12.5 in 100
New Mexico	12.8 in 100
Texas	12.8 in 100
Idaho	13.1 in 100
California	13.3 in 100

Washington	13.6 in 100

Source: Centers for Disease Control.

ATHEISM

Definition: The belief that there is no God.

Despite the fact that daily religious activities are not the major part of many Americans' lives, the belief in a Supreme Being is still very strong around the world.

The Odds: Just over 4 in 5 people in the world believe in God and practice a religion. Among those who do not, 1 in 5 would describe himself as an atheist and 4 in 5 consider themselves to be agnostics. Nearly 3 in 4 of the world's atheists or agnostics live in China.

The following lists represent the proportions of atheists and agnostics to those who practice a religion in various parts of the world:

NONRELIGIOUS OR ATHEISTS

East Asia	1 in 2
USSR	1 in 2
Europe	1 in 8
South Asia	1 in 52
North America	1 in 13
Latin America	1 in 29
Oceania	1 in 8
Africa	1 in 343

ATHEISTS

East Asia	1 in 11
USSR	1 in 5
Europe	1 in 29
South Asia	1 in 51
North America	1 in 275
Latin America	1 in 187
Oceania	1 in 52
Africa	1 in 4,470

NONRELIGIOUS

East Asia	1 in 11
USSR	1 in 2
Europe	1 in 10
South Asia	1 in 65
North America	1 in 14
Latin America	1 in 34
Oceania	1 in 9
Africa	1 in 344

Source: *The World Christian Encyclopedia.*

Also See: Religious Beliefs, Jews.

AUTOMOBILES

3-Car Families

Definition: Group of individuals with common ancestry and garages.

Americans love their cars. This is a culture in which the automobile has become such an integral part that it even generates its own mythology. Having a car, or at least access to one, many regard as essential in our society and it is interesting to note where most of the cars are. The following are the top ten metropolitan areas with three cars or more per family and the odds of occurrence in American society:

Oklahoma City	1 in 5
Dallas	1 in 5
Kansas City	1 in 6
Phoenix	11 in 50
Tucson	19 in 100
Denver	11 in 50
Sacramento	1 in 5
San Diego	1 in 5
San Antonio	9 in 50
Seattle	1 in 5

Source: The Best and Worst of Everything.

AUTOMOBILE ACCIDENTS

Definition: Any occurrence while an automobile is operating which results in fatal or serious injury to persons or appreciable damage to the vehicle.

The Odds: The chance of being killed in an automobile accident on any given excursion is 1 in 4 million, less than the chance of being killed while mowing the lawn.

However, the odds increase significantly when we think not in terms of a single trip but in terms of the average number of automobile trips taken in a lifetime, approximately 50,000. With this in mind, it has been determined that about 1 in 140 people dies in an automobile accident; 1 in 3 is hurt seriously enough to be disabled for at least a day. Considering the increasingly mobile population, it's not surprising that automobile accidents are the leading cause of death for people between the ages of 5 and 34.

Who, When, Where: The greatest chances are that an automobile accident will occur in July, when 1 in 10 do. Most take place in California, where over 5,000 occur annually. Odds are 3 in 4 that the victim will be male. The state with the highest mileage-death-rate (number of fatalities per miles driven) is Arizona, where on average 4.5 deaths occur for every million miles driven.

MOST DEATHS

California	5,223
Texas	3,568
Florida	2,875
New York	2,114

HIGHEST MILEAGE DEATH RATES

Deaths per Million Vehicle Miles

Arizona	4.5
Mississippi	4.0
New Mexico	4.0
South Carolina	3.7

Source: National Highway Safety Board.

Also See: Automobile Safety, Travel.

AUTOMOBILES
The Have-nots

Definition: Individuals who don't give a fig how much snow is on the roads.

Living in a city makes it impractical as well as difficult to own a car. Storage, insurance, and other associated costs for city residents are much higher all around than for those in rural areas. And you might as well forget about parking, unless you're willing to pay for a spot which costs as much as a house elsewhere. Moreover, with easy mass transit available, it is more cost effective to rent a car when the necessity arises, rather than meet the costs of ownership.

The following is a list of cities which have the fewest cars per household and the odds of such occurrences; the order reflects the relative odds of each city:

New York	9 in 25
Philadelphia	11 in 50
Chicago	1 in 5
Baltimore	1 in 5
Boston	1 in 5
Buffalo	19 in 100
Miami	9 in 50
Cincinnati	1 in 6
Milwaukee	1 in 6
San Francisco	1 in 7

Source: The Best and Worst of Everything.

AUTOMOBILE OWNERSHIP

Definition: Taxes aside, the largest guzzler of paychecks around the world, next to rent or mortgage payments.

America is a car culture, make no bumpers about that. We like to rove, roar, rave and rock 'n roll in our bitchin' Camaros, 4x4s and Model Ts. It is little surprise, then, that we lead the world in per-capita car ownership. There are slightly more than 160 million cars in the U.S., or one car per each 1.6 people. On the other hand, rush hour in such auto-deprived countries as Bangladesh, Rwanda and the Maldive Islands are a breeze.

The Odds: The following list represents the proportions of the population who own or lease an automobile.

TOP TEN COUNTRIES

United States	66 in 100
Canada	52 in 100
Switzerland	44 in 100
Iceland	43 in 100
France	43 in 100
Sweden	42 in 100
Luxembourg	41 in 100
Germany (West)	38 in 100
Norway	38 in 100
Qatar	37 in 100

BOTTOM TEN COUNTRIES

Bangladesh	6 in 10,000
Rwanda	7 in 10,000
Maldive Islands	10 in 10,000
Vietnam	1 in 10,000
Ethiopia	2 in 10,000
Nepal	14 in 10,000
Mali	15 in 10,000
China (PRC)	17 in 10,000
Burundi	20 in 10,000

India   23 in 10,000

Source: United Nations.

AUTOMOBILE SAFETY

Makes and Models

The right vehicle makes a difference. The safest car, according to the experts is the Mercedes SDL/SEL series, followed by the Saab 900. Other safe cars include station wagons and minivans. Passengers in smaller cars are much more likely than those in larger cars to be injured in an accident. Among the 202 car makes and models manufactured between 1986 and 1988, model years which were tracked, only four small cars had an injury rate lower than the average. More than 50 percent of all small cars had a significantly higher than average number of injuries. The most dangerous cars in an accident, according to the study's figures, are the Hyundai Excel, the Isuzu I-Mark and the Chevrolet Sprint.

Source: Highway Loss Data Institute.

Also See: Automobile Accident, Death, Travel.

AUTOMOBILE THEFT

Definition: An occurrence which takes place the day before you decide to invest in car alarm system.

Can you picture someone else behind the wheel of your cherished new car, your prized possession, taking a whiff of that new-car smell? It happens all the time. Motor vehicle theft account for the highest losses from crime in the U.S. and is second only to violent crimes in its sheer numbers.

The Odds: Given the present rate of auto thefts in the 1990s, the odds will be approximately 1 in 125 that your car will be stolen in any given year. On the brighter side, the odds are 2 in 3 that the cops will find your car and you will get it back. Most of the time it will have been stripped of your favorite toys including sporting accessories, and high-tech radios, not to mention the more mundane, yet other untraceable parts such as batteries, tires and engine components.

Following is a list of the models the car thieves prefer over all others. Tops on the list are high-performance sports-car models, but, surprisingly, thieves also love the look, the feel and the *safety* of the ultimate Yuppie-mobiles, the Volvo 740 and 760.

MOST STOLEN 1990 MODELS

Order of Thieves' Preferences

1. Nissan 300ZX
2. Ford Mustang
3. Volkswagen Jetta 4-door
4. Cadillac Brougham

5. Mercury Cougar
6. Nissan Maxima
7. Honda Civic CRX
8. Volvo 740
9. Volvo 760 4-door

10. Ford Thunderbird

Source: Highway Loss Data Institute.

Also See: Automobile Ownership.

B b

BACHELOR'S DEGREES

Fields of Study

Definition: A sheep skin which certifies that you know enough about something to be more dangerous than effective.

Have a college education to pay for? What will your money go toward? Today's degree seeker will earn a certificate that will enable him, at least on paper, to become much better at managing, advertising and selling products than at actually developing and building them, much better at dancing and acting than at discovering and inventing.

A few decades ago, the American higher educational system saw a renaissance of Liberal Arts study. In these pragmatic, economically-troubled times, it is not surprising that these sublime but financially unrewarding pursuits have once again declined in popularity. With spiraling tuition costs, today's aver-age student is asking for an education which will bring immediate, tangible results.

The Odds: Today's undergraduates are three times more likely to earn degrees in business management than in engineering. They are twice as likely to earn a bachelor's de-gree in the visual and performing arts than in the physical sciences.

The following list represents the proportions of bachelor's degrees earned in various fields of study:

Business /Manag't	1 in 4
Social Sciences	1 in 10
Education	1 in 11
Engineering	1 in 11
Health Sciences	1 in 16
Communications	1 in 22
Psychology	1 in 23
Letters	1 in 25
Life Sciences	1 in 28
The Arts	1 in 28

Source: U.S. Department of Education.

Also See: Educational Attainment.

BACKACHE

Definition: A pain, usually in the lower part of the back, caused by a strain in a muscle or ligament, or, more seriously, by short leg, a disk problem, a collapsed vertebrae from a fall, an unstable vertebrae that shifts back and forth over a vertebrae beneath it, or a tumor.

The Odds: How likely is it that when, at age 40, you join the one and a half million to two million persons annually who see a doctor for this excruciating ailment, that that ailment is going to be serious enough for surgery or rehabilitation? A look at your profile in the mirror is one indication. Rounded shoulders? Caved-in chest? Arms hanging slightly forward of the knees? You have it. Poor posture. The actual odds of your backache being due to this reason is 4 in 5. But they are only 1 in 5 that you will go on to serious treatment for short leg, slipped disk, a tumor, etc. While lower back pain from poor posture is often crippling for a while, accounting for the most days lost at work because of illness, it is an easily treatable ailment, mostly with exercise to strengthen the back and the abdomen, and by correcting that poor posture you picked up as a kid.

It is worthwhile knowing that back pain is an excuse many men and women use to avoid sex with each other, while actually no matter how serious the back problem becomes, sex is possible and partners can find many ways to enjoy it without further injuring the back. And speaking of poor posture, some occupations induce it no matter how straight the person stands when away from their jobs, most notably musicians. The odds on a piano player winding up with lower back pain is 1 in 3; a guitarist, 2 in 3; and a harpist 3 in 4.

Source: *Freedom from Backache*, Lawrence W. Friedman, M.D., and Lawrence Galton; Columbia University College of Physicians and Surgeons, *Complete Home Medical Guide*.

BAGGAGE LOSS

Airline Losers

Definition: The state in which your tooth brush is somewhere between London and Louisville.

Where has all the baggage gone? The frequency of losing your luggage is one of the most frustrating of all foul-ups. Southwest Airlines, the carrier which is best at getting your bags where they are supposed to, benefits from the fact that it carries a large number of travelers such as businessmen on trips of relatively short duration, thus keeping the overall number of checked bags per passenger down. *The*

Odds: Given that many travelers carry on their bags, or have none, the average air traveler checks an average of approximately one bag. On U.S. carriers, 1 in 176 passengers will temporarily lose their luggage. Airlines estimate that better than 9 in 10 lost bags are eventually recovered, usually within 24 hours.

Given the above statistics, the following list represents the proportions of passengers whose baggage is temporarily lost by the major U.S. carriers:

America West	1 in 116
TWA	1 in 132
Northwest	1 in 155
Delta	1 in 167
USAir	1 in 168
United	1 in 177
Eastern	1 in 181
American	1 in 201
Pan Am	1 in 220
Continental	1 in 225
Southwest	1 in 356

Source: U.S. Department of Transportation.

BALDNESS

Definition: **The state in which men have the ability to shine a flashlight on their head and have the beam bounce to the ceiling, illuminating the room better than natural light. [Probable source for modern word *headlight*.]**

Each epoch in American history has its most famous baldies, from Benjamin Franklin and George Washington, right on up to NBC weather wizard Willard Scott. In the U.S., there are approximately 30 million bald men, toupees,

wigs and hair transplants not withstanding.

How do these men and others develop their distinctive pates? No one knows for sure what causes baldness, though it is suspected to be hereditary and linked on the maternal side of the family. A mother frequently passes on her father's baldness to her son, but there are too many cases in which the hairlines of siblings do not match. One brother can be as bald as a doorknob, yet the other can have a mop of hair.

The Odds: Some 1 in 5 men are bald. About 1 in 4 women between the ages of 25 and 54 will suffer noticeable hair loss.

The following list represents the proportions of men who experience significant hair loss by the time they reach various ages:

20 to 29	1 in 5
30 to 39	3 in 10
40 to 49	2 in 5
50 to 59	1 in 2
60 to 60	2 in 3
70 to 79	3 in 4

Though it might not be much consolation to dead men, if you still have hair at death, it will remain on your corpse hundreds of years after you enter the Pearly Gates. Heavens!

Source: Almanac of the American People, Tom and Nancy Biaracree, Facts on File.

Also See: Hair Color.

BANKING

Definition: 1) Money given to a bank to save for you at a small return 2) banking as a profession.

The Odds: The U.S. is the largest banking nation in the world? Think again. Times have changed since the U.S. influence in banking circles began to crumble in the 1960s from bad loans and the ascendancy of Japan, which was to become the largest trading partner of almost every country on Earth and the most solid banking nation in the world. So with that to contend with, and Germany's financial might, what are the odds of an American bank breaking into the list of the top 50 banks in deposits in the world? Poor, sad to say. The answer is a sickly 1 in 25. That's right. Only two American banks make the list, Citibank (23rd) and Bank of America (50th), while 21 Japanese banks dominate the list, led by Dai-Ichi Kangyo Bank Ltd. of Tokyo, the world's largest bank. What's up? you might ask. How can a nation with less than half the population of the U.S. produce banking institutions so formidable? First, the Japanese are the most savings-minded people around, and with good reason. They spend less per capita on social security, welfare and public service than anybody in any other industrial country, and so must depend on their savings to carry them through sickness and old age. Second, banking in Japan is highly centralized. The U.S., with 3,000 banks worthy of note, finds its savings spread around those 3,000 banks, while the Japanese concentrate their savings in two handfuls of banks in Tokyo and their nationwide branches. So much for top 50 lists. Other nations that top the U.S. on the list:

Germany	1 in 7
France	1 in 12
United Kingdom	1 in 12
Switzerland	1 in 17
Netherlands	1 in 17
Italy	1 in 17

Source: 1991 Information Please Almanac; Moody's Bank and Finance Manual; The Rise of Modern Japan, W.G. Beasley.

BANKRUPTCY

Business Failures

Definition: The state in which a company becomes insolvent and can no longer continue to do business.

Entrepreneurship is a key component of the American character, and in sum, that trait underlies much of this nation's historical success in the world's financial arena. Inherent in the establishment of a commercial enterprise, however, is personal financial risk. Although the eighties were marked by economic recovery and growth, the high attrition rate among new businesses in the nineties is a harbinger of tougher times.

The Odds: Approximately 7 in 10 businesses will declare bankruptcy or become insolvent over a 10 year period. Though various poor economic conditions are often a regional phenomenon, certain areas tend to have a greater proclivity for their business to go belly up. The following list represents the states with the highest percentages of business bankruptcies and the odds that an average business will become bankrupt in one year:

Colorado	1 in 40
Arizona	1 in 48
Alaska	1 in 50
Texas	1 in 53
Utah	1 in 61
Louisiana	1 in 64
Washington	1 in 71
California	1 in 72
Idaho	1 in 75
Nevada	1 in 76

Source: Dun and Bradstreet Corporation.

BASEBALL

Getting to First Base

Definition: 1) The process of getting to the first base of 3 on a baseball diamond; 2) [*Slang*] a term, usually used by a male, which describes his progress in the act of seducing a female.

The formula used to derive the following list adds together a player's total number of bases gained through hits, walks and steals over his career, then divides that number by the total number of games played. The result yields the average number of bases gained per game for each player, and multiplying that number by 150 gives an index of the offensive productivity of a player over the course of a regular season. The statistic favors powerful home run hitters, since a homer earns four bases for every swing of the bat, while a single accounts for only one base. The list is led by three power hitters – Ruth, Gehrig and Williams – but the interesting members of this top ten club are

35

Rickey Henderson and Ty Cobb, players shorter on power but longer on speed. The prowess of Henderson and Cobb in swiping bases adds greatly to their offensive threat.

The Odds: The average hitter in an average major league game will get on base about 1 of every three times at bat, hence it could be said the odds are 1 in 3 he will get to first base. Some past hitters were so proficient at the plate that the odds they would get on base in any given game were as follows:

Babe Ruth	3.2 to 1
Lou Gehrig	3.1 to 1
Ted Williams	3.0 to 1
Rickey Henderson	2.9 to 1
Jimmy Foxx	2.8 to 1
Mickey Mantle	2.7 to 1
Ty Cobb	2.6 to 1
Willie Mays	2.6 to 1
Stan Musial	2.6 to 1
Hank Aaron	2.6 to 1

Source: New York Times.

BASEBALL

Clutch Hitter

Definition: 1) The man at bat in a baseball game with runners in scoring position and two outs. 2) The man in the locker room after the game with one of the following on his face: a smile or egg.

When the game's on the line, who would major league managers most like to see at the plate? According to the numbers, Will Clark of the San Francisco Giants is likely to be their pick. He is the best clutch hitter in baseball. Clark has batted .380 with runners in scoring position and two outs over the past three seasons. Teammates often refer to the "sneer" Clark gets on his face in tight situations as "the Clint Eastwood look." This is the "controlled aggression" managers are looking for, concentration rather than wildness. Other factors that make up a great clutch hitter include competitive spirit, the ability to intimidate a pitcher, and the flair for the dramatic.

The Odds: An average major league players will get a hit approximately 1 of every 4 times at bat. During the seasons of 1988 to 1990 the most outstanding hitters got hits when at bat in the following proportions during the clutch:

Will Clark S.F. Giants	1 in 2.63
Kirby Puckett Minnesota Twins	1 in 3.16
Barry Larkin Cincinnati Reds	1 in 3.16
Tim Raines Montreal Expos	1 in 3.17
Pedro Guerrero Dodgers, Cardinals	1 in 3.18
Eric Davis Reds	1 in 3.18
Paul Molitor Brewers	1 in 3.22
Steve Sax	1 in 3.28

Dodgers, Yankees

Alvin Davis   1 in 3.22
  Seattle Mariners

Andre Dawson   1 in 3.336
  Chicago Cubs

Source: STATS, Inc.

BASEBALL "HIT"

Getting Bonked

Definition: An incident in which a fan is struck by a baseball while attending a game.

The Odds: Every year, approximately 5 sports fans per team suffer serious injuries from being struck by a stray ball. The average attendance for a major league baseball team is 1.5 million per season. Thus the odds of getting pegged come to approximately 1 in 300,000 or some 130 yearly injuries. In the past decade, however, baseball attendance has skyrocketed. The Los Angeles Dodgers, New York Mets and St. Louis Cardinals all recently surpassed the 3 million mark for a season. How does this affect the odds of getting struck?

As the density of human bodies in the park increases, the chances of an individual being struck by a ball rise accordingly. But *your* chances remain about the same, since you will have more bodies to hide behind. Other factors to take into account include the size of the stadium, its amount of foul territory, and the distance of the seat from the batter's box. You're in much greater danger sitting in the first row behind the dugout at Wrigley Field, where you're extremely close to the batter and where dozens of foul balls zing by every game, than in an outfield upper-deck seat in Toronto's Sky Dome, unreachable by all but the likes of super-sluggers Jose Canseco and Bo Jackson.

Source: Original research by editors.

BASKETBALL GRADS

Graduation Rates of Collegiate Hoopsters

Definition: How the intellectual achievement of collegiate basketball players compares to their height in feet and inches.

It is no wonder that collegiate basketball players have lower graduation rates than other students, including athletes in other sports. The dozens of games and extended seasons take their toll on scholarly achievements.

The Odds: Only 3 in 10 college basketball players earn a diploma, compared to 1 in 2 for the main student body. Among other athletes, the 50 percent graduation rate is the same.

The following list represents the proportions of college basketball players who earn diplomas from the universities they play for in various NCAA leagues:

Big Ten	43.9 in 100
Pac 10	40.6 in 100
Mid-American	40.0 in 100
Big 8	34.8 in 100
Independents	33.3 in 100
ACC	32.0 in 100
Southwest	23.5 in 100
Big West	18.9 in 100
Western	17.6 in 100
SEC	14.0 in 100

Source: Chronicle of Higher Education.

Also See: Football Grads, Jock Graduations.

BEACH BUMS?

Life by the Shore

Definition: People who live within 50 miles of coastal shorelines.

Not everyone can jump in the car and go to the beach. Pools, rivers, ponds, and creeks will have to do for most Americans who want to go swimming or sunbathing.

The Odds: The number of people who live within an hour's drive of real sand beaches on the ocean or the Great Lakes has increased two-fold from 60 million in 1940 to 130 million in 1990. The odds, however, that an average American will live an hour away from the shoreline, have stayed relatively the same, 1 in 2.

The following list represents the proportions of the U.S. population who live within an hour's drive (50 miles) of various major shorelines:

Altantic Ocean	2 in 9
Pacific Ocean	1 in 8
Great Lakes	1 in 8
Gulf of Mexico	1 in 16

Source: U.S. Bureau of the Census, Statistical Abstracts.

BICYCLE ACCIDENT

Definition: 1) An unintentional or unexpected happening which results in the injury, harm or death of the rider of a bicycle, 2) An individual who is conceived while his parents were on a bicycle outing.

The Odds: For boys, the odds of accidental death in a bicycle accident peak between the ages of ten and twelve at 1 in 40,000. For girls, fatal accidents peak slightly earlier when the odds of accidental death are slightly more than 1 in 200,000. For both groups, the odds of death decline to the miniscule by the time they reach their mid-twenties. If the accident results in death, the odds are 9 to 1 that an automobile was involved. Minor accidents are usually the result of falls which are rarely reported and therefore hard to predict. The odds are 2 to 1 that accidents which do happen will happen in between May and September. Likewise, the chances are great that any collisions will occur between the hours of 3:00 p.m. and 8:00 p.m. when children are out of school and riding their bicycles around the neighborhood.

Source: Baker, Susan P. et al, *The Injury Fact Book*, Lexington Books, 1984

BIG TEN EGGHEADS

Ph.D.s Degrees from Big Ten Universities

Definition: The nerds, dweebs and nebbishes who are laboriously doing library projects while the rest of the campus is partying. Though most think of the Big Ten schools as undergraduate diplomamills, they produce a fair number of Ph.D.s from among their undergraduates, especially in sheer numbers. The numbers are not as great in terms of the percentage of the undergraduate student body that eventually earns Ph.D.s, but that is understandable, given the public mandate of these schools, and their somewhat more open admissions policies.

The Odds: At Big Ten schools, 1 in 23 students will earn a Ph.D. Less than 1 in 100 undergraduates go on to a doctoral degree in the humanities. At Purdue, only 1 in 1,000 baccalaureates eventually are conferred a Ph.D. in a humanities discipline.

The following list represents the odds that the average undergraduate will eventually earn a Ph.D. degree:

Michigan	1 in 18
Illinois	1 in 19
Wisconsin	1 in 19
Northwestern	1 in 21
Purdue	1 in 23
Minnesota	1 in 26
Iowa	1 in 27
Ohio State	1 in 28
Indiana	1 in 31
Michigan State	1 in 32

Source: "Analysis of Leading Undergraduate Sources of Ph.D.s, Adjusted for Institutional Size," Great Lakes Colleges Association.

Also See: Basketball Grads, Football Grads.

BIRTH CONTROL EFFECTIVENESS

Definition: Brinksmanship in sex, where, by deliberate attempts to control or prevent conception, one hopes to know where the brink is.

The Odds: Here again, as in so many avenues of life, men get the better deal. Of the thirteen generally used birth control methods in use today, not counting natural family planning methods like the calendar method, the temperature method and the mucous inspection method, men are called upon to use only three, the condom, vasectomy and withdrawal. The rest are the responsibility of the woman, and so are the detrimental side effects. Which of the thirteen methods present the most favorable odds against pregnancy, and which present the most unfavorable? According to Better Homes and Gardens' *Woman's Health and Medical Guide*, the Intrauterine Device (IUD) and the condom with spermicides are the safest, with the probability of pregnancy only 1 in 10. Least effective are lactation, while the mother is feeding her new-born baby and before menstruation returns, and douching. The same source says that up to 4 in 10 women will become pregnant if they rely on these methods unless another method is used simultaneously. Women must remember, though, that IUDs pose certain detrimental side effects, chiefly the possibility of infections, more frequent menstrual cramps, and tubal scarring. Men using condoms merely withdraw as soon as orgasm occurs due to the possibility of the condom sliding off as the erection subsides, making the act less of a pleasure for the woman.

Also See: Coitus Interruptus, Contraception, Teen Pregnancies.

BIRTH'N BABIES

Definition: The extent to which a woman of childbearing age keeps her figure and her sanity.

Population growth is a daunting global problem, for its solution lies in the individual discretion of billions of individual souls. In this era, a birth rate of 25 per 1,000 population per annum has been identified as the upper limit at which society can function without disruption.

Currently, 121 of the world's 166 nations exceed this rate. The group of African nations which have the world's highest birth rates is the same basic group which has the world's highest infant mortality rate and its lowest life expectancy. Intensive birth control counseling and education could alleviate the problem, but U.S. opposition to abortion and other family planning counseling means that this country's vast resources cannot be mobilized against the problems of excessive birth rates either here or in the rest of the world.

Conversely, it is the nations of Europe, particularly northern Europe, which have the lowest birth rate, with a continental birth rate of 13.8 births per thousand inhabitants. They are followed by the U.S.S.R. with 18.3 births per thousand and then Oceania, North America, Asia, South America and finally Africa, which has a birth rate of 45.2 births per thousand.

The Odds: The list below represents the proportions of women who give birth during one year.

TOP TEN COUNTRIES

Malawi	5.3 in 100

Niger	5.1 in 100
Rwanda	5.1 in 100
Nigeria	5.1 in 100
Benin	5.1 in 100
Tanzania	5.0 in 100
Mali	5.0 in 100
Uganda	5.0 in 100
Mauritania	5.0 in 100
Ethiopia	4.9 in 100

BOTTOM TEN COUNTRIES

Sweden	1 in 100
Germany	1.1 in 100
Switzerland	1.1 in 100
Denmark	1.1 in 100
Luxembourg	1.1 in 100
Italy	1.2 in 100
Netherlands	1.2 in 100
Norway	1.1 in 100
Hungary	1.2 in 100
Belgium	1.2 in 100

Source: World Resources 1988-89, A Report by The World Resources Institute and The International Institute for Environment and Development in collaboration with The United Nations Environment Programme, Basic Books, Inc., New York.

Also See: Motherhood, Teen Pregnancies.

BIRTHDAYS

The Big Ones!

Definition: Particular anniversaries of one's birth which mark milestones in life (i.e. a 65th birthday).

On an average day in America 673,693 individuals are having their birthday. Some 3 million birthday gifts are purchased each day. Hummm, does that mean the average birthday boy or girl gets 5 presents? More or less, it does, but statistically speaking, no one knows how many gifts are hoarded.

The Odds: Special birthdays occur in the following proportions in the population:

Turn 40	1 in 61
Turn 18	1 in 68

Become teenagers	1 in 76
Turn 65	1 in 122
Turn 100	1 in 19,229

BIRTHDAYS
Matching

Definition: The incidence of two people in any given group being born on the same date, though not necessarily in the same year.

The Odds: The odds of two people in any group having matching birthdays are surprisingly good. If you were a betting person, you could probably make some money off of these odds. In a group of twenty-four randomly selected individuals, the chances are slightly better than even that at least two of the group will have the same birthday. If forty people are brought together the odds in favor of matching birthdays are 9 to 1. Of course, if the group contains 366 or more random individuals, it is almost certain that at least two will have matching birthdays.

Matching within one day: The odds are even better if you are looking for people born within a day of each other. Gather together fourteen randomly selected people and the odds are better than even that two of them will be born within a day of each other.

Source: Encyclopedia Brittanica, What The Odds Are, New York Times, February 27, 1990.

BIRTH DEFECTS

Definition: Deformities or illnesses passed to an infant through families, occurring spontaneously or caused by problems in the passing of genetic material.

The Odds: The following disorders are among the most common or dreaded of all birth defects:

Hemophilia: Women who carry hemophilia have a 1 in 2 chance of passing it to their sons.

Duchenne's Muscular Dystrophy (DMD): The odds of being born with muscular dystrophy are approximately 3 in 10,000 for boys.

Down's Syndrome Trisomy 21 Down's syndrome, as it is most commonly referred to, occurs in 1 of 600 live births. The odds of Down's Syndrome are 100 times greater when a mother is in her mid-forties than it is when the mother is in her mid-twenties.

Source: Encyclopedia Britannica.

BIRTHS, ILLEGITIMATE
Global Rates

Definition: Bringing forth a child out of wedlock.

Less-and-less, unwed mothers carry the social stigma they once did, especially among middle class whites, where more women elect to have children without the benefit of marriage. In other regions of the world, illegitimate births are more the rule, rather than an exception. Such relaxed behavior is prevalent even in tourist meccas like Barbados and Antigua, despite the perceived conservative sexual practices of their inhabitants. Indeed, the ten leading nations in illegitimate births are all Caribbean or Central American countries.

The Odds: The following list represents the top ten countries in proportions of illegitimate births and the incidences of them among the general populations.

Guinea-Bissau	9 in 10
St. Kitts-Nevis-Anguilla	8 in 10
Sao Tome- Principe	8 in 10
Antigua	3 in 4
Montserrat	3 in 4
Barbados	7 in 10
Grenada	7 in 10
Panama	7 in 10
El Salvador	7 in 10
Dominican Repub.	2 in 3

Source: U.N. Demographic Yearbook.

Also See: Birth n' Babies, Motherhood, Teen Pregnancies.

BIRTH RATES

American Cities

Definition: A relative measure of the peace and quiet found in homes from New York to California.

In the beginning, God said go forth and multiply, but these days, most of us are doing our procreation at or near home. And from these carnal conjurings come the young folk, who in turn stick close to the hearth for many years.

The Odds: Birth rates differ enormously among women, depending on age and geographic location, however, on average, 1 in 25 women in American will give birth during a given year. Following are the odds that an average citizen of various American cities will have a child in any given year.

TOP TEN CITIES

Miami, FL	36 in 1,000
Sacramento, CA	32 in 1,000
Santa Ana, CA	31 in 1,000
Fresno, CA	27 in 1,000
Riverside, CA	25 in 1,000
Anchorage, AK	22 in 1,000
El Paso, TX	22 in 1,000
Aurora, CO	22 in 1,000
Houston, TX	22 in 1,000
Wichita, KS	22 in 1,000

BOTTOM TEN CITIES

San Francisco, CA	14 in 1,000
Pittsburgh, PA	14 in 1,000
Seattle, WA	14 in 1,000
St. Petersburg, FL	14 in 1,000
Louisville, KY	15 in 1,000
Boston, MA	15 in 1,000
Philadelphia, PA	15 in 1,000

Pittsburgh, PA	15 in 1,000
Charlotte, NC	15 in 1,000
New York, NY	15 in 1,000

Source: U.S. Census Bureau.

BIRTH CIRCUM- STANCE

Definition: Emergence from the mother's womb of a new American citizen who, with his first breath, will be some $40,000 in debt by involuntarily assuming his share of the national deficit.

The Odds: Each day, approximately 10,500 babies are born in America. What fate befalls this innocent life moments before his birth? The list below represents the occurrences of various events or circumstances which befall the average new born.

Cesarean Section	1 in 4
Unwed Mother	1 in 5
Gifted Intelligence	1 in 10
Delivery by Midwife	1 in 38
Delivery by Quack	1 in 50
Superior Intelligence	1 in 50
Retardation	1 in 50
Death before 1st Birthday	1 in 100
Birth away from Hospital	1 in 107
Muscular Dystrophy	1 in 333
Down's Syndrome	1 in 600
First Order Genius	1 in 1,000

Source: Compiled research by editors.

Also See: Birth Defects, Genius, Intelligence, Pregnancy.

BLACK POPULATION

American Cities

Definition: The relative number of citizens of African ancestry found in American cities.

Populations of black Americans are most concentrated in urban areas, especially those of the South and industrial North. Large migrations of blacks from the South to such cities as New York, Chicago and Baltimore took place at the end of the 19th and beginning of the 20th century, as these oppressed populations sought economic opportunities and greater acceptance in the North. Jobs, they found, in the booming industrial heartland; the battle for civil rights is still being fought.

The Odds: The following list represents the ratios of blacks to non-blacks in metropolitan areas with the greatest percentage of black Americans.

TOP 10 CITIES

Memphis	41 in 100
New Orleans	33 in 100
Norfolk-Newport News, VA	29 in 100
Washington, D.C.	27 in 100

New York	26 in 100
Baltimore	26 in 100
Newark, NJ	24 in 100
Chicago	23 in 100
Atlanta	23 in 100
Charlotte-Rock Hill, NC-SC	21 in 100

Source: *The Best and Worst of Everything.*

BOMBING INCIDENT

Definition: An occurrence in which an incendiary device is used to blow something or someone to smithereens.

In our violent society, shooting, stabbings, muggings and mutilations are everyday occurrences. To truly stand out, an act of mayhem must arrive with a bang. Despite the esoteric reputation of the bomb as a practical weapon of violence, the Bureau of Alcohol, Tobacco and Firearms reports thousands of bombings each year. These, then, are the most explosive states in the union, measured by annual number of bombing incidents. California may be the land of sun and surf, but it is also the state with the most incendiarists in the nation, almost 200 per year.

The Odds: The following list represents the number of bombings in one year relative to the population in the ten states with the most bombing incidents.

Colorado	1 in 93,000
Florida	1 in 126,000
Washington	1 in 128,000
California	1 in 129,900
Illinois	1 in 165,000
Virginia	1 in 176,000
Ohio	1 in 202,000
Michigan	1 in 249,000
Texas	1 in 268,000
New York	1 in 366,000

Source: U.S. Bureau of Alcohol, Tobacco and Firearms.

BOMB TARGETS

Definition: Places and circumstances in which you are a sitting duck.

One often hears of explosions in war-torn locales like Beirut and El Salvador, but we hardly think of our nation as a likely site for such explosive action. In point of fact, though, America is a highly incendiary culture, which saw more than 880 separate bombing incidents in 1989 alone.

The Odds: The list below represents the most dangerous risks and the odds that a mad bomber will blow you to kingdom-come.

Residential Properties	1 in 4
Cars	1 in 7
Homes	1 in 10
Businesses	1 in 13
Schools	1 in 15
Individuals	1 in 18
Commercial Postal	1 in 25

Entertain. Events	1 in 33
Other Vehicles	1 in 38
Other	1 in 98

Source: F.B.I. Uniform Crime Reports.

BOOK PUBLISHING

Where the Line is Drawn

Definition: The process by which a manuscript of book length is printed and distributed for consumption by readers.

For decades past, publishers would publish between 40,000 and 45,000 books each year, though millions are written. The annual quantity reached its peak in 1988, when 55,483 were published, less than the 55,446 in 1989. With the book industry in turmoil, due to the poor economic conditions of the early nineties, the number dropped to 44,218 in 1990. In 1991, it is es-timated that about 40,000 were published.

Despite its defeats in other intellectual, political and commercial arenas, the United States remains the world's most prolific publisher and consumer of printed materials. Although, as a nation, we demonstrate an enormous interest in the sometimes insubstantial field of fiction, our foremost demand is for practical tomes on sociology and economics.

The Odds: It is not known for sure how many books are written or submitted for publication. Industry estimates are that for every book written, somewhere between 1 in 50 and 1 in 100 which are actually submitted for consideration, are published annually.

The following list represents the proportions of the 10 most popular book subjects published in the U.S. by major American publishers:

Sociol./Economics	1 in 5
Fiction	1 in 7
Juvenile	1 in 8
Medicine	1 in 10
Science	1 in 11
Religion	1 in 14
Technology	1 in 12
Biography	1 in 17
Literature	1 in 17
Philos./Psychology	1 in 20

Source: Publishers Weekly.

BOXING UPSETS

Heavyweight Division

Definition: When canaries slay eagles before millions of pigeons who forfeit a week's pay to watch from ringside.

Just as shuttle flights had become routine, almost boring affairs, not even worth covering live by the networks, Tyson's title fights had become predictable early-round knockouts, hardly meriting a few paragraphs in the morning sports pages.

The Douglas/Tyson Upset: Like the flight of the *Challenger,* with its teacher-in-space theme, Tyson's bout with Buster Douglas needed some gimmick to attract any interest at all, this being the Tokyo locale. The Vegas odds-maker had given Douglas only a 45-to-1 chance to wrest the title from "Iron Mike" Tyson, known for his vicious punches and his violent character, both in and out of the ring. But when the smoke cleared in Tokyo, Tyson had tumbled from boxing's firmament with a stunning, *Challenger*-like plunge in the 10th round, and folks had to stand up and take notice. The shine was off the Tyson myth, and a new folk hero had emerged in Douglas.

Although Douglas turned out to be a one-punch wonder — after bulking up to a full-figured 246 pounds, he was easily dispatched by Evander Holyfield in his first title defense — the unlikely hero from Ohio had scored the biggest upset in boxing history.

The following list represents other top upsets, with their pre-fight odds:

Buster Douglas/ Mike Tyson	45 to 1
Muhammad Ali/ G. Foreman	10 to 1
James Braddock/ Max Baer	10 to 1
Cassius Clay/ Sonny Liston	7 to 1
Leon Spinks/ Muhammad Ali	6 to 1
Jersey Joe Walcott/ E. Charles	6 to 1
Ingemar Johansson/ F. Patterson	4 to 1
James Corbett/ John L. Sullivan	4 to 1
George Foreman/ Joe Frazier	3 to 1
Gene Tunney/ Jack Dempsey	11 to 5

Source: National Sports Review.

BRAIN TUMOR

Definition: An abnormal or diseased swelling located between the brain and the skull; especially a more or less circumscribed overgrowth of new tissue that serves no useful purpose and differs in structure from the part in which it grows.

The Odds: Only 1 in 25,000 Americans develops a brain tumor each year, therefore the odds are 24,999 to 1 against developing a brain tumor in any given year. Among the approximately 10,000 Americans who develop brain tumors each year, the odds are 4 to 1 that the tumor will be malignant, that is, cancerous. Only 1 in 5 brain tumors are benign. For patients diagnosed with malignant glioblastomas, one of the most invasive of cancerous brain tumors, the odds are 20 to 1 against surviving for even five years. On the other hand, the odds are 9 to 1 in favor of being cured of benign meningiomas, which are noncancerous tumors of the brain's outer membrane.

The Surgery Option: At one time, brain surgery was looked upon as a very dangerous activity. Today, some risk remains. However, when operated on by a competent surgeon, the odds in favor of surviving brain surgery are 33 to 1.

Source: Dajer, Tony, *Discover,* July, 1990.

BREAST CANCER

Definition: A malignant and invasive growth or tumor which tends to recur after excision and may move to other sites within the body.

The Odds: Sadly, 1 in 9 American women will contract breast cancer during her life-time, according to the American Cancer Society. To put this in real terms, more than 13 million of approximately 125 million women will find a lump in their breasts between adolescence and death.

This is an increase over the American Cancer Society's projections in the late 1980s when it reported that 1 in 10 women would contract breast cancer during her life-time. Some cast doubt on the new projection by speculating that the increase in breast cancers is merely a statistical aberration caused by more women having mammograms at an earlier age. Others contend that the rate of breast cancers has really increased. Breast cancer is not specific to women in particular age groups; however the likelihood of breast cancer does increase among women who bear no live children before the age of thirty and among older women in general.

Source: American Cancer Society.

BREAST IMPLANTS

Definition: A medical procedure undergone by some women to boost their egos and blouses at the same time.

A noted spokesman for the American Society of Plastic and Reconstructive Surgeons, Dennis Lynch, noted that nearly 2 in 3 women (who have undergone a mastectomy) would choose breast implants for cosmetic reasons. Though the procedure normally has few complications, problems do exist.

The Dangers: A California woman in her early fifties underwent implant surgery eight years after having a double mastectomy. Shortly after her operation she reported rashes, fever and pain. The cause was diagnosed as a hardening of the implant coupled by one traveling up and the other down, a horrifying sight. Eventually she had four bouts of corrective surgery. To make matters worse, cancer returned to her body and a hysterectomy became necessary. Doctors performing the operation found silicone which leaked from her implants into her uterus and ovaries. The woman presently has silicone in her liver, which cannot be removed.

The Odds: In the U.S., 1 in 65 women will elect to have a breast implant. Approximately 1 in 25 implants will cause some form of complications. Hardening of the scar tissue is the most common, usually involving an old prostheses, which accounts for 1 in 5 problems. New devices are estimated to cause problems for 1 in 20 to 1 in 25 women, most of which are not serious.

Source: Nation Center for Health Statistics survey estimate.

Also See: Medical Implants.

BUCKET DROWNINGS

Infant Deaths

Definition: A fluke, yet not uncommon accident in which a toddler drowns while exploring a pail of water.

In the past eight years some 200 children have lost their lives while innocently satisfying their understandable curiosity about a bucket filled with water, a wonderful, but dangerous play things for a small child. Most of the victims were between the ages of 8 and 12 months. A Cook County (Illinois) medical examiner estimated that 1 in 4 drownings of infants were in buckets.

The Case of Michael and His Grandmother: In a Silver Springs, Md., apartment, Michael's grandmother kept a bucket in the bathroom for years. When Michael was born, his mother would fill it with water and bleach once or twice each week to clean the 10- month-old boy's clothes. One afternoon, Michael crawled into the bathroom and over to the bucket, just to look into the intriguing looking thing by the toilet. Carelessly, the toddler knocked over a roll of toilet paper which fell into the bucket. He then crawled in the bucket to retrieve the roll.

Fifteen minutes later, his aunt and grandmother found the lifeless infant, drowned in 4 inches of water.

The Odds: A tragedy which is a long shot is perhaps the most difficult to deal with. The odds that your baby could become another Michael is approximately 120,000 to 1. About four times less likely than bucket drownings of infants is suffocation caused by infant bean bag cushions. Though the odds of such an occurrence are 475,000 to 1, between 1987 and 1991, 33 mothers had to live with the reality that it happened to their child.

Source: Knight-Ridder *Tribune News*, September 22, 1991.

BUNT, SACRIFICE

Definition: In baseball, moving a runner along one base by the batter tapping the ball weakly in the infield, normally resulting in the batter being out.

Routinely, the bunt is used in tie games, especially in late innings, or in games in which one team leads by a mere run. The idea of the bunt is to sacrifice the potential for a big inning in order to increase the chances of scoring at least one run, either to break a tie or for "insurance." A look at the numbers will tell us whether the bunt really increases the odds of scoring a run, and at what cost.

The Odds: In his article, "Investigations of Strategies in Baseball," G.R. Lindsey com-

piled statistics for several hundred games played over a two-year period. His study yielded the following situations:

MAN ON	OUTS	%
1st	0	.396
2nd	1	.390
2nd	0	.619
3rd	1	.693
1st, 2nd	0	.605
2nd, 3rd	1	.730

A look at the first line tells us that when there was a runner at first and no outs, a run scored on average 396 times out of 1,000; the average inning produced .813 runs. But, if the manager chooses to sacrifice the next hitter, he will in most cases see the situation in the second line—a runner on second with one out. And we can see by the figures that, on average, the inning will now result in a run 390 times out of 1,000. The difference being insignificant given the sample, the bunting strategy can be seen to be statistically no different from letting the hitter swing away—the odds are about the same at 4 in 10. Moreover, the manager who chooses to bunt in this situation is giving up the opportunity of a "big inning" to a dramatic degree. Over the course of 1,000 innings, the non-bunting team would on average score 141 more runs than the bunting team.

However, with no outs and a runner on second, the manager looking for just one run is advised to bunt the runner over. The odds of the run scoring from second with no outs are about 619 in 1,000, while the odds of the man scoring from third with one out increase to 693 in 1,000. However, with that sacrifice, the manager is again giving up the chance for a big inning. The average number of runs scored in the inning without the bunt is 1.194, while bunting decreases the average number of runs scored to .980.

The only case in which the manager can increase his odds both of scoring at least one run and of having a big inning is that in which he bunts runners over from first and second with no outs. That strategy increases the odds of scoring by about 12 percent; in addition, the average number of runs that score with players on 2nd and 3rd and one out is greater than with 1st and 2nd and no outs.

These considerations, of course, do not take into account a number of idiosyncrasies. Pitchers are much less likely to get a hit than are other hitters; thus it is more advisable for them to bunt. On the other hand, even in late innings with the game on the line, it is clearly better for a manager to allow his better hitters to swing away rather than have them bunt.

Source: "Statistics, Sports, and Some Other Things," Robert Hooke, in *Statistics: A Guide to the Unknown,* Holden-Day, Inc., San Francisco.

BUS ACCIDENTS

Definition: Incidents in which a long tubular passenger vehicle collides with a movable or immovable object such as a traffic cop, a highway divider or your toes.

The Odds: The safest mode of transport is bus travel. Buses average .4 deaths per billion passenger miles. Given these ratios, the odds of being killed on an average bus trip of 5 miles is 1 in 500 million. In terms of fatalities per trip, buses are about 100 times safer than automobiles.

Greyhound, America's Largest: Not long ago, the long distance bus company's accident rates were up 60 perent over the previous year. A 1990 strike had forced them to hire replacement drivers; however they have logged 113 million fewer miles in 1990 than in 1989, but have had 22 more accidents. The company's reported accident rate was 0.90 per million miles in 1990, up from 0.56 in 1989. Given these rates, the odds that you will be in an accident on one of their buses with a replacement driver is highly in favor of the passenger and you are pretty safe compared to other ways to get there!

Source: Federal Highway Administration

C c

CABLE TV

Definition: An idiot box fed by an intelligent wire.

Once upon a time, it seemed that the networks were all but invincible, and a free, clear signal was thought of as a God-given right. But progress, and commercialism, can't be stopped, and the penetration of pay cable channels has made deep inroads into traditional broadcast markets. Although cable is still looked on by many as a low-level luxury, over the next decade, a battle will be played out for supremacy of the screen.

The following list represents the odds that an average household in various cities is wired for cable.

TOP TEN CABLE CITIES

Pittsburgh	51 in 100
San Francisco-Oakland	44 in 100
Philadelphia	42 in 100
Houston	36 in 100
Atlanta	33 in 100
Cleveland-Akron	33 in 100
Miami-Fort Lauderdale	30 in 100
Tampa-St. Pete.-Sarasota	30 in 100
New York	30 in 100

Source: A.C. Nielsen.

CANCER
Annual Diagnosis

Definition: A disease, often curable, in which an abnormal cellular growth destroys healthy tissues.

Cancer is one of the most feared diseases which affect mankind, though, if diagnosed early, it is frequently curable, despite the fact that it is the number two leading cause of death behind heart disease.

For women, the most prevalent cancers are of the breast, cervix, colon, corpus uterus, lung and ovary. Men suffer most from cancers of the lung, stomach, colon, mouth, prostate, esophagus and liver. Breast cancer is not un-

52

known in men; several hundred American males are stricken each year.

The Odds: Though 1 in 5 people in the U.S. will die of cancer, those who prefer to worry about it years before it happens may take a pause. Odds are high that in the next 12 months the average person is safe. The following list represents the most common types of malignant cancer found throughout the world and the approximate odds that an individual will diagnosed with it in one year:

Stomach	1 in 7,600
Lung	1 in 7,500
Breast	1 in 8,700
Colon/Rectum	1 in 8,700
Cervix	1 in 10,700
Mouth/Pharynx	1 in 13,200
Esophagus	1 in 16,100
Liver	1 in 20,000
Lymphoma	1 in 20,200
Prostrate	1 in 21,300
Bladder	1 in 22,800

With the immediate odds of being diagnosed with cancer so high, an additional reprieve should be known. In the U.S., 4 in 10 patients diagnosed with cancer will survive at least another five years.

Source: Environmental Data Report, United Nations Environment Programme, 1989.

CANDIDATE DUMPING

Definition: A state of mind of a voter who decides not to cast his vote for a particular candidate because the aspirant has been caught with his pants down or his hand in someone else's pockets. *The Odds:* 3 to 1 if it is found out the candidate has accepted funds from special interest groups pressuring him to vote a certain way. Slightly less than 2 to 1 if it is found he once failed to pay his income taxes. 13 to 7 if it is found he or she had a drinking problem. 9 in 20 if it was revealed that he or she was a homosexual and slightly more than 1 in 3 would dump their candidate if it were revealed he had had an extramarital affair. Did Gary Hart make a mistake? After Gary Hart was photographed with Donna Rice on his lap, he withdrew from the 1984 Democratic race. With only 1 in 3 voters likely to vote against him for such a lapse, he could have stayed in the race and may very well have won despite his amorous adventures.

Source: Future Vision, The 189 Most Important Trends of the 1990s, Sourcebooks Trade, 1991.

CAR CRASH FATALITIES

By Makes and Models

Definition: The relative safety of your life while driving automobiles of various manufactures.

Muscle cars are an unmatched driving experience for exhilaration – and death. They are owned predominantly by young males – the most accident prone of all drivers. Also among the top ten are a number of models with less muscle but also less size – sub-compacts like the Chevy Chevette and Sprint and the Honda Civic. Airbags, as they become increasingly available, might have a dramatic effect on the death rates in either muscle cars or sub-compacts.

The Odds: Slightly more than 1 in 125 Americans will meet St. Peter in a car-related accident. If you are a passenger or driver in a high-performance small car, the odds are double what they are in an average car and four times greater than in a larger 4-door model. It is fair to say that the make-up of the driver is the key factor in car model fatality rates, rather than the car itself.

The following list represents the odds of being killed in the makes and models with the highest and lowest fatality rates per car:

MOST FATALITIES

Chevrolet Corvette	1 in 1,923
Chevrolet Camaro	1 in 2,041
Dodge Charger/ Shelby	1 in 2,222
Ford Mustang	1 in 2,273
Nissan 300ZX	1 in 2,381
Chevrolet Chevette 4-door	1 in 2,439
Chevrolet Sprint 2-door	1 in 2,439
Honda Civic CRX	1 in 2,564
Pontiac Firebird	1 in 2,632
Plymouth Turismo	1 in 2,778
Pontiac Fiero	1 in 2,778

FEWEST FATALITIES

Audi 5000 4-door	1 in 9,091
Cadillac Fleetwood DeVille 4-door	1 in 9,091
Cadillac Fleetwood DeVille 2-door	1 in 9,091
Chevrolet Cavalier Station Wagon	1 in 9,091
Olds Cutlass Ciera Station Wagon	1 in 9,091
Toyota Cressida 4-door	1 in 9,091
Volkswagen Jetta 4-door	1 in 9,091
Lincoln Town Car	1 in 12,500
Ford Taurus Station Wagon	1 in 14,286
Volvo 740/760 4-door	1 in 16,667

While it may seem that the previous lists indicate lower than average odds of dying in an automobile related accident (1 in 125) even for the cars with the most fatalities, several factors need to be taken into account. The average car has a 5 year life, yet the average American has an average life of some 70 years. Hence, over a lifetime, the odds of being killed in the cars with the most fatalities are about 4 times greater than in an car with average fatality rates. This translates to the fact that those who ride in almost exclusively small, high performance cars are facing approximately 1 in 30-35 odds of dying in a car crash. Those who ride only occasionally in dangerous cars face average odds of being killed in crash.

Source: Insurance Institute for Highway Safety.

Also See: Accidents.

CARROTS AND HEART DISEASE

Definition: The former, Bugs Bunny's favorite dinner; the latter, a medical condition, often fatal for millions.

Heart Disease is not funny business, but some of the funniest characters of cartoonland may be the least at risk from suffering from it. Carrots and Spinach, Popeye's delight, can prevent many ailments and fatalities caused by heart disease.

The Odds: Daily intake of fruits and vegetables high in beta carotene — namely, carrots, spinach and apricots — are thought to reduce the odds of suffering debilitating effects of cardiovascular ailments including heart attacks and strokes. Vitamin E, too, which is found in many fruits and vegetables, is suspected to lower risks.

A 1991 study of 87,245 women pointed to the finding that those who took in carotene and vitamin E had 30 percent fewer strokes and had 22 percent fewer heart attacks. Women whose intake exceeded 100 milligrams of vitamin E daily had 36 percent fewer heart attacks than women who took in less than 30 milligrams.

The study is considered evidence that carotene and vitamin E

prevents cholesterol from oxidizing and clogging or blocking arteries. Strokes and heart attacks are caused by reduced or sudden blockages of the blood to the heart and brain.

Source: Nurses Health Study of 87,245 women.

Also See: Heart Disease, Heart Attack.

CHILD ABUSE

Definition: The mistreatment of a boy or girl in a way which is physically or emotionally damaging.

Each year more cases are reported of child abuse. In the U.S., 2.5 million children are abused, physically, sexually or otherwise, an increase of 22 percent since since 1985. Since 1986, an annual average of almost 1,200 children die in neglect or abuse-related incidents.

Perhaps due to so many celebrities admitting to being abused as children, the issue is now frequently in the media and part of the U.S. social consciousness. Oprah Winfrey and Rosanne Barr are two of the most vocal spokespersons. Winfrey has paid former Illinois governor James Thompson, now an attorney in private practice, to draw up a bill and to lobby in Washington for passage.

The Odds: In the U.S. 1 in 100 children will be criminally abused or neglected. Approximately 1 in 2,000 of them will die as a result. Death rates are growing at an alarming rate. The following list represents abuse and neglect related fatalities of children in various years:

1985	878
1986	1,075
1987	1,142
1988	1,181
1989	1,203
1990	1,211

Child psychologists are reporting that things parents say to their children can cause damage as much as sexual and physical abuse. Parents represent the ideal for many children and those who are put down severely by these ultimate authority figures can suffer deep emotional scars.

ANNUAL FATALITIES IN U.S.

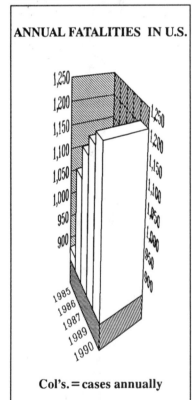

Col's. = cases annually

The following list represents the proportions in the U.S. of various types of child abuse:

Neglect	1 in 2
Physical	1 in 4
Sexual	1 in 7
Emotional	1 in 11
Other	1 in 25

Source: National Committee to Prevent Child Abuse, Senator Joseph Biden's office.

CHILD MISCHIEF

Definition: The shenanigans, mishaps, misfortunes and misdeeds of the future leaders of America.

There are about 50 million Americans under the age of 13 who light firecrackers, pull up little girls' dresses, smear Mommy's make-up all over the bed and otherwise misbehave in socially unacceptable ways. One can only wonder how they get away with so much, given the restraints adults put on their activities. Some 31 million are in school, 3 million are in day-care centers and the remainder are being watched, for the most part, by their mothers. Teachers and moms must be lousy policemen. Consider the gamut of activities these, the most closely watched of all, get into.

The Odds: Chances that the following will occur in an average year are as follows:

Spanking in School	1 in 15
Reported Missing	1 in 29
Run Aways (any kind)	1 in 50
Abductions	1 in 73
Run Aways (with illegal acts)	1 in 267
Run Aways (with prostitution)	1 in 467

Source: *On an Average Day*, Tom Heymann.

CHILDREN IN JAIL

Definition: Kids in the slammer.

Each year nearly 2 million individuals under age 18 are arrested. Generally, these childhood brushes with the law are fleeting, although they may not appear so at the time. Too often in our fragmented society, however, adolescent pranksterism proves to be a dark portent of twisted, pathological deeds in our "children's" future. Kids are turning to crime at a much earlier age and at a most alarming rate in many states of the Union.

The Odds: In one year approximately 1 in 35 Americans under the age of 18 will be arrested. An alarming 1 in 6 arrests involve juveniles.

The following list represents the proportions of the juveniles in prisons or jails in the ten states with the highest ratios:

District of Col.	1 in 101
California	1 in 154
Nevada	1 in 158
Alaska	1 in 164
Kansas	1 in 1,767
South Dakota	1 in 1,796
Nebraska	1 in 1,802
Pennsylvania	1 in 2,283
Oregon	1 in 2,370

Source: U.S. Department of Justice.

Also See: Juvenile Delinquency.

CHILD LABOR

Definition: The practice of making children part of the labor force.

The U.S. and most Western developed nations banned child labor in the early days of the labor movement. In many developing countries, however, children are still hard at work. A nation that sends a child to do an adult's work is certainly underdeveloped, in the deepest sense of that word. Yet, no matter how we decry the participation of unformed juveniles in the workforce, that participation is an indisputable reality in the vast majority of world nations.

The Odds: In troubled, impoverished sections of Asia, nearly 1 in 3 all workers are under the age of 15. The following list represents the odds that an average child will have to go to work:

TOP TEN COUNTRIES

Bhutan	42 in 100
Mali	42 in 100
Rwanda	42 in 100
Upper Volta	40 in 100
Nepal	37 in 100
Central African Republic	37 in 100

Madagascar	37 in 100
Botswana	34 in 100
Ivory Coast	34 in 100
Burundi	31 in 100

Source: U.N. Committee on Children.

CHILDLESS-NESS

Definition: The condition of having perpetual piece, quiet and ample savings.

Childlessness often refers to older women and their partners, who through inability, circumstance or choice have reached the end of their child bearing years without any live offspring.

The Odds: Among adults born during the baby boom, the odds are 4 to 1 against reaching old age without parenting any children. Despite the fact that only 1 in 100 individuals regard childlessness as the ideal condition, about 20 percent will go through life without becoming parents. This means the odds are better than 1 in 5 that you will not have children, even if you want them! Why? The high rate of divorce means that couples are often not together long enough to procreate. Some couples are sterile and others bow to financial considerations. The odds are 32 to 1 that men and women want more than one child yet the odds

are 1 in 4 that they will stop after their first offspring.

Source: Russel, Cheryl, *100 Predictions For The Baby Boom*, Plenum Press, New York.

Also See: Condoms; Infertility.

CHILD SUPPORT
Bringing up Baby

Definition: A monthly payment a divorced or estranged parent, usually the father, is required to submit to the parent with custody of the child.

Child support is a fact of life in America where 2 in 5 marriages end in divorce. The problem is further aggravated by the fact that many unwed fathers are required to pay support. The average payment in 1990 was as follows for the following groups of recipients.

Overall	$2,995
Divorced or Separated	$3,268
Never Married	$1,888
White Mothers	$3,132
Black Mothers	$2,263
Hispanic Mothers	$2,965

The Odds: There is a 1 in 2 chance that the average man who is required to pay child support will deliver less than required by a court ruling. Some 1 in 4 pay nothing at all. A head of a public welfare association speculated that in most cases the shortfall or lack of payments is caused by the man's inability to pay.

Men are more likely to pay if they have been granted visitation rights. Fathers were also more likely to pay if they live in the same state as the mother. Among mothers who were never married to the father, 6 in 10 were classified as poor in 1989 when the official poverty line for a mother of 2 was designated as an income of $9,885 or below.

The following list represents the ratios paid under various circumstances:

OVERALL PAYMENTS

Pay as ordered	1 in 2
Pay less than ordered	1 in 2
Pay nothing	1 in 4

JOINT CUSTODY SETTLEMENTS

Paid	4 in 5

VISITATION RIGHTS SETTLEMENTS

Paid	9 in 10

Source: The Chicago Tribune, October 11, 1991.

Also See: Divorce.

CITY SLICKERS

Around the World

Definition: The masses of humanity with dirt in their lungs, rather on their shoes.

Progress is a two-edged sword. On the blunt edge, expansion, development and growth prolong and enhance living. On the sharp side, though, they destroy natural beauty, disrupt the built-in harmonies of human existence and foster poverty, claustrophobia and violence.

The Odds: In the United States, 77 in 100 people make their home in urban centers. In hamlet nations like Monaco, every last man makes his stand in the houses of progress. The following list represents the odds that the average citizens of the most urbanized nations will live in the city rather the country:

Monaco	100%
Singapore	100%
Malta	94 in 100
United Kingdom	91 in 100
Hong Kong	90 in 100
Australia	89 in 100
Israel	89 in 100
Kuwait	88 in 100
Sweden	87 in 100
West Germany	85 in 100

Source: U.N. Demographic Handbook.

Also See: Country Bumpkins.

CLERGY-WOMEN

Definition: A female who is officially ordained as a spiritual leader of a church, synagogue or any congregation of worshipers.

Of the three major Western religions, only Catholicism does not permit women in the clergy. Judaism, only as recently as the 1980s, allowed women in the Reform Rabbinate. Protestants have the best record as far as equal opportunity employment in the clergy. Some 20,000 protestant ministers are ordained in the U.S. and Canada where 1 in 12 ministers are women.

Source: Yearbook of American and Canadian Churches.

COCAINE EMERGENCIES

City Rates

Definition: The relative measurements of visits to emergency rooms for cocaine-related incidents.

For many years, cocaine was popularly regarded as a sophisticated, even luxurious recreational drug. In this decade, we have recognized the ugliness and enormity of the threat posed by this substance. Now it remains for us to reverse the stranglehold powdered and crystallized ("crack") cocaine have taken on the nation's health and pockets. Cocaine ravages not just its addicts, but the communities that must support them.

The following list gives the cities with the worst cocaine epidemics in the country, as measured by the number of hospital emergency room visits in the population in which cocaine was a contributing factor in the victim's debility.

TOP TEN COCAINE CITIES

New York	1 in 1,300
Philadelphia	1 in 3,600
Washington, D.C	1 in 137
Chicago	1 in 720
Detroit	1 in 259
New Orleans	1 in 171
Los Angeles	1 in 1,123
Atlanta	1 in 256
Baltimore	1 in 488
Boston	1 in 428

Source: "Overview of Selected Drug Trends," NIDA Drug Abuse Warning Network.

COCAINE SMUGGLING

Definition: Importing nose candy into the United States, by undercover means.

The Odds: So you want to be a big drug trafficker? Unfortunately, the odds of getting away with it are on your side. If you're willing to make the big investment into cargo planes, high-speed boats, and couriers, chances are your investment will pay off big. According to the U.S. Coast Guard, American law enforcement agencies succeed in stopping only about 5 to 7 percent of all cocaine shipments entering the U.S. from abroad. That makes the odds about 16 to 1 in favor of the bad guys in the endless war between narco-traffickers and the forces arrayed against them.

The main problem, according to the men enlisted to combat cocaine smuggling, is lack of adequate means to detect drug boats and planes. The Coast Guard, for instance, relies heavily on radar detection to locate suspected shipments, but can call on only two E-2C radar planes for the entire Gulf Coast. In addition to the wide range of sea and coast that each plane must protect, the planes combine for an average of only 2,000 hours a year, meaning that more than three-quarters of the time, the U.S. has no radar planes aloft specifically to track suspected drug shipments. The Coast Guard can also call on nine tracking planes, six helicopters and four radar balloons in the Gulf and Caribbean region, but these resources are simply outmatched by the flood of illicit drugs coming from Mexico and South America. The Coast Guard seized only about 12,000 pounds of cocaine a year, a small proportion of the total that washes up on these shores, or drops from the sky. When the British were about to invade Massachusetts, Paul Revere waited for the signal in the Old North Church, "one if by land, two if by sea." These days, the new invaders are using both routes to deliver their deadly cargo.

Source: U.S. Coast Guard; *New York Times.*

COHABITATION

Definition: Shacking up.

There was a time when women of social graces would never admit to living with their boyfriends. Men who would make similar admissions might loose their lease or even their job. Today, no one blinks an eye. Cohabitation is no longer an admission, it is almost an official status, as significant socially as family status or marital status. Social researchers maintain that cohabitation is so common now that it might offset the declining marriage rates of the 1990s.

The Odds: In the late 1960s and early 1970s, 1 in 11 adults lived together before their first marriage. Today 9 in 20 adults (almost half) cohabitate before their first marriage. Adults under the age of 30 are twice as likely to cohabitiate as those over 30.

The trend among young adults is profound in America. The younger a woman is, the more likely she is to live with her male lover before marriage. This option clearly rivals marriage as a living arrangement. The incidence of a woman who was born in the 1940s marrying before age 25 was 8 in 10. The incidence of cohabitation among this group of women was a rare 1 in 33. The rate of marriage for women born in the 1960s, is only 6 in 10. More than 1 in 3 of these younger women cohabitate before marriage.

Source: American Demographics.

Also See: Marriage.

COITUS INTERRUPTUS

Definition: Withdrawal before orgasm in lovemaking, the oldest method of birth control and one of the least effective, as it relies on self-control on the part of the man at a time when he is least able to do so.

The Odds: Doctors at Columbia Hospital in New York City in their *Complete Home Medical Guide* call coitus interruptus a "highly unreliable" method of birth control. *The Merck Manual,* the doctor's bible, says that the method used over a long period of time can lead to psycho-sexual difficulties for both partners. The fact is, however, that coitus interruptus is always available to any couple under any circumstances, is free, and can be used without a doctor laying a hand on either party. So what are the odds against using this method to prevent pregnancy? One in 5, says Better Homes and Gardens' *Woman's Health and Medical Guide,* and not only because the man might not withdraw, but because the woman might not allow him to, plus the fact that some ejaculatory fluid may escape into the vagina during foreplay and before ejaculation. Further, it is a psychological strain for both partners as the woman wonders, "Has he come yet?" and the man wonders exactly when he should withdraw.

Also See: Birth Control Effectiveness, Condom Failures, Contraceptive Methods.

COLLEGE ADMISSION

Definition: The process of being accepted to an accredited institution of higher learning.

The Odds: Admission ratios may surprise you. They are published in guides such as *The Right College.* At Harvard 1 in 7 applicants are accepted, but only 1 in 15 applicants are accepted at Stetson University in Florida. The University of California at Berkeley is less competitive than Harvey Mudd College in the same state. Your chances of admission are better at some extremely highly-regarded schools that aren't as well known among the general populace as the Ivy League schools. For instance, among top-tier colleges, Dartmouth accepts only 1 in 9 applicants; the University of Chicago accepts almost 1 out of 2 applicants (45 percent).

The following list represents the "most competitive" universities and the proportions of applicants who get accepted to them:

Naval Academy	1 in 8
Harvard	1 in 7
Stanford	1 in 7
Yale	1 in 6
Georgetown	1 in 5
Duke	1 in 5
Columbia	3 in 10
Univ. of Virginia	2 in 10
Notre Dame	4 in 10
U. of Michigan	9 in 20

Improving the Odds: Legacies have an improved chance. The child of an alumnus may be twice as likely to be accepted as a comparable applicant without a "legacy connection," so consider your parents' schools.

Source: The Right College.

COLLEGE, MINORITIES

Definition: The enrollment of Blacks and Hispanics at institutions of higher learning.

Minority Americans have made substantial educational strides through the good offices of such organizations as the United Negro College Fund and through minority scholarship and assistance programs offered by federal and state governments. Whether such assistance will be permitted to continue, however, is in question, as the Bush administration challenges such assistance as discriminatory.

The Odds: Slightly more than 1 in 3 Americans attend college (37 percent). Slightly less than 1 in 5 Americans graduate. Among blacks, 1 in 4 attend college, and 1 in 10 graduate. Among Hispanics 1 in 5 attend, and 1 in 12 graduate. Some cities have an disproportionately high enrollment of minorities. The following list represents the proportions of minority enrollment in the ten cities with the highest ratios:

D.C.	19 in 20
Hawaii	7 in 10
California	1 in 3
Mississippi	1 in 3
New Mexico	3 in 10
New York	3 in 10
Louisiana	1 in 4
Maryland	1 in 4
Texas	1 in 4
New Jersey	1 in 5

Source: U.S. Dept. of Education.

COLLEGE ADMISSION

Minorities

Definition: The successful act of a minority kid convincing the Dean of Admissions that he will not drink, party, or goof around like the rest of the more affluent white students on campus.

Women now earn more college degrees than men. As early as 1975, they were earning three-quarters as many college degrees as men. Despite the improved odds that a college education brings, minorities have not achieved the same success ratios due to discrimination in the workplace which favors promoting men over women.

The Odds: One's ethnic background is certainly a factor. Many schools have voluntary affirmative action admissions policies and consciously recruit minority applicants. The odds at Brown University, for example, are 1 in 3, if you are a black applicant, compared with only 1 in 5 if you are a white applicant. Schools also often have special scholarships for ethnic groups, usually funded by an alumnus of the same heritage.

Improving the Odds: State-supported schools are almost a cinch to get into. A fine school like Purdue University in West Lafayette, Indiana accepts 84% of those applying, black and white. On the other hand, many schools regard geographic diversity among their student body as an enhancement to the collegiate experience. Hence, consider applying to institutions in a part of the country somewhat distant from your high school.

Consider choosing a good high school. Yes, there is a choice. It is often possible to switch your public school district; call them for their individual policies or consult *Public Schools USA* (Williamson Publishing, $17.95). The quality of one's high school itself plays a large role in college admissions. Private schools like Andover or Exeter obviously contribute to one's impression, but even public schools are appraised by admissions offices; and public schools have "reputations" just like the posh academies. A good school provides the opportunity for ambitious students to take Advanced Placement and other higher-level courses, which admissions officers weigh more heavily when reviewing an applicant's credentials. Also, there are some private schools that do not release class rank, which must be considered an advantage for three-quarters of their students.

Admissions committees love joiners. Most high school clubs and community organizations and a surprising number of career-field organizations with impressive names have no prerequisites to join. In fact, it is amazing that some of the most highly-regarded professional associations will accept members only on the basis of good character, interest in the profession or sometimes just the ability to write out a check for a $50 membership fee.

Source: Original research by editors.

CONDOM FAILURE

Definition: The frightful discovery that the blessed thing didn't work.

You hate 'em, but you use 'em. In the old days, the purchasing of a condom was a male right of passage. Remember the dreaded first trip to Mr. Jones's drugstore? You leafed through a bunch of magazines, feigned interest in various pharmaceutical products, fondled the shaving cream and the rock candy. Then, your nerve up, you approached the counter and made the dreaded request, your casual demeanor belying the sweaty palms and palpitating heart, from your fear that this gentle drugstore owner, who used to serve you malts at the counter when your legs didn't even reach the floor, would think you a sex fiend. Then again, maybe you just stole your rubbers from your older brother.

Those innocent days are gone. Now, in the age of AIDS and of teen pregnancy, condoms have come out of hiding. No longer are they behind the counter at most drugstores; rather, they sit on the shelf with the other respectable products. A number of schools are even distributing condoms to high school students to promote their use.

The Odds—Pregnancy: Condoms have been proven to be an effective contraceptive device when used properly, especially in conjunction with a spermicide. In addition, they are perhaps the most convenient contraceptive to use—no prescriptions, no trips to the gynecologist, no parental knowledge. But despite this convenience, the major fear among users is that the condom is unreliable. Just how safe is a condom for preventing pregnancy and the transmission of disease?

Condom effectiveness is determined by two factors—the user and the products. Pregnancy prevention rates for condoms vary depending on the user—studies show that average pregnancy rates for condom users are about 10 to 15 per 100 women in a year of use. Some smaller studies with select groups of women have yielded pregnancy rates as low as 0.4 per 100. Larger samplings must take into account couples who use condoms inconsistently or incorrectly. One large U.S. study of unmarried white women aged 20 to 24 resulted in 23 pregnancies per 100 women in the first year of use, while married white women age 25 to 34 had only 11 per 100.

The Odds—Disease: In addition to protection against pregnancy, condoms also help prevent the transmission of disease. Condom awareness increased with the herpes scare of the 1970s, and has grown even greater with the coming of the AIDS epidemic. Condoms prevent the transmission of disease by means of their impermeability—even the smallest sexually-transmitted disease, the 0.1-micron HIV virus, cannot pass through a latex condom. Although disease prevention is harder to track than pregnancy, a World Health Organization study estimates that condoms reduce the risk of developing gonorrhea, trichomoniasis and chlamydia by 33%; the same study found that condom use halves the risk of HIV transmission. In addition, protection from the former leads to protection from the latter, since people with STDs (sexually transmitted diseases) that cause genital ulcers are anywhere from two to seven times more likely to become infected with the HIV virus.

The Odds—Breakage: The greatest fear among condom users is breakage. Just what are the odds that your protection will rupture? Once again, studies offer varied results, ranging from 1 in 100 to 1 in 8 for vaginal intercourse. Condom breakage can often be attributed to inexperience, insufficient or incorrect lubrication, or simple age of the condom. Breakage from manufacturer's defects is much less common. The International Organization of Standards (ISO) has established standards for condoms for resistance to breakage (using tensile and air-burst tests), as well as for holes and leakage. In a tested batch of 200 condoms, defects are not permitted over 3.5% for weakness, 1% for water leakage, and 8% for incorrect dimensions. Thus your odds of getting a condom that cannot pass the weakness test are at most 1 in 28; for leakage, the odds are 1 in 100. Most condoms sold on the market meet or exceed these standards.

Even if your condom does break, though, pregnancy or infection is not necessarily inevitable. One U.S. study reported 430 condom breaks resulting in 19 pregnancies, for pregnancy odds on a broken condom of 1 in 23.

Source: "Condoms—Now More than Ever," *Population Reports*, Population Information Program, Johns Hopkins University, September, 1990.

Also See: Birth Control; Condom Usage Around the World.

CONDOMS
Usage Around the World

Definition: A helmet on your soldier in the war on venereal diseases and unwanted pregnancies.

Armor, sheath, mackee, rubber, pigskin, prophylactic—its names have changed over the years, but the same trustworthy condom has been around since English authors discussed being "sheathed" while having intercourse with London prostitutes during the late 18th century. Modern authors from Nabakov to Philip Roth have made the "mackee" the subject of both comic and serious discourse. In view of the AIDS crisis and the protection condoms provide against disease, worldwide condom use is again on the upswing.

The Odds: The following list represents usage for married couples only. Dates of information gathering vary according to country.

TOP USERS BY NATION

Japan	9 in 20
Finland	1 in 3
Denmark	1 in 4
Sweden	1 in 4
Singapore	1 in 4
Costa Rica	1 in 5
United Kingdom	1 in 4
Norway	1 in 6
Trinidad/Tobago	1 in 7
Poland	1 in 7
Czechoslovakia	1 in 8
Hong Kong	1 in 8
Mauritius	1 in 9

Source: World Resources 1988-89, A Report by The World Resources Institute and The International Institute for Environment and Development in collaboration with The United Nations.

Also See: AIDS, Birth Control, Condom Failures.

CONGRESS ATTENDANCE

Definition: How an elected official goes to his job and doesn't do a lick of work.

"I slept late!" is a favorite excuse for not going to work. What's yours? If you are a Congressperson, odds are you will officially list the reason as "prior engagement."

The Odds: Given their poor attendance history, the odds are as follows that these Congressmen will be present at a session of Congress.

James Florio, NJ	1 in 5
Jim Courter, NJ	1 in 4
Robert Garcia, NY	1 in 2
Cardiss Collins, IL	1 in 2
Guy Molinari, NY	2 in 3
John Conyers, MI	2 in 3
Henry Hyde, IL	7 in 10
Gus Yatron, PA	7 in 10
John Bryant, TX	7 in 10
Jack Brooks, TX	7 in 10

To be fair, Hyde, Collins, Yatron and Brooks all owed at least some of their absences to illnesses or deaths in the family. Similarly, both Florio and Garcia switched jobs in the middle of their terms. Florio was elected governor of New Jersey and Molinari took the job of Staten Island Borough President. Finally, poor Robert Garcia of New York owed at least some of his absences to his trial and conviction on charges of extortion and conspiracy.

A few Congressmen never miss a session. Gold stars for perfect attendance go to the following: Charles Bennet (Florida), Larry Combest (Texas), Dale Kildee (Michigan), Sander Levin (Michigan), Tom McMillen (Maryland), William Natch (Kentucky), Timothy Penny (Minnesota), Thomas Petri (Wisconsin), Christopher Shays (Connecticut), Gene Taylor (Mississippi), James Traficant (Ohio), Harold Volkmer (Missouri).

Source: Congressional Quarterly 1990 Almanac.

CONTRACEPTIVE METHODS
Most Popular

Definition: A sexually oriented practice which allows heterosexual couples to have more fun than babies.

In this age of hysteria over the AIDS epidemic, more couples are using contraception, which by definition, is a technique aimed at avoiding pregnancy, rather than prevention of disease. Some methods of contraception, however, decrease the chances of spreading venereal diseases. Sterilization, the most common method of contraception is not one of them, since it does not prevent the exchange of body fluids, but it does mean the end of the ability to procreate.

The Odds: Nearly 1 in 3 American couples practice some form of contraception. Near 4 in 10 use some form of sterilization and among them, 7 in 10 opt for female sterilization and 3 in 10 rely on vasectomies. This figure can be attributed in some part to the aging of the female population. In the period from 1982 to 1988, the number of women aged 15 to 24 dropped by 1.5 million and the number aged 25 to 44, those more likely to opt for non-reversible birth control methods, rose by nearly 5.4 million. The decline of IUD use also contributes to the higher number of women relying on sterilization.

Use of the pill, which had declined in the late 1970s for health concerns, has also become more popular, due to its high rate of effectiveness and convenience. Condom use has increased rapidly among teenagers and single women, but the pill remains the method of choice for the younger set.

The following list represents the most common forms of contraception and the proportions of Americans who practice them:

Sterilization	1 in 4
Pill	1 in 3
Condom	1 in 7
Diaphragm	1 in 18
Abstinence	1 in 43
Withdrawal	1 in 45
Other	1 in 48
IUD	1 in 50

Foam   1 in 91

Source: "Contraceptive Practices in the United States", 1982-1988," *Family Planning Perspectives*, September/October 1990.

Also See: Birth Control, Effectiveness; Coitus Interruptus; Rhythm System.

COSMETIC SURGERY

Definition: The rebuilding of face or body by the miracle of the surgeon's knife. A series of procedures tempered only by your ability to suffer discomfort and pay bills which can often be bigger than your old nose.

Being ugly is an affliction which has no social or economic boundaries. Though movies stars and the rich do it frequently, cosmetic or "plastic" surgery is, no doubt, needed by millions more with floppy ears, banana noses, ham-fat thighs and beer barrel butts.

The Odds: Because cosmetic surgery is "elective," the chance you will experience it depends on your ability to withstand the procedures and pay for them. Below are the proportions of average Americans who undergo various types of cosmetic surgery:

Aesthetic Surgery (any kind)	1 in 6
Hair Transplant (men)	1 in 547
Face Lift (all genders)	1 in 50
Face Lift (women)	1 in 29
Face Lift (men)	1 in 245
Nose Job (all genders)	1 in 37
Nose Job (women)	1 in 31
Nose Job (men)	1 in 78
Breast Lift (women)	1 in 101
Breast Augmentation (women)	1 in 19

Source: American Association of Plastic and Reconstructive Surgeons.

COUNTRY BUMPKINS
Around the World

Definition: A hayseed who sits around chew'n the rag in an indistinguishable language.

The world's most rural countries are secluded places where Western influences seldom reach. The lives of their people are insular and completely disconnected from much of the world. Most are farmers or nomadic shepherd peoples. In Bhutan, which is a tiny country at the foot of the Himalayas, barely 53,000 of the one-million inhabitants live in towns or cities. The numbers are scarcely different in any of the African nations near the top of the list. In Kampuchea (Cambodia) in South East Asia, the Khmer Rouge brutally forced many city dwellers into the countryside, systematically killing millions in the process.

The Odds: The following list represents the proportions of the population who live down on the farm or in remote areas.

Bhutan	94.7 in 100
Cape Verde	94.3 in 100
Burundi	92.7 in 100
Rwanda	92.3 in 100
Burkina Faso	91.0 in 100
Nepal	91.4 in 100
Oman	89.4 in 100
Solomon Islands	89.4 in 100
Kampuchea	
(Cambodia)	88.4 in 100
Ethiopia	87.1 in 100

Source: The United Nations.

CRAPS

Definition: Game of chance involving two dice, a table, and a lot of disposable income.

Except for blackjack, in which players who know the optimal strategy actually have a slight advantage over the house, craps is the game the novice gambler should turn to in a casino for the best odds. In craps, the player rolls two dice. Seven or 11 on the first roll wins; a 2, 3 or 12 on the first roll loses whatever the bet is. If the player hits any of the other possibilities, he rolls again until he either hits his first number ("makes his point" and wins the bet) or rolls a 7 ("craps out" and loses). Winning by either hitting 7 or 11 on the first roll or making the point is called "passing."

The Odds: It's fairly easy to figure the odds in craps, since the odds on dice are easily determined. The odds of "passing" are a combination of the odds of hitting 7 or 11 and the odds of making a point. Below are the various odds for dice throws and for making the point.

ODDS ON A DICE THROW

2 or 12	1 in 36
3 or 11	1 in 18
4	1 in 12
10	1 in 3
5	1 in 9
9	2 in 5
6	5 in 36
8	5 in 11
7	1 in 6

The odds on passing are the sum of the probabilities of all of the possible ways of passing: that is, the odds on hitting 7 or 11, the odds on throwing 4 or 10 and making the point, throwing 5 or 9 and making the point, and throwing 6 or 8 and making the point.

THE ODDS ON PASSING ARE AS FOLLOWS:

7 or 11: 2 in 9

If you don't roll 7 or 11 on the first throw, the probability of making your point is 244/495 or about 49.3%. The odds against the pass are 251 to 244, giving the house an advantage of $7 on every $495 played.

Breaking the Bank at the Desert Inn: One day in June, 1950, a man walked up to a craps table at the Desert Inn in Las Vegas and proceeded to make 28 passes in a row, in an incredible roll lasting nearly one and a half hours. Side bettors at the table cheered on the anonymous roller at every turn. As the run of luck continued, people began to be drawn to the table; by the end, they were packed four deep, with those in the back offering up to $500 for a spot in the front row, and a chance to bet. Among the gamblers was Zeppo Marx, who pulled in $28,000; the owner of a competing casino, Gus Greenbaum, raked in $48,000; another professional gambler won $9,000. The house lost a reported $150,000. The anonymous roller, a conservative gambler, took home only $750.

According to our calculations above, the odds on 28 straight passes are 244/495 raised to the 28th power, or a little less than 40 million to 1.

Source: John D. McGervey, *Probabilities in Everyday Life*, Ivy Books, New York; Warren Weaver, *Lady Luck: The Theory of Probability*, Anchor Books, New York.

CREDIT RATINGS

Definition: A classification of credit risk based on a person's financial resources, payment patterns, and history of meeting prior financial obligations; usually provided to businesses by commercial credit ratings bureaus.

The Odds: You are one of the 185 million adults in the U.S. whose name is listed with one of the three major credit bureaus in the country. You would like to change your Visa or Mastercard account from a bank that charges you 21 percent interest to one that will charge you only 18 percent, so you fill out an application to the new bank and mail it in. Eventually you get back a letter from the bank rejecting your application for reasons stated, followed by a long list of reasons with boxes for check marks. Your check mark says "income not verifiable." Is this possible, you say, thinking of your annual salary of $25,000 for driving a bus?

Sad to say, it is possible, and it happens all the time, according to surveys on the accuracy of credit bureau reports. You thereupon become 1 in 12,800 annually who ask a credit bureau for a copy of their report — and, if you are lucky, one of the 1 in 120 who will get a correction. Overall, what are the odds on you having inaccuracies in your credit bureau file? According to one study, taken by Consolidated Information Bureau of New York City, those odds are 4 in 10, a figure naturally disputed by the credit bureaus, who themselves cannot provide figures to dispute this study.

Source: Consumer Reports, May 1991.

CRIME CAPITALS

Most Dangerous Cities

Definition: Places where you had better not make eye contact with weirdos.

New York, which tops the list for most total crimes and is perceived by many across the country as crime-ridden, is, in actuality, relatively safe compared to many cities.

The Odds: The following list represents the odds that an average citizen will be the victim of a crime in one year.

Atlanta	1 in 52
Miami	1 in 61
Newark	1 in 72
St. Louis	1 in 90
Chicago	1 in 90
Los Angeles	1 in 93
New York	1 in 94
Detroit	1 in 96
Boston	1 in 101
Portland, OR	1 in 104

Source: Federal Bureau of Investigation; U.S. Census Bureau.

Also See: Murder, Violence, Urban Crime.

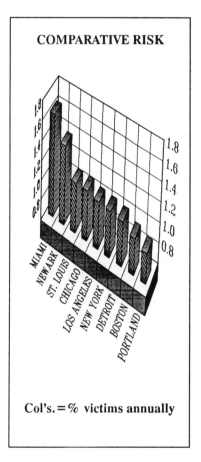

COMPARATIVE RISK

Col's. = % victims annually

73

D d

DATING

Definition: The process by which guys who like girls who like guys, meet girls who like guys who like girls.

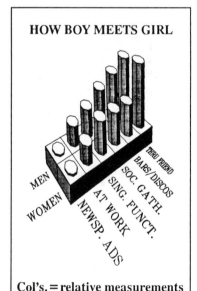

HOW BOY MEETS GIRL

MEN
WOMEN
THRU FRIEND
BARS/DISCOS
SOC. GATH.
SING. FUNCT.
AT WORK
NEWSP. ADS

Col's. = relative measurements

Though the singles bars, or "meat markets," that flourished in the seventies and eighties are a long way from dead, men and women are no longer using them as much to pick up dates. By the late eighties, some 6 in 10 met their dates in "traditional" ways — through friends, family, social events and work.

The Odds: The following list from *Singles, the New Americans* represents how singles meet dates and the proportions among men and women who pair up in various ways:

	MEN	WOMEN
Through Friends	3 in 10	1 in 3
Social Gath's.	1 in 5	1 in 6
Bars & Discos	1 in 4	1 in 6
Singles Funct's.	1 in 7	1 in 6
At work	1 in 10	1 in 11
Newsp'r. Ads	1 in 100	Same

WHAT ATTRACTS WOMEN

Unlike men who are drawn more by the sexual anatomy of the female, women are attracted by the upper torso and, most of all, by the most obvious physical characteristics. The following list from *Sex, A User's Manual* represents what women find most attractive on a man and the proportion who like the various male body parts the best:

Face	11 in 20
Hair	1 in 13
Shoulders	1 in 14
Chest	1 in 16
Hands	1 in 25

Women also like men for their achievements, status and intelligence.

FAVORITE BODY PARTS
ON OPPOSITE SEX (BY PERCENT OF PREFERENCE)

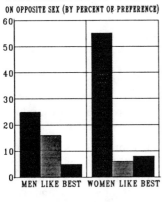

WHAT ATTRACTS MEN

Men are attracted most by the erotic. The following list from the same report as above represents what men find most attractive on women and the proportions who like the various female body parts the best:

Face	1 in 4
Legs	1 in 4

Bust	1 in 6
Hair	1 in 20
Butt	1 in 25

The things they like the best in women are physical attractiveness, erotic powers and affection.

Source: Almanac of the American People, Tom and Nancy Biracree, Facts on File.

DAYS OFF
Unofficial Work Holidays

Definition: Certain days at the office or factory on which everyone is bitching that no one else had to come to work today.

It is a federal law that government offices be closed on many holidays. The option to close is left to employers in the private sector. Major celebrations which are officially designated as "national holidays" include New Year's Day, Memorial Day, Independence Day, Labor Day, Thanksgiving and Christmas.

The Odds: Some unofficial holidays are observed as days off in the following proportions.

Martin Luther King Jr. Day	1 in 6
Columbus Day	1 in 6
Presidents Day	9 in 20

Source: The Bureau of National Affairs.

DEATH

Definition: The day which marks the end of the following: heartburn, headaches, breathing, taxes, cheeseburgers, and all else you abhor or adore.

The inevitability of death sets in at an average age of three to four years. How and when you do it is another matter. Most people envision death as taking place on the weekend and in a hospital bed. The sad truth is that death occurs in about equal proportion each day of the week and many take place in the most unexpected places.

The Odds: Each year slightly more than 2.1 million of Americans' leases on life expire, which is about .9 percent of those who were alive in the last 12 month period. The odds on making it to the next year then, are about 118 to 1 for the average American and odds of dying this year are approximately 1 in 119. The odds that you will die of the following causes are as follows:

Heart Disease	1 in 3
Cancer	1 in 5
Strokes	1 in 14
Accidents	1 in 23
Pulmonary Disease	1 in 29
Pneumonia	1 in 32
Diabetes	1 in 58
Suicide	1 in 73
Liver Ailments	1 in 83
AIDS	1 in 84

Source: National Safety Council

Also See: Accidents, Automobile Accidents, Falls, Deaths, Longevity, Shark Attacks.

DEATH RATES
Major U.S. Cities

Definition: The places at which citizens have the greatest odds of meeting their maker.

Death, funnily enough, is a fact of life. In the era of mass communication, with printed and broadcast obituaries and crime reports cascading at all times, mortality is everyday news. There simply is no place to hide from eternity. Some spots, though, are slightly more alive than others. However, we wouldn't suggest moving to one of the lower death-rate cities in an attempt to escape the Grim Reaper; these death rates are more a matter of demographics than geography.

The Odds: Those living in places with a high percentage of senior citizens or families living below the poverty line are more likely to have a date with St. Peter. The list below represents the odds that citizens will croak in the following cities.

TOP TEN DEATH RATES

St. Petersburg	1 in 55
Sacramento	1 in 66
St. Louis	1 in 69
Pittsburgh	1 in 74
Buffalo	1 in 74
Miami	1 in 76
Louisville	1 in 79
Baltimore	1 in 79
Cleveland	1 in 80
Cincinnati	1 in 81

BOTTOM 10 DEATH RATES

Anchorage	1 in 323
Arlington, TX	1 in 244
Aurora, CO	1 in 227
Virginia Beach	1 in 222
San Jose, CA	1 in 179
El Paso, TX	1 in 175
Austin, TX	1 in 167
Colorado Springs	1 in 159
Santa Ana, CA	1 in 154
Anaheim, CA	1 in 147

Souce: U.S. Census Bureau.

Also See Below.

DEATH POST-PONEMENT

Definition: The ability to fend off the Grim Reaper until after a significant event.

Think the day of your death is a random event? Think again. Believe it or not, those romantic novels and movies in which characters hold out until the return of a son from the war or the birth of a grand-daughter seem actually to be grounded in fact. Studies have shown that the odds of dying are significantly less in the month preceding that of the birth

of close relative, and are subsequently higher in the month following the birth month. Additionally, further studies have shown that Jewish people on average are likely to hold out until after Passover, and that elderly Chinese women tend to hang on until after the Harvest Moon Festival, in which older women play a significant role, taking charge of preparing elaborate meals and directing daughters and daughters-in-law. This holiday is one of the rare occasions in traditionally male-dominated Chinese society in which the women plays the central role – the festival, in fact, is sometimes called "an old woman's holiday."

The Odds — Birthdays and Death-days: Statistician David Philips found a definite dip in the number of deaths in the months immediately preceding that of birth. Assuming the two events, month of birth and month of death, were independent of one another, one would expect the odds against dying in any particular month preceding or following that of birth to be 11 to 1. In fact, the odds are more like 13 to 1.

Examining the birth and mortality figures for 1,251 Americans listed in *Who Was Who in America*, Philips found that 86 died in the month before the birth month, as opposed to the expected 104 (1251/12). Thus, there were about 17 percent fewer deaths in the month leading up to the one containing a birthday. To put it another way, 17 people defied the odds and staved off death until they could celebrate their birthday. Correspondingly, the data shows that 472 of the 1,251 died in the three months following their birth months, or 11 percent *more* than one would expect if dates of birth and death were unrelated.

Another study, by Philipps and Daniel Smith, showed that Chinese women don't shed their mortal coil until after the Harvest Moon Festival. In the study of figures for a group of Chinese women 75 or older, the death rate in the week preceding the Festival was only 65 percent of the expected rate, while deaths in the week immediately following the holiday shot up 35 percent above expected — strangely making up almost exactly for the dip preceding the holiday. Philipps also notes a dip in Jewish deaths before Passover and the Day of Atonement, and a drop in U.S. deaths before Presidential elections.

There is, in addition, interesting anecdotal evidence of the power to hold out until significant events, the most famous of which is that both Thomas Jefferson and John Adams died on July 4th, 1826 — exactly fifty years after the signing of the Declaration of Independence. Coincidence, you say? Not according to Jefferson's physician, who reports the founding father's last words — "Is it the Fourth?"

Source: David P. Philips, "Death-day and Birthday: An Unexpected Connection," in *Statistics: A Guide to the Unknown,* Holden-Day, Inc., San Francisco; David P. Philips and Daniel G. Smith, "Postponement of Death Until Symbolically Meaningful Occasions," *Journal of the American Medical Association,* April 11, 1990.

DEATH RATES
Around the World

In a statistic which should surprise no one, the desperately poor countries of Africa have the world's highest death rates. What is a surprise however, is the low figure presented by certain wealthy oil producing states and two unspectacular yet relatively peaceful players in Central America (figures from Kuwait are from before the Persian Gulf war).

The Odds: Interestingly, no "developed" countries are in the bottom 20 of lowest death rates. Perhaps it is the strain of modern life and the toll of meat and other fatty foods. Americans, who have annual odds of dying of 9 in 1,000, die at a rate faster than all but four countries in our hemisphere. In the Americas, we are surpassed only by politically repressive Haiti, and desperately poor Bolivia, Peru and Uruguay.

The following list represents the proportions of the population who will die in one year:

HIGHEST ANNUAL ODDS

Sierra Leone	27.6 in 1,000
Gambia	26.9 in 1,000
Afghanistan	23.9 in 1,000
Somalia	22.6 in 1,000
Ethiopia	22.3 in 1,000
Guinea	21.9 in 1,000
Niger	20.9 in 1,000
Mali	20.8 in 1,000
Angola	20.6 in 1,000
Central African Republic	20.1 in 1,000

LOWEST ANNUAL ODDS

Kuwait	3.1 in 1,000
Bahrain	4.0 in 1,000
Costa Rica	4.2 in 1,000
United Arab Emirates	4.2 in 1,000
Qatar	4.3 in 1,000
Fiji	5.0 in 1,000
Panama	5.2 in 1,000
Albania	5.4 in 1,000
Guyana	5.4 in 1,000
Venezuela	5.4 in 1,000
Korea, Dem. People's Rep.	5.4 in 1,000

Source: *World Resources 1988-89,* A Report by The World Resources Institute and The International Institute for Environment and Development in collaboration with The United Nations Environment Programme, Basic Books, Inc., New York.

Also See: Death

DEATH WITH DIGNITY

Acceptable Suicide

Definition: The voluntary decision to commit suicide, usually made by a terminally ill individual.

Michigan is the only state which permits a terminally ill patient to take his own life with the assistance of a physician. There is, however, a growing public outcry that those who are destined to die painfully and in the reasonably immediate future should be allowed to "die with dignity".

The Odds: Some 2 in 3 people will die with some pain from the effects of the leading killers: heart disease (1 in 3), cancer (1 in 5) and pulmonary and respiratory diseases (1 in 14). Currently it is society's right, not the individual's, to decide if they may elect to die with dignity when the pain becomes unbearable.

Since the collective will eventually determine who will ultimately have the right to decide, a look at a public opinion poll on acceptable suicide may be the best barometer of your right to decide on death with dignity in the future.

The following list represents what people in the U.S. think are acceptable moral grounds for a person to commit suicide:

In Pain,
No Improvement	2 in 3
Incurable Disease	3 in 5
Heavy Burden on Family	1 in 3
Under Any Circumstance	1 in 16

Source: 1990 Gallop poll of 1,018 adults.

Also See: Death, Suicide.

DENTAL CARIES

Definition: Tooth decay brought on by plaque, diet, susceptible tooth surfaces, and transmission such as a parent kissing a child, primarily affecting children and young adults, but a problem throughout life.

The Odds: With more than half the population of the U.S. enjoying the benefits of fluoride in their drinking water, dentrifices, and mouthwashes, the dawn of a cavity-free nation is in sight, with its attendant savings in money. It is estimated that for every dollar spent on fluoridation, $50 is

saved in dental bills. The results to our children are inestimable, especially children of low-income families, 70 percent of whom may never see a dentist. At the present time, says Columbia University doctors' *Complete Home Medical Guide*, the odds on your children developing cavities while growing up are 1 in 50, and this is principally because of the ever-growing use of fluoride in our drinking water. The fear that fluoride can cause cancer, birth defects, or any other side-effect condition has been dispelled after fifty years of research on the subject by health authorities. According to Dr. Sheldon Saul Hendler's *The Doctors' Vitamin and Mineral Encyclopedia*, the Dr. Strangelove notion that adding fluoride to our drinking water was a Communist plot to poison the U.S. is "utter nonsense." The fluoride that critics feared was one used to kill rats, insects and mice, a poisonous organic fluoride, which is not the inorganic fluoride used in the nation's drinking water. In fact, children could even use topical applications of fluoride gels or solutions obtainable from their dentists to build up a high enough level of fluoride on the surface of their tooth enamel to practically defy any any attack of cavity-causing acids on them.

CAVITIES IN CHILDREN

Under Age 10	1 in 80
Age 17 and Older	1 in 6

Source: Compiled research by editors.

DIETARY CONSCIENCE

Definition: The act or process of determining the most important nutritional concern of an individual.

Recent findings relating to weight control and health indicate that what you eat is far more important than how much you eat. The individual decisions are somewhat gender-related when it comes to calories, but there is relatively little variation in other nutritional decisions.

The following lists represents the most common concerns relating to nutritional intakes:

Calories (Men)	9 in 100
Calories (Wom.)	15 in 100
Cholesterol (Men)	22 in 100
Cholesterol (Wom.)	24 in 100
Fat (Men)	19 in 100
Fat (Wom.)	23 in 100
Vitamins/ Minerals (Men)	23 in 100
Vitamins/ Minerals (Women)	20 in 100

Source: The American Dietetic Association poll of 1,000 adults aged 25 and up.

Also See: Dieting.

DIETING

Definition: Something we do in hopes to get the following results: 1) get the opposite sex to pay more attention to us 2) fit into our clothes 3) be temporarily chic at a ladies-only luncheon, no matter how fat you intend to be in the future.

Looking physically fit is regarded by many as a prerequisite of social acceptance. Each year Americans spend $13 billion on athletic wear, $730 million on home exercise equipment and $4.7 billion for health-club memberships. From two-thirds to three-quarters of all Americans say they would like to lose weight and 101 million are on some sort of diet.

The Odds: Dieting is a mania in America—Jenny Craig, Weightwatchers, Ultra Slim Fast, Nutra Systems. They are cultural icons of weight conscious America. Many lose weight with these supervised nutritional plans and self imposed diets. The odds are 7 in 10 that you will lose weight if you carry out the organized plans. Odds are 9 in 10 that the average dieter will gain his weight loss back. The following groups at any given time will be on a diet in the following proportions:

Average U.S.	1 in 2.5
Average U.S. Man	1 in 3
Average U.S. Wom.	1 in 2
Average U.S.	
Adolescent Girl	1 in 6

Source: Compiled research by editors.

DISTRUST

Definition: The over-whelming feeling that another individual will rob you of everything but your eyeballs if you turn you back on him.

While it is unrealistic and inequitable to judge a person solely by his occupation, some jobs have been stigmatized by the actions of their worst practitioners. In occupations like car salesman, the economic temptation to distort or dispense with hard truths is enormous. Similar forces come to bear on our elected officials from lobbyists, co-opting opponents and vocally gifted constituents.

The Odds: Below are the odds that various professionals will be trusted "in high faith" by the average person.

Car Salesman	1 in 100
Advtg. Practitioners	1 in 100
State Officeholders	1 in 100
Insurance Salesmen	1 in 50
Stockbrokers	1 in 50
Bus. Executives	1 in 50
Congressman	1 in 50
Local Politician	1 in 50
Union Leaders	1 in 33
Real Estate Agents	1 in 33

Source: The Gallup Report, #279, 1988.

DIVORCE

Also See: Trust.

DIVORCE

Definition: The sure cure for a sick marriage.

Most people think that divorce is a way of life that is unique to the twentieth century. It is, but primarily in America, which has one of the world's highest divorce rates. Elsewhere, divorces are not as common, and in some countries, such as Italy or many Latin American nations, marriage breakups are almost unheard of.

The Odds: Divorce rates peaked in 1973, when the number of divorces almost exceeded the number of marriages. At that time it was projected that 9 in 20 marriages would end in divorce and some thought the odds were headed as high as 1 in 2 within a few years. A look back reveals that the divorce rate has been declining steadily and a more realistic estimate is that 2 in 5 marriages will breakup.

AGE FACTORS

Younger couples have the highest odds of getting the big D. In 1985, 3 in 5 women and 1 in 2 men who got divorced were under the age of 30. Among the marriages of those couples, 1 in 8 lasted one year or less and 3 in 10 lasted three years or less.

The following list represents the proportions of divorces at various stages of marriage:

1 to 5 Years	9 in 20
6 to 9 Years	1 in 5
10 to 15 Years	1 in 6
15 to 19	1 in 11
20 to 24	1 in 18
25 to 29	1 in 33
30 Plus	1 in 32

RACIAL FACTORS

Blacks are more than twice as likely as whites to get divorced. Americans of Hispanic origin conform to the American norm, despite their primarily Catholic religion which strictly prohibits divorce. The following list represents the proportions of divorces among the races in one year:

All Races	1 in 9
Whites	1 in 8
Blacks	1 in 4
Hispanics	1 in 8

MARRIAGE DURATIONS

The average first marriage lasts 27 years and the average marriage lasts 23 years. The average marriage ending with the death of a spouse lasts 43 years. Happily, 1 in 8 couples will celebrate a 50th anniversary. The following list represents the median years of marriage at divorce:

First Marriage	7.5
Second Marriage	4.8
Third Marriage or beyond	3.5

Source: Compiled research by editors.

Also See: Marriage, Prison Escapes.

DOG BITE FATALITIES

Definition: Circumstances in which a dog mistakes your jugular vein for his puppy chow.

Man's best friend? No doubt about the old adage when you consider that a person is one-thousand times more likely to be killed by his fellow man than a dog. To be fair, more often than not the owners of the offending dogs are to blame for negligence in the upbringing, treatment and care of their animals. Deadly dogs are not born—they are created by their owners.

The Odds: The chance that you will be killed by a dog is approximately 700,000 to 1. Some dogs are more deadly than others. A pit bull terrier is four times more likely to kill you than the sturdy, supportive German Shepherd and the lovable, fiery-eyed Malamute. The St. Bernard, ever genial and compassionate on stage and screen, drops several notches in esteem as well, as he is revealed as one of nature's most consummate man-eaters.

The following list gives the dog breeds responsible for the highest number of fatal attacks over a ten-year period from 1979 to 1989 and the proportions of deaths caused by them:

Pit Bull	37 in 10 million
Germ. Shep.	9 in 10 million
Husky	7 in 10 million
Malamute	6 in 10 million
Doberman	5 in 10 million
Rottweiler	5 in 10 million
Grt. Dane	4 in 10 million
St. Bernard	4 in 10 million

Source: Journal of the American Medical Association.

DOING IT

English Style

Definition: The staid, conservative way to roll around in the sheets, according to the rules of Canterbury.

Do the Brits have their own way of having a jolly good sexual romp? Some say so, but more and more, the rules and preferences are changing as Queen Victoria fades from living memories and into the history books.

The Odds: So where do the chaps bring their birds when they are ready to tickle their feathers? The following list represents the most common places they do it and the proportions of Britons who do it there:

In the Bedroom	96%
In the Living Room	84%
In the Bathroom	58%
On the Beach	21%
In Swimming Pools	12%
In the Sea	7%

And how about the Royal Family, where do they do it? In Buckingham Palace, of course.

Source: The London Sunday Express poll of 749 Britons.

DRINKING ARRESTS

Definition: Circumstances of being thrown into the tank when you're out on a binge.

Sending an authoritative, chastening message to the America's habitual drunk drivers is a national priority. Overall, the U.S. has been slowing down, sobering up and getting smart. To secure our roads for our children and our streets for ourselves will be a test of our resolve in the coming decade.

The Odds: The following list represents the ratio of arrests in one year for alcohol abuse relative to the population in the ten states with the highest cases:

California	1 in 39
Texas	1 in 37
New York	1 in 98
Pennsylvania	1 in 79
Illinois	1 in 85
Florida	1 in 77
Virginia	1 in 45
Michigan	1 in 69
Ohio	1 in 99
Wisconsin	1 in 59

Source: U.S. Department of Health and Human Services.

DRINKING PROBLEMS

Definition: The sorrows found at the bottoms of beer cans, shot glasses and little brown bottles.

Drinking is a problem with which we will not dispense, anymore than we would consider dispensing alcoholic beverages in elementary schools. We have made one attempt at prohibition and — noting its failure — resigned ourselves to the inevitability of alcoholism, alcohol-related traffic fatalities and liver diseases.

The Odds: Approximately 1 in 3 Americans have some problems at one point in their life associated with imbibing too much alcohol. The following list represents the most common problems and the proportions found in problem drinkers aged 12 to 80:

Mean/Aggressive	1 in 5
Memory Loss	1 in 7
Drink too Fast	1 in 7
Argue Heatedly	1 in 9
Pressured by Mate to Quit	1 in 9
Solitary Drunkenness	1 in 11
Fears of Drinking	1 in 12
Can't Stop Drinking	1 in 14
Keep Drinking after Resolutions to Stop	1 in 15
Pressured by Relative to Quit	1 in 15

Source: U.S. Dept. of Health and Human Services, National Institute on Drug Abuse.

Also See: Alcoholism, Teen Drinking.

DROPOUTS

Definition: People who withdraw from established social endeavors to follow another lifestyle; especially, students who give up high school before graduation.

The Odds: Many of us think of the word "dropout" as coming into general usage during the flower children dropout days of the sixties and early seventies. Actually, it is uniquely an American word that first surfaced in 1925, so long ago in fact, that a panel on English usage now considers it usable in both formal speech and writing, but would prefer to see it used only in journalism. In any event, it is a word that scares the bejesus out of teachers and parents, and with good reason in this era, when even college graduates do not always find the work they studied to do. So, parents and teachers, what are the odds of your children or charges getting through the often emotionally charged high school years, and thus becoming eligible to go on to college? The odds on dropping out for 16-year-olds is 1 in 17, down from a high of 1 in 11 in

1980; for 18-year-olds, it zooms precipitously to 1 in 7, down from a high of 1 in 6 in 1980. As if those figures are not alarming enough, the odds are 1 in 10 for the total school population including 14- and 15-year-olds and various race groups.

HIGHEST DROPOUT RATES

Washington, D.C.	1 in 2
Florida	1 in 3
Georgia	1 in 3
Dropouts by Race:	
White 16-year-olds	1 in 16
White 18-year-olds	1 in 7
Black 16-year-olds	1 in 20
Black 18-year-olds	1 in 6

Source: National Center for Education Statistics; U.S. Department of Education; U.S. Bureau of the Census.

DROWNING

Infants And Toddlers

Definition: Suffocation of a child while submersed in water.

The Odds: Drowning is the second leading accidental cause of death among children aged 1 to 14. The odds for a child in that age group drowning are about 20,000 to 1 annually; about 45 percent of those deaths are among toddlers—infants one to two years old. Researchers have identified the major culprits in toddler drownings as swimming pools, accounting for 55 percent to 80 percent of all deaths, and bathtubs, accounting for 25 percent to 31 percent of such fatalities.

But there is another risky household contraption that one might not normally consider a severe danger. A recent study showed that of 49 drowning deaths among infants and toddlers in Cook County, Illinois, between 1985 and 1989 occurred in 5-gallon industrial buckets— the kind used for mopping the floor, as a catch under a leaking sink, a flush for a broken toilet, or even a storage container for fish. In all cases, the toddler had been left unattended, for anywhere from 1 minute to several hours. Infants were found head-down in the buckets; some had drowned in a bucket as little as 10 percent full of water. The U.S. Consumer Product Safety Commission reviewed data on infant drownings and found 67 other cases of similar drownings in a three-year period. Other household hazards for toddler drownings include toilet bowls and humidifiers.

Infants just learning to crawl or walk are extremely curious about their environment—and dangerous! With a high center of gravity due to the relatively large head, the toddler can easily fall into a seemingly innocuous bucket or other floor-standing container.

Source: "Accidental Toddler Drowning in 5-Gallon Buckets," *Journal of the American Medical Association*, April 11, 1990.

Also See: Bucket Drowning.

DRUG EMERGENCIES

Definition: A medical emergency in which the victim doesn't really care where he is, as long as he is high and feeling no pain.

The Odds: Each day thousands are admitted to emergency rooms for drug-related incidents. During an average year the odds that an average American will experience such an ordeal is 1 in 2,500. For those who wind up flat on their back, but high as a kite in an emergency room, odds are it will be associated with the following substances.

Marijuana	1 in 21
Aspirin	1 in 19
PCP	1 in 18
Valium	1 in 13
Cocaine	1 in 78
Heroin or Morphine	1 in 7
Alcohol	1 in 5

Of those admitted to emergency rooms for drug-related treatment, 1 in 29 will die.

Source: National Institute on Drug Abuse.

DRUG TESTING

How Likely?

Definition: The process by which your boss makes you, among other things, pee in a bottle and submit it for approval.

The privacy of your urine is no longer as sacrosanct as it once was. The eighties may go down in history as the decade in which U.S. industry and government decided to take an avid interest in urology. The right to privacy has been on the wane through much of the post-war epoch, and now, with the employer's right to examine an employee's urine, it has perhaps hit its all-time low.

The Odds: By the end of the 1980s, when the practice of employee drug testing was at an all-time high, almost in 1 in 10 employees were working at companies which either required a urine test or required some sort of disclosure about drug intake.

The following list represents the odds in various industries that an employee will be required to take a drug test:

Mining	1 in 5
Utilities	1 in 6
Transportation	1 in 7
Manufacturing	1 in 10
Wholesale Trade	1 in 19
Finance/Real Est.	1 in 33
Construction	1 in 43
Services	1 in 71
Retail Trade	1 in 143

Source: Bureau of Labor Statistics, Survey of Employer Anti-Drug Programs, 1989.

E e

EARTHQUAKES

Predictions

Definition: 1) The forecast that a noticeable tremor in the earth will take place; 2) A barometer of the relative value of a California insurance agent's commissions.

In 1811 and 1812, the worst series of earthquakes in American history struck along the New Madrid fault in Missouri. Over the course of three months, three massive tremors, registering a phenomenal 8.4 to 8.8 on the Richter scale, released energy equivalent to 12,000 Hiroshimas or 150 million tons of TNT. In 1990 a new shock wave swept through the town of New Madrid. Iben Browning, a climatologist from Sandia Park, New Mexico, recently predicted a "50-50" chance of a powerful earthquake striking the area on December 3, 1990. Some people in New Madrid and environs took trips that day, and at least 9 school districts in three states canceled classes. Insurers were swamped with inquiries about earthquake insurance — as if they would grant insurance on such short odds.

The Odds: Scientists disputed Browning's projection, which was based on correlations between tidal forces and tremors. There simply is no means as of yet for predicting earthquakes with such accuracy. Arch Johnston, director of the Tennessee earthquake information center at Memphis State University, reckoned the likelihood of a magnitude 7.6 quake in the New Madrid area as only 7 to 9 percent before the year 2000, but gave even odds that a tremors of magnitude 6 to 6.5 will hit within that period. That is as accurate as any scientist is willing to get about wagering on earthquakes. Given Johnston's scientific projection, the odds could be calculated at 46,000 to 1 against the quake on December 3.

Oh, two more things. The quake never happened and Browning died two months later.

Source: Compiled research by editors.

ECONOMIC FORECASTING

Definition: The art and science of gazing into a crystal ball and seeing the economic future.

The Odds: A poll taken from a 1987 survey of executives of major corporations revealed that they believe the U.S. was only slightly more likely to avert a depression than it was to have one. They assess the odds are 100% that no major depression will occur during the coming decade and 49 to 51 that we will suffer a major financial crisis. On inflation/deflation the executives give inflation caused by the budget deficit and deflation (where the value of money increases and greenbacks grow more scarce) equal odds. Both are set at 47 to 53.

Interest rates behind the budget deficit are a problem. When interest rates are high, the government ends up paying billions more on its debt. When interest rates are low, few want to buy government securities. Executives say there is a 43 to 57 chance that future interest rates will be lower than they are today. The executives say the chances of social problems slowing the growth of the U.S. economy are 2 in 5.

Source: Weidenbaum, Murray; *Rendezvous With Reality,* Basic Books, Inc.

ECONOMIC TRENDS

Definition: The outside forces that determine if you can buy a new suit or dress at the mall on Saturday afternoon.

The Odds: The following odds come from a 1987 survey of executives of major corporations:

Savings: Executives lay 13 to 7 odds that Americans will continue saving less money than the rest of the developed world.

Education: There are 6 in 10 odds that the good education the baby boom received will have a positive effect on the economy.

Labor Shortages: Despite government predictions of a coming labor shortage, executives will give only a 1 in 4 chance of such a contingency actually happening.

Executives are beginning to realize that wider social issues such as education, discrimination and crime affect the business world. The collectively polled business people are giving more than 2 in 5 odds that social problems will slow the growth of the American economy.

Source: Weidenbaum, Murray *Rendezvous With Reality*, Basic Books, Inc.

EDUCATIONAL ATTAINMENT

College Educations

Definition: The rate at which people think they know everything, the underlying principle being the less education you have, the more you think you know.

The list of big cities with the best-educated populace is lead by Austin, home of the University of Texas, and the West Coast meccas of San Francisco and Seattle. Washington, with its preponderance of white-collar workers – lawyers and bureaucrats – also scores high. The cities in which educational attainment is lowest are primarily Northeastern urban centers that also suffer from other blights – unemployment, high crime, an entrenched underclass. These factors are part of the continued cycle of poverty that keeps educational, and ultimately social, opportunity out of reach for many inner city residents. In Newark, a mere 6.3 percent of the population has reached a college-degree level of education.

The Odds: Approximately 1 in 5 Americans have either completed college or attended college for 4 years or more. The list below represents the odds that the average citizen in the following cities has attended 16 or more years of school.

TOP TEN CITIES

Austin, TX	31 in 100
San Francisco	28 in 100
Seattle	28 in 100
Washington, DC	27 in 100
Arlington, TX	27 in 100
Lexington, KY	25 in 100
Baton Rouge	25 in 100
Aurora, CO	25 in 100
Albuquerque	25 in 100
Denver	25 in 100

BOTTOM TEN CITIES

Newark	6 in 100
Cleveland	6 in 100
Detroit	8 in 100
St. Louis	10 in 100
Philadelphia	11 in 100
Buffalo	11 in 100
Baltimore	11 in 100
Jersey City, NJ	11 in 100
Santa Ana, CA	12 in 100
Toledo	12 in 100

Source: U.S. Bureau of the Census.

EGGS, BUSTED

Definition: The roundish reproductive body produced by the female chicken, consisting of the ovum and albumen, which we fry, boil, poach, scramble, shirr and use in baking, salad dressings and soups, and its case, or shell, which we use for compost, to add to bird food, to clear up cloudy coffee, or, as most of us do, throw away.

The Odds: How often have you neglected to check in the store and brought home a carton of eggs only to find one or more broken? What are the odds? They would be zero if we were talking about the eggs from the extinct elephant birds of Madagascar, which had a capacity of two gallons each, but from the U.S. Leghorn's puny 2-ouncer, we often find a surprise in the carton. Before World War II, this was not much of a problem for shoppers who brought home their eggs in a brown paper bag carefully put there by the grocer. With the advent of cartons just after the war, however, this nagging little problem began hectoring egg lovers, until today, according to interviews with grocers and egg distributors, you can expect to find one cracked egg in every 24 cartons. The odds rise dramatically once the eggs are put on display. Then, with careless shoppers leaning on the cartons to reach for something else on the shelf above, placing cans on them, changing their minds on whether they want jumbo, medium or small eggs, and dropping the cartons back on the stack, the odds shoot up to 1 in 10, and sometimes, in wilder neighborhoods, 1 in 5. What do you do when you find you have brought home a cracked egg? Freeze it immediately, and when you want a hard-boiled egg, take it out of the freezer and boil the hell out of it.

Source: Egg Nutrition Council; interviews.

ELDERLY CARE
Who will take care of Ma & Pa?

Definition: The act of being the responsible party for one's parent or parents when, due to age-related illnesses, they are no longer functioning well enough to live independently.

Few children ever imagined that they would eventually have to care for their parents in a fashion similar to how they cared for them decades earlier. Care for the elderly is now common, mainly due to the fact that life expectancy has risen 50% in the twentieth century, from age 50 to 75.

The Odds: In previous times, most older Americans lived with their grown children. Today approximately 1 in 3 elderly live with children. According to a Florida research team, it is the daughter who usually takes the burden. In families with a male and a female offspring, daughters are 3.2 times more likely to take the reigns than the son.

Source: Journal of Gerontology.

Also See: Longevity.

EMBEZZLEMENT

Definition: The act of proving the proverb that a fool and his money are soon parted.

In the past, the public has been lenient in its assessment of bunco artists, embezzlers and other white collar criminals. With the disastrous convergences of the savings and loan crisis now manifestly obvious to all, the nation is now taking a much dimmer and more punishing view of fiduciary pilferage.

The Odds: Unlike many crimes which are ubiquitous, embezzlement tends to be highly regionalized. A good embezzler knows to go where the money is, not just where the fools are, which he knows are everywhere. The following list represents the proportions of embezzlement and bank fraud crimes in one year, relative to the population, in the ten states with the highest rates:

California	1 in 10,300
Texas	1 in 13,300
Florida	1 in 11,800
New York	1 in 24,900
New Jersey	1 in 13,400
Georgia	1 in 9,900
Ohio	1 in 21,100
Pennsylvania	1 in 23,500
Illinois	1 in 26,200
Maryland	1 in 12,700

Source: F.B.I. Bank Crime Statistics.

ENERGY SOURCES

National Fuels

Definition: The origin of fuels used to power the nation.

Wheaties aside, most energy in the U.S. is produced by fossil fuels. Fully 1 in 3 of all U.S. dollars spent abroad is for oil, which is the chief source of energy in the U.S. and much of the world.

The Odds: The list below represents the ratios of energy sources used in America.

Oil	2 in 5
Coal /Natural Gas	1 in 4
Renewables	1 in 14
Nuclear	1 in 14
Other	1 in 5

Source: Interior Department.

Also See: Oil Consumption.

ENTERTAINERS

Definition: Professional singers, dancers, actors, musicians, comedians, TV performers and the like, whose talents are so great or personalities so strong that they are recognized around the world.

The Odds: Is it important to be born in the right place in order to achieve the status of celebrityhood? In the entertainment field, it certainly doesn't hurt to claim America's blessed shores as your birthright. Bruce Willis (Germany), Liv Ullman (Japan), Ursula Andress (Switzerland), and Jennifer O'Neill (Brazil), all surmounted stupendous odds to make *The World Almanac and Book of Facts* compilation of 1,895 entertainment figures who are universally known, while Karl Malden (Chicago), Cloris Leachman (Des Moines, Iowa), and Stacy Keach (Savannah, Georgia) quite easily made the grade, swept along in the avalanche of American talent that dominates the list. English being almost a universal language in the entertainment world today, entertainers born in the U.S. are more likely to have their images beamed through the airwaves than persons in other countries – American stars have a 1 in 2 chance of being known globally. Their closest competitors are from Great Britain, which, though producing outstanding talent, manages only 1 in 14 odds of achieving truly worldwide fame. The remainder of the list is filled out by Canada at 1 in 36; France, 1 in 79; Italy, 1 in 82; Germany, 1 in 119; Ireland, 1 in 126; Australia and Sweden, 1 in 146, and Russia, at 1 in 189.

Source: Compiled research by editors.

ENVIRONMENT-ALISTS

Definition: A movement which gained momentum in the eighties which professed that grass, moss and leaves were more natural ground coverings than paper cups and beer cans.

No question about it, America has gone green. From the massive celebrations of Earth Day to the mass effort to save the California redwoods, people are standing up for old Mother Earth. Leading the way are America's environmental organizations. Some of these organizations lobby the government for increased protection for wildlife or specific habitats, others work to inform the public and confront polluting businesses, while still others are actively involved in saving or restoring threatened lands.

The Odds: Recent polls show that the majority of Americans considers themselves environmentalists. Despite the popular sentiment, only 1 in 25 Americans belongs to a nationally organized environmental constituency. The following list represents the largest environmental groups and the proportions of Americans who are members:

Nat'l. Wildlife Fed.	1 in 44
Greenpeace	1 in 179
Sierra Club	1 in 452
National Audubon Society	1 in 484
The Wilderness Society	1 in 757
Environ. Defense Fund	1 in 2,000
Nat'l. Resources Defense Council	1 in 2,000
National Parks and Conservation Assoc.	1 in 2,500
Def'ders of Wildlife	1 in 3,125
Friends of the Earth	1 in 5,000
Izaak Walton League	1 in 5,000
Environmental Action	1 in 12,500
League of Conservation Voters	1 in 16,667

Source: Congressional Quarterly: Current American Government Fall 1990 Guide.

ENVIRONMENT-ALISM

Definition: The philosophy of protecting air, water, animals, plants and other natural resources from the effects of pollution, overpopulation and the other consequences of man's domination of the planet.

The Odds: The odds that the average person will participate in environmentally conscious activities is getting better all the time. Three of 5 Americans will recycle bottles or aluminum cans regularly and almost 1 in 2 will bring newspapers to collection sites. Almost 7 in 10 will reduce the use of gas and or electricity in their homes and 11 in 20 will cut household water use during droughts. Finally, 1 in 5 people will regularly change products because of environmental concerns while another 1 in 5 will do so occasionally.

Improving the Odds: Only 1 in 5 Americans will regularly reduce auto emissions by car-pooling and taking public transportation. Less than 1 in 12 people will actually take part in a meeting or activity involved with environmental issues.

Source: Future Vision, The 189 Most Important Trends of the 1990s, Sourcebooks Trade, 1991.

EROTICISM

Fantastic Behavior

Definition: Not exactly sex, but better than being a priest or a nun.

What to do when you just can't get it? Dream about it. Do it yourself. Or whisper some trash in the ears of shoppers at the mall. If it gets you off, it's better than taking a cold shower.

The Odds: The following list represents the proportions of people who engage in various forms of erotic behavior according to two studies, *Do You Do it with the Lights on?* and *The Kinsey Report:*

Male Masturbation	9 in 10
Fem. Masturbation	3 in 5
Male Wet Dreams	8 in 10
Fem. Wet Dreams	1 in 3
Strip Tease for Spouse	2 in 3
Shower with Partner	9 in 10
Fantasize about Wife	9 in 10
Fantasize about Friend's Wife	2 in 3
Fantasize about Secretary	2 in 5

Source: Compiled research by editors.

EXECUTIVE ANXIETIES

Boy do I have a Headache!

Definition: The plagues that effect the minds of the lieutenants of business and industry.

With the new worry of accusations of sexual harassment which could bring down many a boss, it seems to be the last thing on the executive mind. Rather, most worry about getting booted, for a variety of reasons.

The Odds: Executives at large firms may have a good reason to be insecure about their jobs. At one time or another, 3 in 4 will get laid off or fired. A poll which spanned two years found the following worries among 200 executives at the largest 1,000 firms:

	1989	1991
Being Fired	6%	20%
Losing Job due to merger/ acquisition	54%	55%
Burnout	25%	13%

Fire Insurance: As a response, to the fear of getting fired, 13% more "fire insurance" clauses in employment contracts are being demanded by executives taking on a new job. This provision usually guarantees an executive up to one year of pay if he is fired for any reason. Nice work, if you can get it.

Source: Robert Half International Survey.

Also See: Recession of 1990-92, Job Woes.

EXECUTION

Definition: The act of the state actually invoking capital punishment on a condemned prisoner.

Capital punishment has always been an enormously emotional issue for politically aware Americans. On one hand, most citizens acknowledge the need to establish a strong and chilling deterrent against such heinous crimes as pre-meditated murder and kidnaping. On the other hand, our system is based around the presumption of innocence, the apportionment of mercy and the continuing possibility of redemption. Historically, each state, through its citizens, has grappled individually with these issues. Alaska, Hawaii, Maine, Michigan, Minnesota, North Dakota, Rhode Island and Wisconsin have never seen fit to take a life.

The Odds: Any potential murderer who is keeping track of actual executions of condemned offenders will not be scared off. In

1988, 11 in 2,124 condemned prisoners were put to death. The other 99.5 percent on death row are likely to remain there till they get old and join their victims in the great beyond.

The following list represents the proportions of prisoners on death row who were executed in the ten states with the most condemned prisoners:

Georgia	1 in 91
Texas	3 in 284
California	0 in 299
North Carolina	0 in 80
Florida	2 in 295
Ohio	0 in 88
South Carolina	0 in 36
Mississippi	0 in 48
Pennsylvania	0 in 98
Louisiana	3 in 40

Source: BJS Bulletin, Capital Punishment, 1987.

EXPATRIATION, AMERICAN

Where the Very Disillusioned Go

Definition: U.S. citizens who responded to the latter portion of the "love it or leave it" sentiment.

Some Americans fall so in love with the gentle beaches of Mexico and the quirky back streets of Quebec that they stay. Others decide just to get out of the country for a variety of reasons. One in several hundred Americans decides there are greener pastures elsewhere, so they pack up and leave to become permanent residents or citizens of other nations.

The Odds: The following are the ten countries that have opened their arms the widest to American expatriates. The following list represents the proportions of Americans who expatriated to various countries:

To Mexico	1 in 631
To Canada	1 in 1,063
To the U.K.	1 in 1,582
To the Philippines	1 in 1,603
To West Germany	1 in 1,865
To Italy	1 in 2,906
To Australia	1 in 3,676
To the Dominican Republic	1 in 3,968
To Israel	1 in 3,623
To Spain	1 in 3,623

Source: U.S. Bureau of the Census

EXTRATERRESTRIAL LIFE

Definition: Living organisms which have originated from outer space.

The Odds: What are the odds that those mysterious colored lights up in the sky actually are extraterrestrials? In 1961, astronomer Frank Drake devised a formula for calculating the odds of our making contact with intelligent life from other worlds. The number of possible extraterrestrial civilizations (N), Drake reasoned, would be a product of a string of probabilities for various events in the galaxy. He devised the following equation:

$$N = R \times P \times N \times L \times I \times C \times L$$

This odd looking string of characters translates to the number of extraterrestrial civilizations being equal to the rate at which stars form, times the fraction of stars with planets, times the average number of planets capable of supporting life, times the fraction of planets that actually give rise to life, times the fraction of intelligent species that attempt communication, times the average lifetime of such a civilization.

Astronomers and biologists differ as to the values for each of the elements of the equations. Some claim that we cannot estimate certain factors, such as the probability of a planet giving rise to life. Others say we can.

Given the most optimistic estimates, the Drake equation yields N = 100,000 extraterrestrial civilizations in the galaxy with the means and the desire for interstellar communication. Not bad odds! Now all we have to do is figure out how to make contact.

On the other hand, a more pessimistic approach to calculating the development of intelligent life yields a much more bleak assessment — that we are the only intelligent life in two galaxies. But even so, given that there are 100 billion known galaxies, that still yields 50 billion other intelligent life forms in the universe. However, the vagaries of space make intergalactic contact unimaginable.

Proponents of intelligent ETs point to the billions of stars in our own galaxy. How could we possibly be unique, they ask? Skeptics point to the incredibly complex chain of physical, chemical and biological events that have led to cognitive intelligence on Earth. How could it happen again, just like with us, they say?

Intelligent Commentary: Gerrit Verschuur, writing in *Life* Magazine, comments on the difficulty in communication: "There have been between 500,000 and one billion species on this planet since life began here. If I were to put you on a time machine and drop you at random back then, who could you talk to? Try to talk to an ant. Now try imagining that it's up to the ant to make contact with you."

Source: Original research by editors.

F f

FALLING DOWN

Definition: The state of having once been standing up and now being flat on your butt.

The Odds: Each year 1 in 20 Americans will receive emergency room treatment for fall-related injuries. The odds of serious injury from a fall are the worst for children and the elderly. Children between one and three years of age face 1 in 10 odds they will fall and visit the emergency room. Women aged 75 have a 1 in 83 chance of a fall resulting in a hospital stay while men of the same age have a 1 in 250 chance of the same injury.

For most people, the odds of dying in a fall are extremely small — less than 1 in 200,000. Falls, however, are one of the leading causes of death among the elderly. Among those surviving to age eighty, the odds of dying in a fall are 1 in 2,000. At ninety, the odds of dying in a fall are 1 in 570.

Source: Baker, Susan P., et al, *The Injury Fact Book*, Lexington Books.

Also See: Accidents, Children.

FEDERAL EMPLOYMENT
Top Cities

Definition: Workers who cannot be fired for anything less than killing their boss.

Nearly everyone complains about big government, but few in that teeming majority recognize the irony when they also complain of the scarcity of staff at public facilities and the sloth of service at public-sector glamour spots like the departments of Motor Vehicles and Health. City workers, who engage the public mano-a-mano, are the closest link of 'us' (the citizens) with 'them' (the "leaders").

The Odds: Somewhat over 1 in 13 workers are employed by the Federal Government. The list below represents. the odds that an average citizen works in the public sector.

TOP 10 CITIES

Washington, DC	1 in 14
New York	1 in 18
Richmond, VA	1 in 22
Jersey City, NJ	1 in 23
Baltimore	1 in 24
Norfolk	1 in 25
Anchorage	1 in 26
Nashville	1 in 26
Buffalo	1 in 27
Rochester, NY	1 in 27

Source: U.S. Bureau of the Census.

Also See: Government Workers

FEDERAL LAND

Definition: Acreage, mostly wilderness, which is owned by the tax payers.

The Granddaddy of all property owners is your uncle, Uncle Sam. Of the 2,271,343,360 acres in the United States, the federal government owns a whopping 30%, making it by far the biggest landowner in the country. More than four-fifths of the land in Alaska is under federal control, compared to less than one percent of the land in Iowa. The vast majority of federally owned land is used for national parks, forests and wilderness areas, as well as for military use. The government even makes money in some unexpected ways from its land—for instance, many of the ski resorts in Colorado are located in national forests and are leased from the government by the resort owners.

The Odds: The following lists represents the proportions of federal acreage in the states with the most and least proportions owned by Uncle Sam:

TOP TEN STATES

Alaska	4 in 5
Nevada	4 in 5
Idaho	3 in 5
Utah	3 in 5
Oregon	1 in 2
Wyoming	9 in 20
Arizona	9 in 20
California	9 in 20
New Mexico	1 in 3
Colorado	2 in 7

BOTTOM TEN STATES

Iowa	1 in 227
Rhode Island	1 in 149
Maine	1 in 127
New York	1 in 129
Nebraska	1 in 87
Ohio	1 in 79
Kansas	1 in 76
Illinois	1 in 72
Connecticut	1 in 69

Texas   1 in 62

Source: Public Land Statistics, U.S. Dept. of the Interior.

FERTILITY

Definition: The ability to produce offspring, even if you are trying like hell not to.

The Odds: Among aggregate men and women, the odds are slightly greater than 6 to 1 in favor of couples who want offspring actually producing them. Younger women, however, are more fertile than older ones. For instance women between the ages of 20 and 24 have a 90 percent chance of being fertile while women between 40 and 44 have only a 37 percent chance of bearing children.

Improving the Odds: Artificial insemination and in vitro fertilization have enabled many women to become pregnant who had been deemed infertile in the past. Unfortunately the 10% who say they don't want children do not all fit into 14% who are infertile. The fertility odds for those want children and those who don't are the same. The odds are only 1 in 70 that a woman will be infertile and will not want children.

Source: Russel, Cheryl 100 *Predictions For The Baby Boo*m, Plenum Press, New York

FIRES

Definition: The ignition of combustible material which requires extinguishing by professional fire fighters.

In 1988 there were 2.4 million fires which caused $8.3 billion in property damage and caused 30,800 injuries and 6,215 deaths.

The Odds: In your home the chance of a fire breaking out in any given year is approximately 1 in 200. The odds you will die in a fire in any given year is 1 in 40,200. If you are in anyway caught up in a fire the odds are 1 in 77 that you will be injured.

Odds are that an average fire will be a result of the following causes:

Smoking	3 in 10
Heating Equipment	1 in 6
Arson	1 in 8
Electrical	1 in 10
Children at Play	1 in 12

Source: National Fire Protection Association.

FIRE ALARMS
Big City Action

Definition: A call to action for a company of firemen, regardless of whether it is an actual fire, or a false alarm.

Although every situation is not necessarily extreme (some are false alarms, minor incidents or other easily resolved problems), the chance is always there for the handling of something major. The following engine companies (including both fire & EMT) are the busiest in the nation with the leading company responding to an average 13 calls a day, every day of the year!

BUSIEST ENGINE COMPANIES

The list below represents the number of "runs" in 1990 in the following cities.

New York	4,933
Phoenix	4,753
Cincinnati	4,620
Milwaukee	4,294
Sacramento	3,939
Denver	3,745
Los Angeles	3,671
Tucson	3,587
Washington, D.C.	3,555
Minneapolis	3,533

GREATEST ODDS

The list below represents the ratio of fire alarms to the general population in 1990 in the following cities. The figures shown could be thought of as the odds that the average citizen will be caught up in a fire alarm in one year.

New York	1 in 24
Chicago	1 in 10
Los Angeles	1 in 14
Washington, D.C.	1 in 4
Philadelphia	1 in 11
Houston	1 in 12
Baltimore	1 in 5
Detroit	1 in 7
Dallas	1 in 9
Phoenix	1 in 10

Source: The Best and Worst of Everything.

Also See: Accidents.

FIREWORKS

Definition: 1) Little things that go boom in night, especially on July 4th; 2) A display your boss puts on when you really screw up something.

Approximately 6 in 10 American's will see some sort of fireworks display during any year. A lesser number, estimated to be about 1 in 10 to 1 in 20, will ignite fireworks on their own. The practice has proved to be a dangerous one. Perhaps because of the known danger, odds are very good that you will not be injured. Only about 1 in 40,000 Americans are injured yearly.

Of those who are injured, odds of it resulting from the use of specific fireworks are as follows:

Firecrackers	2 in 5
Sparklers	1 in 20
Bottle Rockets	1 in 9
Fountains	1 in 20
Spinners	1 in 33
Missiles	1 in 100

Source: Consumer Product Safety Commission.

FLIGHT ARRIVALS
On-Time Performance

Definition: The rate at which airplanes drop out of the sky and pop into the gate when they are supposed to.

Worrying about making a tight connection? Want to minimize the risk? Nowadays, the Department of Transportation keeps detailed records of on-time performance for the major domestic carriers, not only overall, but for specific flights. This information is available to travel agents on their computerized booking systems. Each flight gets a score based on its past average on-time performance. Knowing this information will allow travelers to avoid chronically late flights when time is pressing.

The Odds: On average 17 in 20 flights (85 percent) arrive on time. Who are the slow pokes? The following list represents the major airlines and the proportions of their flights arriving within 15 minutes of their scheduled arrival, in a given month (In this case, September 1990, Eastern Airlines was still operating):

Pan Am	89.2 in 100
Eastern	88.1 in 100
AmericaWest	85.6 in 100
American	84.6 in 100
United	83.8 in 100
Northwest	83.2 in 100
Continental	82.7 in 100
USAir	82.5 in 100
TWA	82.2 in 100
Delta	81.9 in 100
Southwest	81.8 in 100

Source: U.S. Dept. of Transportation.

Also See: Airline Screwup

FOOTBALL, COLLEGE
Winning Teams

Definition: Athletes who are enrolled at an accredited institution of higher learning who are winning football games at a pace which usually exceeds that of winning high marks for academic achievement.

The Odds: At least one-hundred games were needed to qualify before the odds were computed on the following list.

Nebraska is the team with the top spot in the odds of winning any given game. The team right behind is Penn State. The odds of a team winning depend not just on the quality of players, but on the ability of the coach to guide his men to victory. Because talent varies from season to season, and coaching is relatively more stable, the following represents the odds that the best teams will win one of their "average" games:

Tom Osborne, Neb.   81 in 100
Joe Paterno,
  Penn State   79 in 100
LaVell Edwards,
  BYU   75 in 100
Pat Dye, Auburn   73 in 100
Bobby Bowden,
  Florida St.   73 in 100
Jackie Sherrill,
  Miss. St.   70 in 100
Dick Sheridan,
  N.C. State   69 in 100
Terry Donahue,
  UCLA   69 in 100
Herb Deromedi,
  Cent. Mich.   68 in 100
Dennis Erickson,
  Miami (Fla.)   68 in 100

Source: Compiled research by editors.

FOOTBALL, COLLEGE

Losing Teams

Definition. Groups of football players who definitely do not get to jump in the sack with the head cheerleader the night of the game.

Measuring futility is never easy, but most of the teams on this list can find more than a miserable winning percentage to be ashamed of. Unlike the winning-most teams, the losers tend to have a greater turnover in coaching. Therefore the record of any coach was not factored into the odds as shown below.

Kansas State, the losingest team in the nation, has had losing records in 65 of the 95 seasons it has fielded a program. The school also shared the record for most consecutive games lost (28) with Virginia through 1981, only to have Big Ten doormat Northwestern come along and extend the standard to 34 before defeating Northern Illinois early the next year. And by failing to make a two-point conversion against Baylor in the last game of the 1990 season, Rice kept hold of the dubious distinction of having gone a record 27 consecutive seasons without a winning one.

The Odds: Based on their records over the past decade, the following list represents the team's odds against winning one of their "average" games.

Kansas St.   37 in 100
Wake Forest   41 in 100
Northwestern   43 in 100
Indiana   44 in 100
UTEP   44 in 100
Kent State   44 in 100
Cal. State-Fullerton 44 in 100
Rice   44 in 100
Colorado State   46 in 100
New Mexico St.   46 in 100

Source: Compiled research by editors.

FOOTBALL GRADS

Graduation Rates of College Players

Definition: Students who graduate by the skin of a pig, rather than by that of their teeth.

If football players have a reputation which is less than scholarly, it may be deserved, at least when it comes to graduating college. Graduation rates of collegiate pig-skinners are significantly below the rest of the student body. On the other hand, when compared to basketball players, football players are veritable whiz kids.

The Odds: Overall, athletes have similar graduation rates to the main student body (1 in 2), but only approximately 2 in 5 football players graduate from the universities they play for. This compares to only 3 in 10 for basketball players, the athletes with the worst graduation rates.

The following list represents the major collegiate athletic leagues and the proportion of football players who earn diplomas:

ACC	55.4 in 100
Independents	51.7 in 100
Big Ten	50.1 in 100
Pac 10	46.6 in 100
Western Ath. Conf.	43.1 in 100
Mid-American 4	2.9 in 100
Big 8	39.4 in 100
Southwest	32.5 in 100
SEC 3	2.2 in 100
Big West	23.8 in 100

The following list represents graduation rates of football players, measured in percent, compared to average students at universities affiliated with major collegiate athletic leagues:

Western	+9.1
Independents	+3.0
Pac	+1 3.
Mid-American	- 3.7
Big	- 8 6.6
Big Ten	- 9.1
ACC	- 10.2
SEC	- 13.2
Big West	- 14.5
Southwest	- 16.8

Source: Chronicle of Higher Education.

Also See: Basketball Grads, Jock Graduations.

FOOTBALL INJURIES

Varsity

Definition: Bruises, breaks and other ills suffered by gorillas-like adolescents trying to take each others' heads off.

The Odds: The chance of injury on the gridiron and the practice field are just about even. Slightly more than half of all high school and college football players are injured each year. The odds of a and college football players are injured each year. The odds of a team sustaining injuries on a daily or semi-daily basis are very good. About 11.3 of every 1,000 athletic encounters results in injury. That is, if a team of 50 practices seventeen times and plays three games it should have eleven or twelve injuries.

Multiple Injuries: The odds of two players being injured on the same day are 1 in 4, three players being injured is 1 in 8 and 4 players being injured is 1 in 16. One in 16 may seem like bad odds but consider that for most teams this means that four players will be injured on game day once every other year.

Source: Vinger, Paul F,. and Earl F. Hoerner, Eds. *Sports Injuries: The Unthwarted Epidemic* 1982.

FOOTBALL HEROES

Can Your Kid Make it to the Super Bowl?

Definition: A young lad hell-bent on using his guts for glory.

It's the dream a many a kid to someday play in the Super Bowl, and to lead his team to a last-minute victory. It's not an easy thing to do.

The Odds: The odds against your high-school player making the pros are 1,175 to 1. A thousand-to-one shot might not sound so far fetched, but consider what it

takes to climb the ladder to the NFL:

The Climb: On average, the odds against a high-school player playing NCAA football are 25 to 1. But even if he's made his college team, his odds are a slim 30 to 1 against being chosen in the NFL draft. Of the 10,000 college players eligible for the draft

every year, only 336 are selected. If drafted, there is about an even chance to make the team — the odds are almost certain for 1st and 2nd round picks but dwindle to about 3 to 1 against players chosen in the last rounds. If not drafted, a college player still has a chance, though, at 500 to 1, not a very good chance, of making an NFL team as a free-agent rookie. In a given year, about 210 rookies make it onto an NFL roster out of the 10,000 or so eligible college players, giving odds of about 47 to 1 against a college jock making the pros.

The Big One: But will he play in a Super Bowl? Given an average NFL career of 6 years, the straight odds of making it to a Super Bowl are a little less than even, giving our high-school player odds of 2,350 to 1 against playing in a Super Bowl. (Of course, the odds are a lot better if he's drafted by a good team than a bad one). The odds of being the starting quarterback are another 45 to 1 against him, or 100,000 to 1; of being the winning quarterback 200,000 to 1. And since odds of a Super Bowl being won in the last two minutes are 8.5 to 1 against, it's about a 2,000,000 to one shot that your high school hero will end up leading his team to a last minute win in the Super Bowl. Keep practicing!

Source: Compiled research by editors.

FORECLOSURE

Definition: A process in which a man with a pencil-thin mustache gets the key to your ranch.

To many, the loss of a family home is an archetypal symbol of failure and disaster. In recessionary times, unfortunately, the relinquishing of one's home through bank foreclosure is a very real possibility.

The Odds: In 1990, nearly 1 in 8 new mortgages were foreclosed on. Older mortgages which reflect lower rates are safer from default. The states with the most foreclosures are also those with some of the fastest-growing populations, so as soon as a house is emptied, it is immediately re-occupied.

The following list represents the proportions of home mortgages which were foreclosed on in the ten states with the highest rates:

Arizona	1 in 8
Texas	1 in 9
Alaska	1 in 12
Wyoming	1 in 12
Colorado	1 in 13
Oklahoma	1 in 15
Arkansas	1 in 17
Louisiana	1 in 18
New Mexico	1 in 22
Mississippi	1 in 29

Source: U.S. Office of Economic Analysis.

FOREIGN BORN

Definition: An American citizen or permanent resident whose birth took place outside the country.

Each year America welcomes between 800,000 and one million immigrants. This is significantly down from yesteryear when, during the early part of the century, immigration was unrestricted. From 1900 to 1925 between 3 and 4 million arrived

annually from other lands to live in America.

The Odds: Today, even with the ebb in immigration, 1 in 9 Americans speaks a language other than English in the home. One in 16 Americans is foreign born. In many of the largest cities the ratios are much higher. In Manhattan 1 in 2 residents is foreign born; in Los Angeles 1 in 3; in Chicago 1 in 4.

Source: Compiled research by editors.

FOREIGN TAKEOVERS

Corporate Transfers

Definition: A circumstance in which your boss just doesn't speak your language.

Everyone decries the transfer of critical U.S. commercial assets into foreign hands, but few are aware of the positive contributions many foreign companies make to our economy through the establishment of domestic subsidiaries. Though the Japanese and their Asian neighbors may take American jobs as they incrementally increase the share of the domestic durable goods markets, they return many of these jobs by establishing U.S. plants to manufacture those very goods.

Among the largest 1,000 U.S. corporations, approximately 1 in 7 dollars of revenue belongs to a foreign owned company which was once in the hands of Americans. Nearly 1 in 15 dollars of the nation's gross national product is produced by foreign owned corporations.

The Odds: What then are the odds that an outlander will take over your workplace? If it does happened at all, it is most likely to be someone who is Canadian, British or Dutch, which represent the nationalities of the three largest acquirers of American assets. The Japanese are seventh on the tally sheet of acquisitions by foreign investors.

The following list represents the proportions of workers who work for foreign companies in the ten states with the highest percentage of foreign-owned businesses:

California	1 in 3
New York	3 in 10
Texas	1 in 5
New Jersey	1 in 6
Pennsylvania	1 in 6
Illinois	1 in 6

North Carolina	1 in 8
Ohio	1 in 8
Georgia	1 in 9
Florida	1 in 9

Source: U.S. Bureau of Economic Analysis.

FOREIGN TRADE

Definition: Imports and exports of goods and services businesses sell to customers in other countries.

The Odds: According to a survey of executives of major corporations, there is a 13 in 20 chance that the U.S. share of world markets will further erode during the 1990s. What should we do? Executives feel the odds are slightly better than even that U.S. import restrictions will increase considerably to deal with mounting foreign competition in our own markets. Crisis in confidence or facing reality, few in business would give odds on America rebounding to its preeminence in the industrial world. Most business leaders believe there is only a 1 in 4 chance that U.S. manufacturers will win back most of the market share they recently lost to foreign competition. Unfortunately for Americans, many business leaders seem to feel we have had our day on the world stage.

Source: Weidenbaum, Murray *Rendezvous With Reality*, Basic Books, Inc.

FRIDAY THE 13TH

Definition: The unluckiest day of the year.

Ever wonder why a pair of dice only goes up to twelve? Well, think about this. What craps player would want to have to make unlucky 13 (Let's not worry about how hard it would be to make seven-sided dice). Thirteen is indeed an unlucky number, at least in the minds of superstitious folk. In fact, it seems that most of the odd prime numbers are believed to hold some supernatural significance. Three, for instance, is the number of the Holy Trinity, five the number of digits on a hand, seven the lucky number, as well as the number of Snow White's dwarves, 11 the number of players the unlucky Minnesota Vikings fielded on the gridiron in their four Super Bowl losses.

But 13 — that number conjures up images of black cats, witches, wizards and goblins. Many tall buildings skip over the 13th floor and go directly from 12 to 14. The professional athlete who chooses the number for his jersey is indeed tempting the fates. And woe to those unlucky souls born on that strange day.

The Odds: Every 28 years, there are 48 Friday the 13ths. This makes the odds against being born on a Friday the 13 about 214 to 1—not bad, but it does mean that there are more than one million Americans carrying around some pretty unlucky birthday baggage with them. In the 1980s, what with Reaganomics and all, you may have thought the country had gone through a particularly long string of bad luck. If so, don't blame it on the calendar— there were only 17 of the ill-boding Fridays in that decade. On the other hand, maybe Hollywood's to blame. In the last ten years, studio moguls added to our bad luck by making seven *Friday the 13th* movies. That makes the chances about 3 in 7 that Hollywood will once again resurrect Jason Vorhees this year. The chances of a particular Friday falling on the 13th are a reasonable 1 in 30.

Source: Research compiled by editors.

FRIENDLY FIRE
Modern U.S. Fatalities

Definition: A circumstance in which a U.S. soldier is unknow-ingly killed or injured by guns, bombs or other types of aggression which are administered by his own troops.

Until the Viet Nam War there was little public awareness of friendly fire fatalities, though among combat troops it was always a known hazard of fighting a war. It has always been assumed that friendly fire was unintentional.

The Odds: In previous conflicts the subject of death by friendly fire was a taboo and no official records were kept and few reports hit the media. This has changed dramatically in wars fought during the age of investigative reporting. In the Viet Nam War is has been estimated that between 7,000 and 8,000 U.S. troops were killed by friendly fire, which accounted for 1 in 7 battle deaths.

Among the total troops committed to the War in the Persian Gulf, 1 in 12,000 fell victim to their own guns. Of the estimated 150 Americans who fought and died in combat during this 1991 war, slightly more than 1 in 3 deaths (35) were caused by friendly fire. There were 72 reports of injuries due to the same.

Incidents in the Gulf: More than 2 in 3 deaths due to friendly fire were among Army troops, who suffered 21 fatalities. The Marines suffered 14 fatalities. There were no known Air Force, Coast Guard or Navy casualties due to friendly fire. Incidents of friendly fire were as follows:

16 ground-to-ground

24 killed, 57 wounded

9 air-to-ground

11 killed, 15 wounded

1 ship-to-ship, 1 shore-to-ship, 1 ground-to-air

no casualties.

Source: U.S. Department of Defense.

Also See: War Casualties.

G g

GAMBLING EXPENSES

Definition: The money spent for a whirl around the casino floor with Lady Luck.

In the 1990s, America has been bitten by the gambling bug. On an almost monthly basis, gambling is being legalized at places as diverse as Midwest riverboats and remote Indian reservations on the Great Plains. Where is all the money going?

The Odds: In 1990 in America, $25.8 billion was spent on eight principle types of legalized gaming. The list below represents the odds, dollar-for-dollar, that it was wagered in various ways:

Lotteries	2 in 4
Casinos	1 in 3
Pari-mutuel Betting	1 in 7
Charitable Games	1 in 21
Bingo	1 in 25
Card Rooms	1 in 40
Indian Reservations	1 in 50
Sports Bookmaking	1 in 206

Source: Christiansen/Cummings Associates of New York CIty, for Gaming and Wagering Business Magazine. *The Statistical Abstract*, 1991

Also See: Craps, Lotteries, Poker.

GENIUS

Definition: An individual with an IQ above 139, as opposed to someone who is simply called one because he has made a lot of money.

Contrary to popular belief, geniuses don't usually wear glasses. They do, however, frequently tend to be excellent physical specimens, less prone to mental disorders, physical weaknesses and body deformities than the general population.

The Odds: Among the general population, the odds are 1 in 250 that any child tested will be revealed to be a genius. Recent intelligence measures have tended to categorize the most intelligent as a "first order genius" which occurs in 1 in every 1,000 births.

ESTIMATED IQS OF HISTORICAL FIGURES

John Stuart Mill	190
Goethe	185
Voltaire	170
Mozart	150
Thomas Jefferson	145
Napoleon	140
Leonardo da Vinci	135
George Washington	130
Les Krantz *	122
Dan Quayle†	106

* Les Krantz is the Editor-in-Chief of *What the Odds Are*.

† Dan Quayle will be the next U.S. President if George Bush gets eaten by a shark (See Shark Attack) or drowns in a bucket (See Bucket Drowning).

Source: Stanford-Binet Inteligence Quotient; List of highest IQs among historical figure: *The Book of Lists*.

Also See: Intelligence.

GENTRIFIC-ATION

Definition: A process which involves the phasing out of the old-stock and minority residents of a city neighborhood by the baby boomers, yuppies and otherwise moneyed class.

Even the poshest of cities have their own unsightly slices of life. Dwellings for servants, em-ployees and other nuts-and-bolts service-oriented folks mar the most uppity and pretentious of urban landscapes. It is these ivoried walls that every marketer wants to breach, and every underclassman aspires to.

The Odds: The following list represents the ten areas with the highest ratios of households earning over $50,000.

HIGHEST RATIOS

Nassau-Suffolk, NY	44 in 100
Stamford-Norwalk-Danbury, CT	43 in 100
Middlebury-Somerset, NJ	43 in 100
San Jose, CA	40 in 100
Washington, D.C.	40 in 100
Bergen-Passaic, NJ	40 in 100
Trenton, NJ	37 in 100
Newark, NJ	36 in 100
Manchester-Nashua, NH	35 in 100
Anaheim-Santa Anna, CA	34 in 100

Source: Sales and Marketing Management, 1990 Survey of Buying Power.

GIRL SCOUTS

Definition: Active members of the Girl Scouts of America, a not-for-profit organization to foster American ideals in young women ages 5 to 17.

Nearly 2,500,000 girls across the country are members of the Girl

Scouts; another 800,000 adults are members.

The Odds: In the U.S., 1 in 9 girls are Scouts. Among younger girls 6 to 8 years of age, 1 in 4 are members and 1 in 7 girls ages 9 to 11 is a Scout. Fourteen percent of all Scout members are minorities. Girls in Missouri are the most likely to be Scouts.

The following list represents proportions of the population who are Scouts in the ten states with the highest number of members:

California	1 in 117
New York	1 in 104
Pennsylvania	1 in 80
Illinois	1 in 78
Ohio	1 in 74
Texas	1 in 101
Michigan	1 in 84
Florida	1 in 109
New Jersey	1 in 82
Missouri	1 in 60

Source: Girl Scouts of the United States of America.

GOVERNMENT REGULATION

Definition: The process by which Federal bureaucrats convince voters that they know more about operating factories and service businesses than the owners do.

The Odds: According to a 1987 survey of executives at major corporations, there is a 9 in 20 chance that government regula-tion will increase over the next decade.

Environmental Regulation: According to the same executives, there is a 3 in 5 chance that environmental regulations will intensify. Though taxes are not regulations per se, they do in some ways effect the ways businesses will perform. On this issue, businessmen believe there is a 7 in 10 chance that the severity of taxation will increase to deal with the deficit. Bearing out the businessmen's predictions, the government has not moved to excessively reregulate problem industries such as airlines and banking. It is only in business's relationship to the environment and not in business practices that the administration has seen fit to intervene

Source: Weidenbaum, Murray *Rendezvous With Reality*, Basic Books, Inc.

GOVERNMENT WORKERS

A Growing Field

Definition: The only workers in the nation who love to see tax increases, which are always directly proportional to their pay raises, increased benefits and decreased work loads.

Read their lips, all 52 million ruby red, fleshy rims of the hungry mouths of the 26 million Americans who work for a federal, state or local government. To fire them is near impossible. To give them raises and increase their benefits is inevitable. To increase their work loads is unthinkable. During the decade 1980-89, their numbers grew twice as fast as the U.S. population. It soared up 18.4 percent.

The Odds: The founding fathers of our nation drew up the U.S. Constitution and the Bill of Rights because they distrusted big governments. During the latter part of the eighteenth century, less than 1 in 1,000 people worked at a government job, mostly military men. Two hundred years later, it all changed. Today, approximately 1 in 4 full-time workers are employed by some form of government at the federal, state or local level. Somewhat over 1 in 13 workers are employed by the federal government.

The following list represents the states with the fastest growth of state and local government jobs:

Wyoming	20.9%
New York	18.9
Kentucky	17.7

There's good news though. Government employment dropped in other places, but only in 4 of 50 states: Alaska, Massachusetts, Maryland and Rhode Island. Unfortunately they are among either the least populous or smallest of the U.S. states. Are you ready for your next tax bill?

Source: U.S. Department of Commerce.

Also See: Federal Employment.

GREENHOUSE EFFECTS

Definition: A general rise in world temperatures caused by increasing concentrations of carbon dioxide (CO_2) and other "green-house gases" (those given off by burning fossil fuels and using repellents, particularly fluorocarbons).

The problem is further hampered by the general removal of trees, especially the tropical rain forests, which previously acted as "sinks" for carbon dioxide, by using it in the process of photosynthesis.

The Odds: According to the Senate testimony of NASA scientist James Hansen, the odds are 99 to 1 that recent temperature increases reflect the impact of greenhouse effects. Green-house gases hold heat in the lower atmosphere allowing temperatures to rise. Though the five warmest years in recorded history occurred during the 1980s and though humanity adds more than 5.5 billion tons of carbon to the atmosphere each year, there is still a 1 in 100 chance that these events are just a fluke.

In the future, according to some experts it is likely that average temperatures will eventually rise three to eight degrees higher than they have been in recent years.

Source: Brown Lester R. et al, *State of The World 1989; A World-watch Institute Report on Progress Toward a Sustainable Society.* W.W. Norton & Co

GUNS

Definition: How people kill each other.

It has been estimated that there are over 30 million handguns owned by American citizens, which is several fold what the U.S. military owns.

The Odds: The following list, which is based on statistics for the period 1985-1989, represents the odds that you will wind up on the right or wrong side of gun:

Own Gun	11 in 25
Killed by Firearm	1 in 4,600
Killed by Handgun	1 in 6,100
Killed by Rifle	1 in 63,000
Killed by Shotgun	1 in 45,000

Source: FBI Uniform Crime Reports.

Also See: Also see Murder, Crime, Killers.

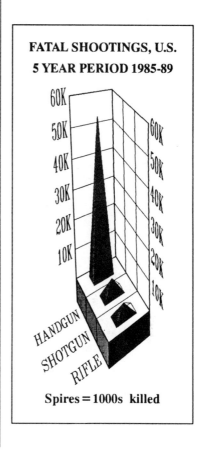

FATAL SHOOTINGS, U.S.

5 YEAR PERIOD 1985-89

Spires = 1000s killed

H h

HAIR COLOR

Definition: The overall hue, tint, tone, and shade of your locks.

What can hair color tell you? Plenty, says red-headed writer for *Town and Country* Magazine, Dan Rottenberg. He cites various studies that point to red heads being smarter. Since seeing is believing, we know they are brighter, at least their locks are, but the rest of his theory is open to question.

The Odds: Because hair color is hereditary, there is at least some predictability. Among Caucasians of European origin, the only major racial subgroup with varied hair colors, the odds are 1 in 4 that a child will have one of his parent's overall hair color. Among other racial groups, hair color is almost invariably very dark brown or black.

The following list represents the odds that a Caucasian American will have various hair colors:

Brown	7 in 10
Blonde	1 in 7
Black	1 in 10
Red	1 in 16
"Rust Red"	1 in 33

Source: Clairol, Inc.

Also See: Baldness.

HEALTH WORRIES

Definition: Fears people have about risks of diseases, infections and dying from natural causes of all kinds.

The Odds: There is no doubt that there are many disasters that can befall innocent victims, but health risks loom high in the minds of the fearful. The highest on the lists of American health scares are as follows.

AIDS	1 in 4
Cancer	1 in 5
Heart Disease	1 in 10

Source: Gallop Organization Poll for the American Association of Blood Banks.

Also See: AIDS, Cancer, Death, Heart Attack, Heart Disease.

HEART ATTACK

Definition: A medical condition brought on when 3 events happen on the same day: 1) your teenager goes joy riding in the family car without a driver's license; 2) your unmarried daughter announces she is pregnant and 3) you have an IRS agent show up at your front door.

Heart attacks may be one of the most joked about afflictions, but in reality they are the number one cause of death in the U.S. (over 500,000 annually), with cancer being in a very close second position (475,000). Individual behavior and nutrition is suspected to be a key factor in whether or not heart disease will result in a fatal heart attack.

The Odds: The overall odds of dying from a heart attack is 1 in 3. The odds of dying immediately when stricken are also 1 in 3. The odds of immediate death can be significantly reduced if treatment is sought the moment symptoms appear, such as simultaneous chest pains, nausea and shortness of breath. Some 1 in 2 heart attack victims is under the age of 65 and 1 in 20 victims is under age 40.

Risk Factors: Smokers, men, low income individuals and those who are overweight are the most at risk. According to *The Almanac of the American People* men earning under $13,000 annually have a 40 percent greater risk than men earning over $28,000. The lowest income women have a 27 percent greater risk than the highest income women. The American Heart Association reports that women have a slight advantage over men in surviving a heart attack.

Source: Compiled research by editors.

Also See: Heart Disease; Heart Attack, Number 2.

HEART ATTACK, No. 2

Not again!

Definition: The recurrence of a sudden affliction also known as myocardial infarction, coronary thrombosis or "a coronary."

The onslaught of a second heart attack is brought on by the same factors that caused the first (see Heart Attack). Though victims of a first heart attack have the advantage of knowing of their heart condition and taking precautions, they are significantly more at risk than those who have never suffered from heart ailments.

The Odds: Those who have had a heart attack are 3 times more likely to be stricken again than the average individual. Victims of heart attacks with high cholesterol levels during or after recovery are 4 times more at risk of having a second attack than heart patients with normal levels of 200 or below. They also are twice as likely to die of other causes.

One of the reasons why so many individuals who have had heart attacks have a second may be that doctors often pay more attention to less significant factors than to high risk ones such as smoking and high blood pressure. Too frequently, doctors fail to check or discuss cholesterol levels with their patients. Heart specialists recommend that if a heart patient is not talked to by his doctor about his cholesterol level, he would be wise to ask.

Source: Framingham (Mass.) Heart Study as reported in *Annals of Internal Medicine.*

Also See: Heart Attack; Heart Disease; Heart Disease, Women.

HEART DISEASE

Definition: Any malady relating to the cardiovascular system, most commonly, high blood pressure, atherosclerosis, angina pectoris and heart attacks.

Over 63 million Americans suffer some form of heart disease. The sickness is thought to be primarily congenital, but individual behavior and nutrition is suspected to be a key factor in how the disease will effort your overall health.

The Odds: According to the American Heart Association, 1 in 4 Americans suffer from some form of heart disease and 1 in 3 Americans can expect to die from a heart-related health problem. Atherosclerosis, a medical term for the clogging of arteries, is the most common cardiovascular ailment causing over 600,000 deaths annually. Some 2 in 3 of these deaths happen unexpectedly, usually related to heart attacks. Slightly less than 1 in 3 deaths related to the clogging of arteries takes the form of a stroke, which occurs when a vessel supplying blood to the brain breaks.

Improving Recovery Odds: Medical surveys have recently shed a whole new light on successfully convalescing. Those with friends and money have a significantly higher rates of recovery. One finding shows that 1 in 2 unmarried patients dies from heart disease. Among married patients, only 1 in 7 will die. Among those with annual incomes less than $10,000 1 in 4 dies. Among patients with incomes of $40,000 or over, 1 in 11 dies.

Source: Beat the Odds by Harold S. Solomon, M.D.; Duke University Medical Center, Durham NC.

Also See: Heart Attack, Second; Heart Disease; Heart Disease; Women, High Blood Pressure.

HEART DISEASE
Among Women

Definition: (see Heart Disease)

Heart disease, and particularly heart attacks, was long thought to be mainly a male problem. The postwar phenomena of better medical record keeping has shown that heart disease among women is not only serious, but there are some significantly different sets of occurrences than those of males. There are also different rates in women based on their race.

The Odds: Women are less likely to die from a heart attack than men. The female rate of death is 47.5 percent compared to 52.5 for males. Ironically, heart attacks of women are twice as likely to be fatal within the first few weeks. One year after a heart attack, 39 percent of women die, compared to 31 percent of men.

Racial differences in women include rates of high blood pressure, which are 1 in 4 among whites and almost 2 in 5 among blacks. Age related deaths from heart attacks among black women is one-and-half times higher than among whites. Deaths from strokes are higher among black women than white women.

Source: American Heart Association.

Also See: Heart Attacks, Heart Disease.

HEROIN DEATHS

Definition: An act in which a type of dope injects another type of dope in his system until the dope is dead.

Although the nation's attention is deservedly focused on the prevalence of crack and and other socially corrosive cocaine derivatives, heroin still poses a deadly threat. In fact, the danger from this drug has now become a two-edged sword, with the very real threat of HIV infection that heroin injectors face from shared needles.

The following list represents the ratio of very much alive citizens to very dead dopes who overdosed on heroin:

Los Angeles	1 in 8,009
Chicago	1 in 13,378
Philadelphia	1 in 7,843
San Francisco	1 in 4,253
Washington, D.C.	1 in 3,717
San Diego	1 in 9,394
Detroit	1 in 10,049
Boston	1 in ,7493
Seattle	1 in 8,964

Source: "Overview of Selected Drug Trends," NIDA Drug Abuse Warning Network.

Also See: Drug Emergencies.

HEROES OF KIDS

Definition: Anyone rich or famous except Pee Wee Herman.

Through the century, heroes have been Tom Mix, Hopalong Cassidy, Babe Ruth, Davy Crockett, President John Kennedy, Rocky, Arnold Schwarzenegger and the list goes on. But what do these heroes really do for a living?

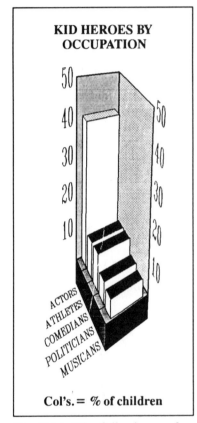

KID HEROES BY OCCUPATION

50
40
30
20
10
50
40
30
20
10

ACTORS
ATHLETES
COMEDIANS
POLITICIANS
MUSICANS

Col's. = % of children

The Odds: The following professions represents the occupations of children's heroes:

Actors	2 in 5
Athletes	1 in 10
Comedians	1 in 10
Musicians	1 in 20
Politicians	1 in 16

Source: Harris Poll.

HIGH SCHOOL DRUGS

Usage Among Seniors

Definition: The use of illicit drugs by upperclassmen in secondary school.

Most high school students pattern their social behavior after upperclassmen, which is why the rate of drug usage among seniors is so disturbing. The 1980s were marked by the re-emergence of traditional (even conservative) values among our youth, yet abuse of legal and illegal recreational drugs remains a problem of monumental proportions.

The Odds: Nearly 9 in 10 American high school seniors reported significant use of alcohol within a span of two months, and nearly 1 in 2 had consumed marijuana or hashish in that same period. The following are the drugs of preference for "high" schoolers and proportions of seniors who have admitted consuming particular substances within the two months prior to the survey:

Alcohol	9 in 10
Marijuana/Hashish	1 in 2
Stimulants	1 in 6
Tranquilizers	1 in 9
Barbiturates	1 in 11
Hallucinogens	1 in 11
Cocaine	1 in 14
Opiates	1 in 16
LSD	1 in 18

Source: "Drug Use, Smoking and Drinking by America's High School Students," U.S. Dept. of Health and Human Services.

HIGH SCHOOL GRADUATION

Definition: Earning a certificate for completion of secondary school, whether you know how to read or not.

Not so many years ago, a high school diploma was an invaluable possession which separated the diligent and employable from the unkempt masses. Just decades later, the value of that degree has eroded enormously, as an undergraduate university education has become the minimum prerequisite for even relatively low-brow positions. This devaluation, however, has made the completion of a high school program all the more critical, because of the tremendous stigma and difficulties the high school dropout faces in the job market.

The Odds: Slightly better than 3 in 4 Americans under the age of 25 complete high school. The lowest rate of completion is among Hispanics, 1 in 2. Among blacks, slightly better than 3 in 5 graduate.

The following list represents the proportions of the population which graduate high school in the states with the highest and lowest graduation rates:

TEN HIGHEST STATES

Minnesota	91.4 in 100
Connecticut	89.8 in 100
North Dakota	89.7 in 100
Nebraska	88.1 in 100
Iowa	87.5 in 100
Montana	87.2 in 100
Wisconsin	86.3 in 100
South Dakota	81.5 in 100
Kansas	81.5 in 100
Wyoming	81.2 in 100

THE LOWEST STATES

Dist. of Columbia	56.8 in 100
Florida	62.0 in 100
Louisiana	62.7 in 100
Georgia	62.7 in 100
Arizona	63.0 in 100
Mississippi	63.3 in 100
New York	64.2 in 100
Texas	64.3 in 100
South Carolina	64.5 in 100
Nevada	65.2 in 100

Source: U.S. Department of Education, Office of Planning, Budget and Evaluation.

HIGHWAY FATALITIES
Global Rates

Definition: The rate at which automobile passengers fly through windshields or get mashed on the upholstery and dash boards of their automobiles.

When it comes to taking to the road in Europe, steer clear of the Mediterranean countries and watch out in Portugal. The Portuguese, normally a quiet, easygoing people, somehow turn into raving lunatics on the roadway, accounting for the highest traffic fatality rate among all developed nations.

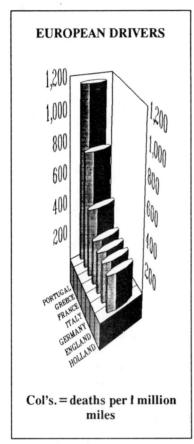

EUROPEAN DRIVERS

Col's. = deaths per 1 million miles

The Odds: In contrast to the death-prone Portuguese drivers, the staid residents of northern climes—Denmark, Germany, the U.K—suffer a fatality rate only about one-quarter that of the Portuguese and a third that of the Greeks.

The following list represents the ratio of deaths to miles driven in the 10 most fatality-prone countries.

Portugal	1,163 in 1,000,000
Greece	764 in 1,000,000
Spain	635 in 1,000,000
France	439 in 1,000,000
Denmark	376 in 1,000,000
Italy	285 in 1,000,000
Germany	265 in 1,000,000
U. K.	255 in 1,000,000
U.S.	248 in 1,000,000
Netherl'ds	236 in 1,000,000

Portugal: Many blame outdated driver's education and testing programs in which Portuguese drivers can receive their licenses without ever taking a car out onto a highway. Others blame drunk driving, excessive speed, poor auto and road conditions in the newly industrialized nation, and a general sense that the road is the best place to relieve tensions.

Source: New York Times.

Also See: Automobile Accidents.

HISPANIC POPULATIONS
U.S. Communities

Definition: The aggregate number of people who trace their ancestry to Spanish-speaking countries, especially Mexico, Puerto Rico, Central and South America.

America has always prided itself on being a nation of immigrants. Such celebration should continue well into the foreseeable future, for America remains a nation of new arrivees. Of course, many of these folks arrive without proper papers or legal pedigree, but in time even these less-than-legal immigrants are assimilated into the fabric of America.

The Odds: Hispanic populations in the U.S. have soared to almost 24 million, making the odds that the average American is of Latin-American origin about 1 in 10. The odds that an Hispanic is an illegal alien is estimated to be between 1 in 15 and 1 in 8.

The lists below represents the ratio of Hispanics to non-Hispanics in various cities.

TOP 10 HISPANIC U.S. CITIES

San Antonio	52 in 100
Miami-Hialeah	45 in 100
Los Angeles- Long Beach	37 in 100
Riverside- San Bernadino, CA	23 in 100
New York	22 in 100
San Jose	22 in 100
Anaheim-Santa Ana	19 in 100
Houston	19 in 100
San Diego	16 in 100
Phoenix	14 in 100

BOTTOM 10 HISPANIC U.S. CITIES

The following list represents the toughest places in the U.S. in which to find a good burrito.

Cincinnati	6 in 1,000
Pittsburgh	6 in 1,000
Columbus	7 in 1,000
Nashville	8 in 1,000
Indianapolis	8 in 1,000
Charlotte- Rockhill-NC-SC	9 in 1,000
Memphis	11 in 1,000
St. Louis	11 in 1,000
Minneapolis-St. Paul,	11 in 1,000
Baltimore	11 in 1,000

Source: Marketing Management, Survey of Buying Power.

Also See: Illegal Aliens.

HIT BY CAR

Definition: 1) Being hit by a car while standing on your own two feet; 2) a song sung by an automobile which makes the Top 40 List.

The Odds: The odds of getting hit are highest for children between 5 and 14. The odds of being in a fatal car-pedestrian accident peaks at age six when 1 in 12,500 boys die and 1 in 25,000 girls fall victim. The vast majority of car-pedestrian cases occur in urban areas. However, the odds of a fatality are higher in the country. Of people hit by cars in rural areas, more than 1 in 8 die. The figure is 1 in 25 in the city.

Playing the Odds: Cross at the intersection! Among adult accident victims who actually die, the odds are 4 to 1 that the accident did not happen at an intersection. Among children younger than 5, the odds are 7 to 1 that he ran into the street away from a crossing. Lay off the sauce. The odds are almost even that fatally injured adults will have blood alcohol concentrations of 0.10 percent or greater.

Source: Baker, Susan P. et al; *The Injury Fact Book*, Lexington Books.

HIV IN BLOOD

Definition: The presence of the HIV virus which causes AIDS in the blood supply.

There are many celebrated cases in which people have contacted AIDS and AID-related syndrome from blood transfusions. The actual occurrences, however, are rare. A decade ago, the risk was greater and many hemophiliacs who required regular transfusions contacted the virus and eventually died as a result. With the risks of contaminated blood now known as being a possible carrier, precautions are now meticulously in place in blood banks.

The Odds: Slightly more than 1 in 2 people wrongly believe that blood transfusions are common causes of AIDS. The calculated risk, however, is thousands-fold less. Risks of infection from a transfusion range from 1 in 40,000 in urban areas to less than 1 in 150,000 in rural America.

Source: USA Today.

Also See: AIDS; AIDS Among Children; AIDS, Riskiest Cities; AIDS Transmission.

HOLE-IN-ONE
The Ultimate Golf Story

Definition: Sinking a tee shot in golf.

A hole in one is every golfer's dream. Sure, you can pile up the birdies and the eagles, you can hit the occasional 300-yard drive, you can polish 'em off at the 19th hole as well as anybody. But to achieve true fame in links lore, you've gotta sink an ace at least once in your life.

The Odds: The Professional Golfers Association (PGA), the keepers of statistics on professional golf, and therefore the ones who should know the most about such things, put the odds of a professional golfer sinking a hole-in-one in a single round of a PGA event at 3,708 to 1. In other words, for every 3,709 rounds of golf played, one of them will contain a hole in one. Since it is next to impossible to score a hole-in-one on a par 4 hole in PGA competition (the vast majority of which are too long even for the longest hitter on the tour even to reach the green from the tee), we can estimate that the average PGA course containing four par-

3 holes at which holes-in-one are possible so the odds of a player sinking the tee shot on any particular par 3 hole are approximately 15,000 to 1.

Believe it or Not Department: Even in the pro ranks, a hole-in-one is a rarity. But even more rare are multiple holes-in-one during the same round of a PGA event. But, how about multiple holes-in-one on the same hole by separate golfers on the same day, within a matter of hours? Amazingly, on June 16, 1989, at the U.S. Open at Oak Hill Country Club in Pittsford, New York, not one but *four* golfers each aced the par-3, 167-yard sixth hole.

Doug Weaver, a pro from Hilton Head, South Carolina, was the first player to shoot at the hole that day. His 7-iron shot landed 15 feet beyond the cup. The back-spin of the ball gently took it down a slope toward the cup, and as the roar of the crowd grew, the ball rolled in the cup for a hole in one. But that simply set the stage for the dramatics to follow.

A little over an hour later, a threesome including 31-year-old Coloradan Mark Wiebe stepped up to the tee. Wiebe promptly dropped his 7-iron tee shot in the cup for the second ace on the hole that day. Less than a half an hour later, Jerry Pate put in his 7-iron shot on the same hole. By that time, word had spread throughout the gallery, and the crowd all around the course was abuzz. In the threesome immedi-ately following Pate's, one can imagine the golfers each grabbing anxiously for their own 7-irons. Sure enough, Zimbabwean Nick Price nailed his tee shot onto the crest of the green about 20 feet from the hole, and the ball spun right back into the hole.

The PGA calculated the odds of any four golfers acing the same hole on the same day as 332,000 to 1. Actually, in the U.S. Open, one would expect the odds to be slightly lower, since it is a premier event that attracts only the top golfers on the tour. Though the hole-in-one may seem like pure luck, pro golfers, who consistently hit the green on par-3 holes, have much better odds of sinking an ace. Indeed, the four who hit the holes-in-one that lucky day had sixteen other aces between them in professional play prior to the fluke at the U.S. Open.

Source: New York Times, June 17, 1989.

HOMELESSNESS

Definition: The condition, usually found among the poor, of having no permanent place to hang their hat.

The "poverty line" in America is defined as an income of $12,674 or less for a family of four. Despite the scarcity of money, only 1 in 48 poor people have no place to call home. In the U.S., 735,000 individuals are homeless.

The Odds: Approximate 1 in 2

homeless persons suffers some form of mental illness. According to *Parade* magazine (October 13, 1991), slightly more than 2 in 3 homeless persons are veterans. The odds it will happen to the average American are as follows:

Homeless (all U.S.) 1 in 340

Homeless (children) 1 in 2,500

Source: Compiled research by editors.

Also See: Poverty.

HOMOSEX-UALITY

Definition: Sexual desire culminating in erotic behavior directed toward a person or persons of one's own sex.

Because there has never been a reliable survey on sexual preferences in the U.S., it is difficult to tally the number of homosexuals. In 1950, *The Kinsey Report* disclosed that as many as 37 percent of Americans have had at least one homosexual experience. Another study claimed

as low as two percent of the population practiced exclusive homosexual behavior.

The Odds: Because of the wide range of estimates of sexual preferences, estimating ratios can only be an educated guess. Most sex researchers estimate that about 1 in 10 American men are homosexual or bisexual. Among women the odds of exclusively homosexual sexual activity are between 1 in 50 and 1 in 33. Among men, the odds of having a more than incidental homosexual experience for at least three years between the ages of 16 and 65 are 1 in 4. For men, the odds of having at least one homosexual experience which leads to orgasm are almost 2 in 5. For women, the odds of having a homosexual experience leading to orgasm are between 1 in 7 and 1 in 8.

Source: Encyclopedia Britannica.

HONKY BASHING

Black Racism in America

Definition: The proclivity of some blacks to think that all whites drive their cars into black ghettos and honk their horns.

Racism in America is commonly associated with the behavior of whites toward blacks. There is, however, a large contingent of blacks who attribute many undesirable traits to whites.

The Odds: Surprisingly, many blacks hold beliefs about moral issues which are different than those held by whites. For example, blacks are twice as likely as whites to believe their spouse is cheating. Blacks are also more likely to believe that most marriages will end in a divorce.

The list below represents the proportion of blacks who attribute various traits to whites:

Racism	1 in 2
Wealth	2 in 9
Greedy	1 in 5
Intelligent	1 in 7
Dangerous	1 in 7

Source: The Day America Told the Truth, James Patterson, Peter Kim.

Also See: Black Racism, White Boys.

HOSPITAL BEDS

Availability

Definition: Places to recline and convalesce under the care of doctors who are too expensive to beckon and nurses who are too busy to make you comfortable.

Ready access to competent emergency care is probably the first medical priority for any community. But to augment the provision of initial care, those communities must marshal the beds and other hospital resources necessary to maintain those whose recovery is not immediate.

The Odds: What are the odds you'll get a hospital bed when you need one? The unfortunate 1 in 7 people who have no health insurance will have trouble getting a hospital bed unless they prepay. Assuming you have the money or the insurance, odds are pretty good you can get a bed in most cities, but the chances are dismal in some places. The lists below indicates the ratio of hospital beds to the population:

BEST CITIES FOR AVAILABILITY

Pittsburgh	1 to 41
St. Louis	1 to 44
Richmond, VA	1 to 46
Buffalo	1 to 51
Birmingham	1 to 54
Cincinnati	1 to 55
Louisville	1 to 58
Rochester, NY	1 to 58
Miami	1 to 60
Minneapolis	1 to 61

WORST CITIES FOR AVAILABILITY

Virginia Beach	1 to 621
San Jose, CA	1 to 395
Arlington, TX	1 to 385
Santa Ana, CA	1 to 319
Los Angeles	1 to 294
Aurora, CO	1 to 288
Mesa, AZ	1 to 264
Anchorage	1 to240
San Diego	1 to 227
El Paso, TX	1 to 208

Source: The Best and Worst of Everything.

"HOT HANDS"

Definition: 1) The belief that the the performance of an athlete is somehow dependent on his last attempt; 2) the specific belief that the odds of a basketball player hitting his next shot are related to whether or not he made his last shot.

Is a player on a streak more likely to hit his next shot than one who isn't streaking? Don't listen to athletes, sportswriters and sports broadcasters, who are notorious for abusing the laws of probability and physics. Ever hear a commentator say that a baseball actually *picks up speed* when it bounces? Impossible, according to the law of physics. How about that a ball carries better in the cold, or in the heat, or when it's humid? Sorry, it ain't so.

The Law of Averages: Perhaps the greatest misunderstanding of probability in sports is the notorious "law of averages." For instance, say Jose Canseco has played 100 games and hit 25 home runs. He is then averaging 1 home run every 4 games. Now Canseco goes through a slump in which he doesn't ding one for twelve games. Is he "due?"

The idea that Canseco is somehow "due" for a home run misuses the idea of statistics. According to the laws of probability, his being at bat at any particular time is entirely unrelated to what he's done in the past. In fact, it's quite likely that he'll go through a slump during which he doesn't hit a home run for a long time. Indeed, a player in the midst of a slump may even hinder his chances of hitting another home run, by "pressing," or trying too hard.

Hitting home runs, or getting base hits, is not like clockwork. A player who averages one home run every four games in the first 100 games would hit about 40 home runs over the course of a 162-game season, if he maintained precisely the pace he did in the first 100 games. But just because he's established that pace in the first part of the season doesn't mean he's somehow been allotted his 40 home runs, which he will undoubtedly collect by the end of the year. Indeed, it's possible our theoretical Canseco may not hit another home run all season; in fact, the specious "law of averages" would tell you exactly this if you looked at his "average" just in the last twelve games. An owner or a general manager can blow a lot of money by abusing statistics. . . and they do!

Basketball Hot Hands: Most basketball players and coaches swear by it—that a player who's hit a couple of shots in a row is more likely to hit his next one. But, with that reasoning, some players might *never* miss.

At least one study has been done to disprove the "hot hands" theory. Stanford University

130

psychologist Amos Tversky and a team of researchers looked at the records of every shot taken by the Philadelphia 76ers over the course of a season and a half. Examining the shots of individual players, their research showed that, on average, a player was slightly more likely to follow up a made shot with a miss — which is what you'd expect, since the 76ers, like most NBA teams, hit less than 50 percent of their shots over the course of a season.

So, for the fan, the athlete, the broadcaster and the sports writer: The Hot Hands Theory is more hot air than reality.

Source: New York Times.

HOUSEHOLD INJURIES

Definition: Mishaps in the privacy of your home at which you may use all the cuss words desired when they occur.

Accidents resulting in injuries are extremely common. Each year 1 in 27 people will be hurt accidentally. Most accidents and injuries happen in or near the home. The list below represents the most common causes and the odds they will occur in an average year:

Drowning in Tub	1 in 685,000
Shaving	1 in 6,585
Mowing Lawn	1 in 3,623
Bath or Shower	1 in 2,232
Chain Saw	1 in 4,464

Fireworks	1 in 19,566

Source: On an Average Day, Tom Heymann.

Also See: Accidents, Death

HUNGER

Definition: 1) The reason so many people consistently eat french fries, hot dogs and hot fudge sundaes knowing full-well it will probably ruin their health; 2) The means by which Jenny Craig and Tommy Lasorda earn their daily bread and chocolate shakes.

Though there is more than enough food to feed the world, hunger is a fact of life in America and throughout the world. Some of the world's populaces have more than enough to fill their stomachs, but still suffer from various forms of malnutrition such as iron, vitamin or calcium deficiencies, and it is not uncommon for hungry individuals to suffer from all three maladies.

The Odds: There are over 1 billion people people who experience hunger. The odds for the average American to go hungary is estimated as 1 in 10. Throughout the world, 1 in 5 people go hungry. In developing countries, 1 in 3 children is so poorly nourished that their physical development is impaired.

Source: The Chicago Tribune, October 16, 1991

Also See: Poverty

HYPERTENSION
(High Blood Pressure)

Definition: A medical condition which results from excess force being generated by your heart as it pumps blood through your vessels. The group defined as having hypertension are those with blood pressure readings above 140 over 90.

Though hypertension is not fatal by itself, it is related to the onslaught of heart attacks and strokes. There are two types of hypertension, secondary hypertension and essential hypertension. The secondary form is caused by conditions ranging from kidney ailments to blocked arteries to complications from birth control pills. Essential hypertension is caused by the many factors your body uses to regulate the force of blood flow. No one knows its exact cause.

The Odds: Slightly more than 1 in 4 Americans has some form of hypertension. Approximately 1 in 25 sufferers of hypertension have the secondary form, and the others have the more common essential form.

Like most forms of heart disease, hypertension risks increase with age. Ironically, young men are at a higher risk than women, but as aging occurs, women are more at risk. The following list represents the rate of occurrence of hypertension among men and women at various age levels:

	Men	Women
18-24	1 in 7	1 in 25
25-34	1 in 5	1 in 16
35-44	1 in 4	1 in 5
45-54	11 in 25	2 in 5
55-64	1 in 2	1 in 2

65+   6 in 10   7 in 10

Recent studies have shown blacks to have a greater risk of suffering from hypertension than whites.

Source: The American Heart Association.

Also See: Heart Attacks, Heart Disease, Kiddy Horseplay, Strokes.

I i

ILLEGAL ALIENS

Definition: Individuals with foreign accents who quiver each time a policeman looks their way.

Each year about 2.3 million foreign nationals, many without proper visas, enter the U.S. with intent to maintain residence. There are severe penalties for companies which choose to hire those who do not come with proper work papers from the Department of Immigration and Naturalization. Employers who are criticized for discriminating against suspicious-looking foreigners in their hiring practices may have good reason. According to the department's statistics, the odds of an undocumented foreign-born worker being illegal is better than 7 in 10.

Each year 1.7 million people are caught trying to cross the border illegally, of which 96.6% are Mexican. Just more than 200,000 people, only 1 in 8, successfully evade eventually getting caught.

In an average year, 600,000 individuals will immigrate illegally, but a disappointing 2 in 5 will stay and achieve citizenship status.

Source: Dept. of Naturalization and Immigration; *On an Average Day,* Heymann.

IMMIGRATION
Who gets in the U.S.?

Definition: The process in which a foreign national is accepted in the U.S. as a permanent resident.

Not everybody who wants to live in the U.S. goes through the immigration process, which is long and tedious and often disappointing. Some 1 in 20 who apply for immigration visas are accepted right away. The others wait, often futilely. Given these odds, it is no wonder that 1 in 4 foreign entrants on U.S. soil are illegal aliens, most of whom are Mexican. Each day thousands try to sneak in, most of whom enter via the Mexican border.

Among those who get in officially with proper immigration papers, are 600,000 to 800,000, depend-

WHO GETS IN?

Col's. = relative proportions

ing on national immigration quotas set at the time.

The Odds: Among legal immigrants, they are found in the following proportions from various countries:

China (Mainland)	1 in 24
India	1 in 23
Dominican Rep.	1 in 23
Vietnam	1 in 20
Cuba	1 in 18
Korea	1 in 17
Philippines	1 in 11
Mexico	1 in 9

Source: U.S. Immigration and Naturalization Service.

Also See: Illegal Aliens, Immigration Sweepstakes.

IMMIGRATION SWEEPSTAKES
Luck of the Irish?

Definition: A high stakes raffle conducted by the U.S. State Department which determines which foreigners will be allowed to reside in the U.S.

There are approximately 20 million foreign nationals who seek to reside in the U.S. each year. Only 1 in 27 are allowed in. The occasional sweepstakes is but one way to get into the country. Most get in by applying for immigration papers and going through a long process of screening and waiting. The formal immigration process is conducted with quotas which change yearly. In past years, Canadians and Europeans had a much higher priority than other groups. In order be fair about giving equal opportunity, the sweepstakes was started in 1990. Because it involves random selection, many low-priority immigrants are granted long term resident visas.

The Odds: If an entrant in the sweepstakes gets his application in on time (1 in 3 don't), the odds of winning residency are 300 to 1. Some 40,000 winners are chosen annually among 12 million who submit applications in a timely fashion. A high proportion are Irish.

It is thought that many of the applicants are illegal aliens who cannot apply for visas or immigration papers.

Source: U.S. State Department.

Also See: Illegal Aliens, Immigration.

INDIAN RESERVATIONS

Tribal Affiliations

Definition: Officially delineated lands which the Federal Government has set aside for the ex-

clusive use of designated Native American tribes ranging from Aleuts to Zunis.

There are over 500 Indian tribes and 278 reservations in the United States. Estimates of the general population of Indians and those who on live on reservations are extremely unreliable. Reservation populations of Indians range from just over 500,000 to as high as 861,000. Perhaps the difficulty is that some Indians list their residences as both in urban areas as well as on a reservation.

The Odds: Somewhere between 1 in 4 and 1 in 2.3 Indians live on reservations. Because U.S. Census data only indicates if an American is "Indian or Native American", the best estimate of tribal affiliations can be drawn from reservation data as compiled by the Bureau of Indian Affairs.

The following list represents the proportions of reservation Indians belonging to the largest tribes and the states in which most of them reside:

TEN LARGEST TRIBES

Navajo	
(AZ, NM, UT)	1 in 5
Cherokee (OK)	1 in 15
Creek (OK)	1 in 16
Choctaw (OK)	1 in 41
Pine Ridge (SD)	1 in 45
Southern Pueblo	
(NM)	1 in 51
Chicksaw (OK)	1 in 78
Rosebud (SD)	1 in 78
Gila River (AZ)	1 in 81
Papago-Sells (AZ)	1 in 86

Proportions of some smaller but well known tribes include Hopi (AZ) 1 in 96, Apache (AZ) 1 in 103, Zuni 1 in 106, Pawnee (OK) 1 in 113, Shawnee (OK, TX) 1 in 120 and Blackfeet (MT) 1 in 121.

Reservation Indians generally have more social problems than average Americans. Over 1 in 3 are unemployed. In some tribes such as the Sioux, jobless rates are as high as 8 in 10. Cherokees have the lowest joblessness, 1 in 5. Poverty rates on reservations average 9 in 20. Education rates are poor as well, with almost 6 in 10 dropping out of high school before graduation versus about 1 in 3 among average Americans.

Source: Bureau of Indian Affairs.

Also See: Native Americans.

INFANT MORTALITY

Definition: The rate at which babies die before their first birthday.

War, famine, lack of pre-natal care, lack of sanitary conditions, lack of proper obstetrical care — the reasons for infant mortality are many. Yet while larger societal problems loom as difficult to solve, young children most often die from diseases which are readily treatable in the West, such as diarrhea, whose dehydrating effects can usually be kept at bay with fluids. Except for Afghanistan, which borders on Pakistan and the Soviet Union, all the countries with the highest infant mortality rate are on the continent of Africa. While many of these countries have recently been involved in wars, others merely struggle with dismal living conditions.

The Odds: The following list represents the proportions of infants who die before reaching their first birthday in the ten nations with the highest and lowest infant mortality rates:

HIGHEST INFANT DEATHS

Afghanistan	1 in 5.5
Sierra Leone	1 in 5.9
Mali	1 in 5.9
Gambia	1 in 6.1
Malawi	1 in 6.5
Somalia	1 in 6.7
Ethiopia	1 in 6.7
Mozambique	1 in 7.1
Burkina Faso	1 in 7.2
Angola	1 in 7.3

LOWEST INFANT DEATHS

Japan	1 in 167
Finland	1 in 167
Iceland	1 in 167
Sweden	1 in 167
Switzerland	1 in 143
Denmark	1 in 143
Netherlands	1 in 143
Norway	1 in 143
France	1 in 125
Luxembourg	1 in 125
Australia	1 in 125

Canada   1 in 125

Source: World Resources 1988-89.

INJURIES TO CHILDREN

Definition: What happens when Junior gets the urge to test his bravado in the backyard, base-

ment and other places where Mom is not present to temper his audacious behavior.

The Odds: Each year nearly 200,000 children are treated for playground injuries, which represents about 1 in 250 of the 50 million Americans under the age of 13. Injuries to children and the odds of occurrences during an average year are shown below.

Death by	
Handgun	1 in 140,000
High Chair	
Injuries	1 in 6,000
Strollers Injuries	1 in 4,300
Crib Injuries	1 in 3,600
Walker or Jumper	
Injuries	1 in 2,400
Playpen Injuries	1 in 1,950
Skateboard Injuries	1 in 600
Bicycles Injuries	1 in 89

Source: U.S. Consumer Product Safety Commission

Also See: Accidents, Deaths

INTEGRATION

Definition: A phenomenon in which members of a racial or ethnic minority are interspersed throughout the community.

The most integrated metropolitan areas in America are those in which black populations are small to begin with, and in which Hispanic populations are either small or are long established in the community.

The Odds: The lists which follow are based on a *USA Today* analysis of U.S. Census Bureau Data:

WHERE THEY LIVE

Whites

Central Cities	1 in 4
Suburbs	1 in 2
Rural	1 in 4

Blacks

Central Cities	6 in 10
Suburbs	1 in 4
Rural	1 in 6

Hispanics

Central Cities	1 in 2
Suburbs	2 in 5
Rural	1 in 10

Asians

Central Cities	9 in 20
Suburbs	9 in 20
Rural	1 in 16

The following list represents an analysis and ranking from the book *The Best and Worst of Everything* which is based on data compiled by Douglas S. Massey and Nancy A. Denton, authors of "Hypersegregation in U.S. Metropolitan Areas," *Demography*, August, 1989.

THE MOST INTEGRATED U.S. CITIES

1. Salt Lake City-Ogden
2. Anaheim-Santa Ana
3. San Jose
4. Nassau-Cephalic, NY
5. Albuquerque
6. Sacramento
7. Fort Lauderdale
8. Norfolk-Virginia Beach
9. Riverside-San Bernardino
10. El Paso

Source: Compiled research by editors.

Also See: Segregation.

INTELLIGENCE

Definition: The wisdom to know that the two most dangerous individuals are the genius and the totally stupid.

The Odds: Recent educational efforts have tended to distinguish between the most intelligent ("first-order genius") which occur in 1 in 1,000 births and the more intelligent (*second-order gifted*) which occur in 1 in 10. By the age 35, gifted children have a 4 in 5 chance of rising to the highest levels in the business and professional worlds.

According to research, the percentage of "very superior" intellects in the general population – those with I.Q. test scores over 130 – is identical to the percentage of "mentally defective" individuals–those with scores below 69. Out of every one-hundred American births, they predict two children will prove to be "very superior" in intellect, while two more will suffer from severe mental deficiencies. The vast majority of children end up having normal intelligence, that is, IQs between 85 and 115.

Improving the Odds: Research has suggested that high intelligence tends to run in families.

Any person wanting to have a genius as an offspring should mate with someone who has a genius in the family. Though most scientists agree that heredity is a factor, many disagree about the relative importance of heredity, environment and education.

Source: Stanford-Binet Intelligence Quotient; the Wechsler Adult Intelligence Scale.

Also See: Genius.

INTERCOURSE

Heterosexual

Definition: Next to baseball, America's favorite pastime.

Over 21 million Americans go to a baseball game at least once each year. Some 150 million Americans (88 percent of adults) engage in sexual intercourse at least once each year. The frequency of playing ball in bed, instead of on the diamond, is 57 times annually for adults. Women have intercourse an average of 51 times annually, versus 66 times for men.

The Odds: While 9 in 10 Americans are sexually active, their activities are as wide as the practice itself. Some 9 in 10 have participated in oral sex; 1 in 4 have participated in interracial sex and 1 in 3 have had intercourse in public places.

The following list represents various ratios for types or situations involving sexual intercourse among American men and women:

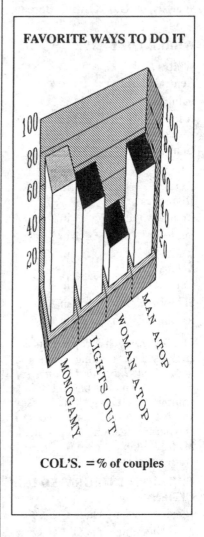

FAVORITE WAYS TO DO IT

MONOGAMY · LIGHTS OUT · WOMAN ATOP · MAN ATOP

COL'S. = % of couples

ADULT PREFERENCES

Missionary Position	6 in 10
Woman on Top	1 in 4
With Lights Off	6 in 10
With Spouse Only	8 in 10

FOR FEMALES

Never Done it*	1 in 3
Premarital	7 in 10
Before Age 20*	2 in 3
Orgasms While Penetrated	1 in 3
Regular Orgasm	6 in 10
Have any Orgasm	9 in 10
Done Anally	1 in 3

FOR MALES

Never Done it	1 in 3
Premarital	8 in 10
Done before Age 20	8 in 10
Performed Cunnilingus	8 in 10
Done with Prostitute	1 in 3

* Figures do not actually add to 100% because of variance in groups surveyed.

Source: Compiled research by editors.

Also See: Marital Fidelity, Teen Sex.

INTERRACIAL MARRIAGE

Definition: The matrimonial union of a male and female of different racial backgrounds.

Interracial marriages were so socially unacceptable, most of the few interracial couples who even dared to share their love, did so without benefit of marriage. Few men of cloth would even consider presiding over such a marriage.

The Odds: After passage of the 1965 Civil Rights Bill, interracial couples began to emerge as legally marrieds. In 1970, only 1 in 145 marriages were interracial. By 1980, 1 in 75 were interracial and by 1990 it increased to 1 in 53. Only 1 in 5 interracial marriages are between blacks and whites. The others are mixtures involving various other races.

The following list represents various interracial marriage situations and the proportions of them among interracially married couples ("Other" refers to Asians, Native Americans, and mixed races):

Black Man and White Woman	1 in 6
White Man and Black Woman	1 in 16
Black Man and Woman (Other)	1 in 38
Black Woman and Man (Other)	1 in 106
White Man and Woman (Other)	1 in 2
White Woman and Man (Other)	1 in 4

Source: U.S. Census Bureau.

IRS AUDIT

The Tax Man Cometh?

Definition: Next to World War III, the most stressful future event.

We know the folks in Utah have are a little different from the rest of the country, but does that make them so suspicious? Apparently the Internal Revenue Service thinks so. Utah taxpayers are at least three times more likely to be audited by the IRS on their federal income tax than any other citizens. In fact, they're ten times more likely to be audited than are the honest folks of Maine, Wisconsin and Hawaii.

The Odds: Overall, less than 1 in 100 of all personal income tax returns were audited by the IRS in 1989. If you are audited, the odds are nearly 3 in 4 that you will be required to pay more taxes. The odds that a taxpayer will be audited differs greatly around the nation. The following list represents the ten states with the highest and lowest incidences of audits and the odds that a citizen in them will meet the tax man:

TEN MOST DANGEROUS STATES

Utah	1 in 21
Nevada	1 in 60
California	1 in 67
Georgia	1 in 73
Missouri	1 in 76
Texas	1 in 80
Massachusetts	1 in 85
Alaska	1 in 89
Montana	1 in 91
Wyoming	1 in 91

TEN SAFEST STATES

Maine	1 in 227
Wisconsin	1 in 227
Hawaii	1 in 222
North Carolina	1 in 208
New Jersey	1 in 204
Oregon	1 in 189
South Carolina	1 in 185
Virginia	1 in 175
Michigan	1 in 175
West Virginia	1 in 169

Source: Research Recommendations, National Inst. of Bus. Mgt.; IRS.

Also See: Heart Attacks.

IVY LEAGUE SCHOLARS

Ph.D. Production

Definition: Rah-rah-sis-boom-bah brain children of the wealthy.

In the opinion of many, there is no better academic credential than a degree from an Ivy League university. But, are the Ivies just high priced diploma mills, or do they really turn out scholars? Some would say the answer lies in the percentage of undergraduates who eventually earn doctoral degrees.

The Odds: Based on the criterion of the percentage of under-graduate degree earners who eventually earn a doctoral degree, tops on the scholarly list is Princeton, where 11.7 percent of the baccalaureates eventually earn a Ph.D. somewhere. This low figure, however, represents a marked change from the tradition in which the Ivy League schools blazed the trail in American scholarship. Princeton ranks only 21st on the overall list of the top-50 institutions for producing the scientists, humanities scholars, life scientists and social scientists that do the all-important research keeping the U.S. on the cutting edge in scientific and scholarly fields, as well as training the next generation of the intellectual elite.

The following list represents the Ivy League universities and the proportions of baccalaureates who eventually earn doctoral degrees:

Princeton	1 in 9
Harvard	1 in 11
Cornell	1 in 11
Yale	1 in 12
Brown	1 in 12
Dartmouth	1 in 13
Columbia	1 in 15
Dartmouth	1 in 21

Source: "An Analysis of Leading Undergraduate Sources of Ph.D.s, Adjusted for Institutional Size," Great Lakes Colleges Association.

J j

JAIL SUICIDES

Definition: Escaping the joint — and all else — on a permanent basis.

Society, as an abstract institution and collection of individuals, wishes to see criminal elements pay for their misdeeds, yet the abortive loss of life through prison suicide is an inarguably tragic and fatal end to an already misspent existence.

The Odds: Though about 1 in 8,000 Americans commit suicide on the outside, in jail, the rate is estimated to be ten times higher. Below are the numbers that spell out this tragedy, measured in the number of suicides among institutionalized people in a single year in various states:

Texas	1 in 700
California	1 in 1,000
Illinois	1 in 600
Ohio	1 in 700
Pennsylvania	1 in 600
Florida	1 in 1,400
Maryland	1 in 1,000

Source: National Study: Population Density Jail Suicides, National Center on Institutions and Alternatives.

Also See: Suicide, Prison Escapes.

JEWS

Definition: People from the ancient tribe of Judah who practice Judaism.

The great waves of immigration from Europe to the United States gave to this country a rich ethnic heritage of peoples and creeds. In fact, the United States is home to more Jewish people than any other country on Earth, Israel included. Tragically, though, the small populations in Europe are more the result of genocide than immigration, as millions of European Jews perished in the Holocaust, and hundreds of thousands more fled to the fledgling state of Israel upon its founding in 1948. The healthy Jewish population in the United States guarantees our continued close ties with and commitment to Israel.

The Odds: The lists following the graph represent the nations with highest and lowest ratios of Jews to Gentiles and proportions of Jews in those nations.

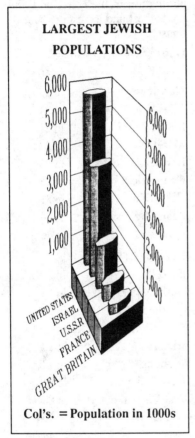

LARGEST JEWISH POPULATIONS

Col's. = Population in 1000s

Great Britain	1 in 178
Canada	1 in 86
Argentina	1 in 147
South Africa	1 in 347
Brazil	1 in 1,500
Australia	1 in 2,011

LOWEST POPULATIONS

Philippines	1 in 588,235
South Korea	1 in 416,666
Egypt	1 in 256,410
Thailand	1 in 181,818
India	1 in 158,730
Iraq	1 in 88,495
Zaire	1 in 84,033
Dominican Rep.	1 in 68,494
Kenya	1 in 59,880
Lebanon	1 in 28,248

Source: American Jewish Year Book, 1990.

JEWS IN THE U.S.

Where To Find Them

Definition: Followers of Judaism who live in America.

European Jews, like other ethnic groups when they came to America, tended to settle first in the metropolitan areas on the East Coast, because of their proximity to Ellis Island, the ability to find work easily, and, eventually, the existence of a well-established Jewish community. New York State leads the nation both in overall Jewish population and in the percent of

HIGHEST POPULATIONS

United States	1 in 44
Israel	1 in 1.24
U.S.S.R.	1 in 203
France	1 in 106

the population that is Jewish: more than ten percent are is Jewish; in New York City, approximately 1 in 4 are. For reasons of practicality and because of real and perceived persecution, areas of the South and the Great Plains contain the fewest Jewish people, both in total numbers and in percentage. So good luck finding a *latke* in Idaho.

The Odds: The U.S., Canada and Israel are the only countries in which the Jews account for more than 1 in 100 citizens. In the U.S., 1 in 44 citizens is Jewish.

The following list represents the ratio of Jews to the general population in the states with the ten highest and lowest concentrations:

TOP TEN STATES

New York	1 in 10
New Jersey	1 in 19
Florida	1 in 21
Massachusetts	1 in 21
Maryland	1 in 22
District of Col.	1 in 25
Connecticut	1 in 28
California	1 in 33
Pennsylvania	1 in 34
Illinois	1 in 45

BOTTOM TEN STATES

Idaho	1 in 2,500
South Dakota	1 in 2,041
Montana	1 in 2,041
Mississippi	1 in 1,250
Arkansas	1 in 1,190
Wyoming	1 in 1,087
North Dakota	1 in 840
West Virginia	1 in 801
Oklahoma	1 in 794
Iowa	1 in 442

Source: American Jewish Year Book, 1990.

Also See: Jews.

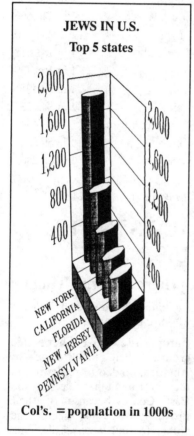

JEWS IN U.S.

Top 5 states

Col's. = population in 1000s

JOB INJURIES

Definition: Harm to an employee while at work which is sufficient enough to require medical attention or loss of time on the job.

Who is taking all the chances while earning a buck? Virtually everyone who gets up in the morning to go to work. Everyday, 5,000 people suffer a disabling injury at work. Who are they, and what do they do? The most dangerous jobs in America do not belong to the cops, firemen, bullfighters or football stars. Surprisingly, it is America's

MOST INJURY-PRONE INDUSTRIES

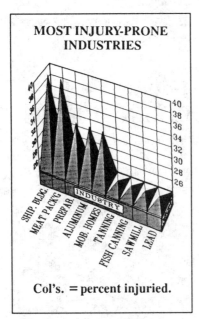

Col's. = percent injuried.

front-line, heavy-industrial factory workers who are most at risk.

The Odds: Each year, job injuries cost industry upwards of $140 billion which accounts for medical expenses and work lost for the 1.8 million workers who are injured. In one year, an average of 1 in 70 workers will be involved in an accident on the job; 1 in 94 of them will die as a result of the mishap.

The following list represents the most dangerous jobs and the proportions of workers in these occupations who will be involved in some sort of disabling accident:

Ship Bldg./ Repair'g	2 in 5
Meat Packing	2 in 5
Metal Sanitary Ware	1 in 3
Prefabricated Wood Buildings	1 in 3
Mobile Homes	3 in 10
Primary Aluminum	3 in 10
Leather Tanning and Finishing	1 in 4
Canned and Cured Seafood	1 in 4
Special Product Sawmills	1 in 4
Primary Lead	1 in 4

Source: U.S. Bureau of Labor Statistics, Occupational Injuries and Illnesses by Industry.

Also See: Accidents, Job Deaths.

JOCK GRADUATIONS

Graduation Rates of Athletes

Definition: A ceremony at which college athletes are awarded diplomas for their intellectual achievements, rather than their athletic prowess.

Football players, and basketball players are notorious for having big hearts on the field or court, but empty heads in the classroom. Is the reputation deserved? If the answer is found by looking at graduation rates, it is not.

The Odds: Only about 1 in 2 students who begin college eventually graduate. Among athletes, the rate is almost exactly the same. Some might argue that universities provide tutors and enforce study hours on their athletes. While that is true at some schools, there is also the intangible incentive an athlete has for sticking around for four years—he can play the game, and maybe even enter the pros. Though a diploma is not required, just being enrolled for four years makes it more likely that a student will graduate.

Graduation rates for athletes are not uniform. Generally, Eastern and Midwestern schools have a better record of awarding diplomas to jocks, about 3 in 5. In the West and South, odds that a jock will leave with a diploma fall to 2 in 5.

The following list represents the major collegiate athletic leagues and the proportions of athletes who graduate with degrees:

Atlantic Coast	66.2 in 100
Independents	59.0 in 100
Big Ten	58.0 in 100
Mid-American Ath. Conf.	54.4 in 100
Pac10	10 52.9 in 100
Western Ath. Conf.	43.1 in 100
Big Ten	42.3 in 100
Southwest Ath. Conf	40.6 in 100
Big West	39.4 in 100
Southeastern (SEC)	36.4 in 100

Source: Chronicle of Higher Education.

Also See: Football Grads, Basketball Grads.

JUVENILE DELINQUENTS

Definition: The name given to 2 million kids whose behavioral problems are with the cops.

Adolescence poses great discomfort and difficulty for teens, parents and society at large. Generally, these difficulties are fleeting, although they may not appear so at the time. Too often in our fragmented era, however, adolescent pranksterism proves to be a dark portent of twisted, pathological deeds in our "children's" future. Kids are turning to crime at a much earlier age and at a most alarming rate in many states of the Union.

The Odds: More than 1 in 6 arrests involve juveniles. Among those youths arrested, odds are, it will be for the following offenses:

AMONG GIRLS

Murder	1 in 3,000
Forcible Rape	1 in 4,200
Robbery	1 in 200
Aggravated Assault	1 in 60
Burglary	1 in 45
Larceny Theft	1 in 4
Motor Vehicle Theft	1 in 55
Arson	1 in 600

AMONG BOYS

Murder	1 in 800
Forcible Rape	1 in 300
Robbery	1 in 60
Aggravated Assault	1 in 40
Burglary	1 in 13
Larceny Theft	1 in 5
Motor Vehicle Theft	1 in 25
Arson	1 in 2,300

Source: FBI Uniform Crime Reports.

K k

KIDDY HORSEPLAY

Minor Misdeeds During Childhood

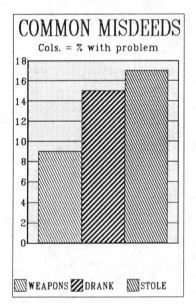

COMMON MISDEEDS

Cols. = % with problem

WEAPONS DRANK STOLE

Definition: The just-under-the wire behavior that juveniles experiment with before the law steps in.

Most adults will confess to a few youthful violations of the law—major and minor—or unethical behavior as a child. The darkly tinted glasses through which we view our youthful horseplay, mischief—even petty criminality—are tokens of those innocent times of life. The security and decency of our society depends on the eventual recognition and repentance of these then-minor missteps.

The Odds: Approximately 1 in 25 children will have some brush with the law before reaching the age of 13. More common antisocial behavior evades the law, being overlooked as problems parents should deal with and not the courts.

The following list represents the most common acts of juvenile delinquency and the proportions of the juvenile population in the U.S. who engage in them:

Kept Change	1 in 6
Drank Liquor	1 in 7
Stole at Job	1 in 11
Carried Weapon	1 in 11

Evaded Payment	1 in 20
Illegal Checks	1 in 50
Fraud	1 in 50
Paid for Sex	1 in 50
Stole From Family	1 in 50
Pressured for Sex	1 in 50

Source: National Youth Survey Project.

Also See: Juvenile Delinquency.

KID STUFF
Potpourri

Definition: The sundry circumstances that children find themselves in while learning the ropes of life.

Children under the age of 13 comprise 20 percent of the American population. While getting acquainted with the do's and don'ts of life they find themselves in many uncomfortable situations ranging from public to reform schools.

The Odds: Below is a potpourri of odds that the average kid will find himself afflicted or blessed by on a typical day:

Watching TV (any given time)	1 in 3
Eating a fast-food hamburger	1 in 29
Homelessness	1 in 650
Spanked at school	1 in 9,000
Reported missing	1 in 10,600
In day-care	1 in 20
Suffer from neglect	1 in 18,000
Suffer from abuse	1 in 27,000
Die	1 in 3.6 mil.

During the course of childhood which the editors of this book have defined as the period from birth to age 13, the odds of the above occurring are obviously greater than those listed, which reflect the odds just on one day.

Source: On an Average Day, Tom Heymann.

Also See: Also see Children, Mischief.

KILLERS ON THE LOOSE

Getting Away With Murder

Definition: Individuals, usually males, who will do any or all of the following: 1) slit your throat for a nickel; 2) bump you off on the freeway for cutting them off; 3) plug you or stick you, if you ask their girl to dance.

Those who think the only time they might see a real killer is at a Jerry Lee Lewis concert may be dead wrong. Each year about 10,000 people in the U.S. kill someone, and a surprisingly high number get away scot-free. Police aren't as adept at snatching the killers as they should be. Prosecutors, aren't too effective either, and judges, amazingly, let many murderers loose on the street for you to unknowingly interact with.

The Odds: Careful records are kept on murders and known murderers, but no one knows for sure who is the killer in an unsolved case, which accounts for 3 in 10 murders. There are also no available statistics on the longevity of murderers once they are released from prison. This means that there is no absolutely verifiable way to know for sure how many murderers you see in an average day. It can be estimated roughly, however, that about 1 in 1,000 people on the street are murderers. That could mean if you hang around Grand Central Station for a few minutes you'll see at least a few go by, maybe more. Airports, sports events and at any large gathering, you are probably not far from a real, live murderer on the loose.

How can this be in the U.S. with our get tough on crime policies? According to a former high official at the FBI's Behavioral Science Unit, the answer is that it evolved over a thirty year period. In 1962, better than 9 in 10 murders were solved and roughly 1 in 14 killers got away with . . . you know what. Thirty years later only 7 in 10 murder cases were solved and roughly 1 in 3 killers escaped the law. These changes translate to the odds of meeting a loose killer increasing 1,200 percent over three decades.

What are the chances a convicted murderer will serve some time? Not very good, according to U.S. District court rulings in the late 1980s. Almost 1 in 3 convicted murderers are not imprisoned.

KILLERS ON THE LOOSE

Each year about 1 in 12,000 people have a fatal meeting with a murderer. Over a lifetime, 1 in 100 of us will have a similar end. Watch out next time you have the opportunity to get in an argument with a complete stranger. He could be stranger than you think, and he could spoil your whole day.

Source: Compiled research by editors.

L l

LADY BOWLERS

Definition: Women whose nights out are spent bowling over wooden pins rather than handsome men.

Although Americans love to watch baseball, football and basketball, when it comes time to actually participate in a sporting activity, millions turn to the oft-maligned, old indoor standby, bowling. Although that sport has acquired a reputation as an after-work tension release for beer-toting good ole boys, in reality, it has achieved remarkable popularity with women. Last year, there were more than 4 million registered members of the Women's International Bowling Congress, belonging to more than 160,000 leagues nationwide.

The Odds: While about 1 in 5 women bowl, the most enthusiastic ones, members of the Bowling Congress, represent 1 in 7 lady bowlers.

The following list represents the number of female bowling leagues in the ten states with the most leagues:

California	16,898
New York	12,564
Ohio	11,992
Michigan	10,734
Illinois	8,568
Wisconsin	8,418
Pennsylvania	7,097
Texas	6,950
Florida	6,252
New Jersey	4,970

Source: Women's International Bowling Congress.

LATE FLIGHTS

Associated Troubles

Definition: The annoying tendency of major airlines to depart or arrive later than scheduled, disrupting travel plans and making passengers late for important business meetings.

Airlines have a hard time with punctuality. When the federal government deregulated domestic air travel, all hell broke loose. New airlines came crawling out of the woodwork. Existing airlines expanded their routes to horn in on once-monopolized destinations. Bargain carriers like People's Express popped up to serve the low-budget flier. Price wars made air travel competitive with trains, buses and cars.

The result is overcrowding at airports and odd scheduling. Carriers at airports like Chicago's O'Hare, the nation's busiest, schedules dozens of flights to land and take-off during very brief periods, such as early morning or early evening. Haggard ground controllers, still reeling from the break-up of their union, are forced to delay some incoming and outgoing flights, simply to maintain a safe buffer between planes. Hence, delays.

Which airlines are most susceptible to delays? A flight is deemed late by the U.S. Department of Transportation if it doesn't arrive within fifteen minutes of schedule. Most airline schedules give planes added time to make the trip. For example, a flight from New York to Chicago may only take 2 hours, but the airline will schedule the flight for 2 1/2 hours, thus giving the flight plenty of leeway for delays.

The Odds: The following list represents are the odds in favor of being on time on any particular flight among the major American carriers:

Southwest	4.5 to 1
Delta	4.5 to 1
TWA	4.6 to 1
USAir	4.7 to 1
Continental	4.8 to 1
Northwest	5.0 to 1
United	6.2 to 1
American	6.5 to 1
America West	6.9 to 1

The O.J. Syndrome: Believe it or not, in addition to the psychological stress caused by late flights, airport delays, traffic congestion and rushing to and from gates to catch planes, doctors have discovered a real, live physical malady that strikes frequent fliers. They've dubbed it "Airport Induced 'Cervical Traction' Radiculopathy." According to the *Journal of the American Medical Association*, eleven busy executives have come down with severe pain and weakness in the cervix. All had evidence of degeneration of cervical disks, and three suffered muscle spasms in the neck. Doctors diagnosed the cause of the disability as (and we are not making this up) "running from one [airport] gate to another, carrying heavy, under-the-seat bags." Hence, playful sawbones have dubbed the disease the "O.J. Syndrome," for the rental car commercials in which the former football star is seen sprinting and hurdling through air terminals. Intermittent traction and the use of wheelchairs resolved the travelers' complaints in every in-

155

stance, the report states. It is unknown whether the travelers filed for worker's compensation pay.

Sources: U.S. Department of Transportation; *Journal of the American Medical Association,* April 18, 1990.

LAWYERS, SLEAZY

Ultimate Shysters

Definition: Attorneys who do not conform to the usual honest, friendly and caring ethic for which the profession is famous.

In the U.S., there are approximately 600,000 individuals with law degrees. Almost 1 in 6 have come to realize they have too much integrity to practice the profession and therefore have given up practicing law to do something honest. Of the 5 in 6 who make their living as lawyers, 1 in 5 each year are named in a complaint by one or more clients; 3 in 5 of the complaints are for drug or alcohol dependencies. There is no known case of a complaint that an attorney was too honest to adequately represent his client.

Source: HALT.

LEFT-HANDED-NESS

Definition: A devastating handicap in playlot baseball which results in at least one team member not being able to borrow a mitt from other players.

The Odds: Approximately 1 in 10 people prefer to use their left hand over the right in at least some tasks. Among children, 1 in 7 are left-handed, but many change over to accommodate the sway of the right-handed world. According to an Irish study, 1 in 20 fetuses suck their right thumb as opposed to the left, leading researchers to believe the same proportion of babies are naturally left-handed.

Source: Compiled research by editors.

LEMONS

Definition: The inevitable bottom of the barrel cars which automobile salesmen always assure you will never get if you buy the model they are selling.

Pay enough money and you won't have a nickel's worth of worry when you drive out of the show room? Maybe a few thousand bucks worth, though. It could be that whirring coming from the engine, the power seats, the tape player, or the rear defogger. You know the story. It happens to everyone. Well, almost everyone.

With today's prices of new cars, buyers want perfect performance and the rate at which they return to the dealers with complaints is astonishing.

The Odds: The following list represents various 1990 models and the ratio of problems per 100 cars during the first 60 to 90 days:

Toyota Cressida	2 in 3
Mercedes-Benz E-Series	7 in 10
Toyota Camry	7 in 10
Lexus LS400	3 in 4
Mercedes-Benz S-Class	3 in 4
Buick LeSabre	4 in 5
Nissan Maxima	9 in 10
Infinity Q45	9 in 10
Toyota Corolla	19 in 20
Mazda Miata	99 in 100

Next, we consider not the integrity of a single model but the overall average initial quality of an operating unit or name-plate. It averages the scores of all the different models you might see in a showroom. The following list represents the most trouble free manufacturers and the ratio of problems per 100 cars during the first 60 to 90 days:

PROBLEMS PER 100 CARS

Lexus	82
Mercedes-Benz	84
Toyota	89
Infiniti	99
Buick	113
Honda	114
Nissan	123
Acura	129
BMW	139
Mazda	139

Source: J.D. Power and Associates 1990 New Car Initial Quality Study.

LEPROSY

Definition: A bacterial infection characterized by the forming of nodules which show through the skin and eventually cause paralysis and death.

Leprosy has all but been eradicated in the United States and most developed countries; and with that eradication, the disease has all but vanished from the public eye. The few who are still afflicted by the illness in the U.S. are cared for just as any other patients. However, leprosy, which calls to mind the darkest images of the Middle Ages, still constitutes a major public health problem in Africa.

The Odds: In Africa, the incidence is more than 1 in 1,000. The numbers, though, have been declining in the last two decades, from 1,685,526 cases in 1966 to 534,720 cases in 1988, in response to the World Health Organization's program of monitoring and treatment of cases of leprosy in Africa.

The following list represents the incidence of the disease in the nations which have the ten highest occurrences:

Congo	1 in 185
Ivory Coast	1 in 235
Gambia	1 in 272
Mali	1 in 297
Cape Verde	1 in 365
Cent'l African Rep.	1 in 369
Madagascar	1 in 391
Guinea-Bissau	1 in 413
Burkina Faso	1 in 444
Benin	1 in 481

Source: Epidemiological Bulletin, World Health Organization, Brazzaville, Congo.

LIABILITY SUITS

Definition: As the baker earns his wages making bread, as the butcher earns his pay cutting meat, so too does the lawyer get his cut of the jury award.

The legal profession has been severely criticized in recent years for "making a federal case" of stubbed toes, bruised egos and anything else for which clients are willing to pay to file suit. What are these disgruntled and sometimes greedy clients filing their suits about?

The Odds: The following list represents the proportions for which the 85,694 liability suits were filed between 1974-86:

Contracts	1 in 15
Real Property	1 in 114
Personal Property	1 in 20
Airplane	1 in 31
Asbestos	1 in 5
Boat	1 in 70
Motor Vehicles	1 in 14
Other	1 in 2

The previously listed types of suits have been growing in frequency at break-neck speed. Over the ten year period 1976-86, there has been a four-fold increase in the filing of liability suits (from 3,414 in 1974 to 12,666 in 1986).

Source: RAND's Institute for Civil Justice.

LIFE EXPECTANCY

Definition: The average number of years a new born baby can expect to be paying taxes.

We citizens of the industrialized world are modern-day

Methuselahs. That is, we live a long time if we don't wrap ourselves around telephone poles in a car crash or succumb to disease and gang warfare. With an American life expectancy of 75

Unfortunately, the disparity between life expectancy in the industrialized world and life expectancy in the rest of the world indicates more about the generally awful nutritional,

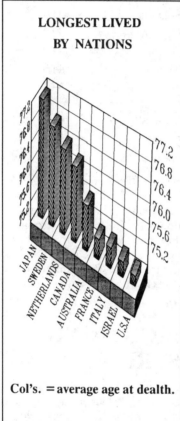

LONGEST LIVED BY NATIONS

Col's. = average age at dealth.

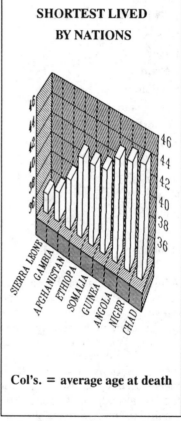

SHORTEST LIVED BY NATIONS

Col's. = average age at death

years, a kid who is ten in 1992 will probably live to see the goings-on in 2057. Some in Japan and Iceland are living a full sixteen years longer than the world's aveage life expectancy, which is 61.1 years.

sanitary and economic conditions most humans live with than it does about the good living conditions in a few advanced countries.

The Odds: Since life expectancy is customarily expressed as the average number of years of average people, true odds cannot be calculated. It is interesting, however to see the following list which represents the countries with the highest and lowest figures which are expressed below in years:

TEN LONGEST EXPECT-ANCIES

Japan	77.2
Iceland	77.1
Sweden	76.8
Switzerland	76.5
Netherlands	76.5
Norway	76.4
Canada	76.3
Australia	75.7
France	75.2
Italy	75.2
Israel	75.1
Denmark	75.1

While we've all seen the pictures of West African starvation on television, sometimes statistics can be even more startling than pictures. Twelve of the world's 13 lowest life expectancies are in African nations. If you are 18 in Sierra Leone, statistically, your life is already half over. You would be lucky to reach the ripe old age of 42 in Ethiopia and Somalia, countries long locked in a bloody war and lately wracked by famine and drought. In Chad, the former French colony and the scene of many armed struggles, 45 years is all you'd have to look forward to.

TEN SHORTEST EXPECTAN-CIES

Sierra Leone	36.0
Gambia	37.0
Afghanistan	39.0
Ethiopia	41.9
Somalia	41.9
Guinea	42.2
Angola	44.0
Mali	44.0
Niger	44.5
Central African Republic	45.0
Chad	45.0
Guinea-Bissau	45.0

Source: *World Resources 1988-89*, A Report by The World Resources Institute and The International Institute for Environment and Development in collaboration with The United Nations Environment Programme, Basic Books, Inc., New York.

Also See: Death Rates

LIGHTNING STRIKE

Definition: A visible bolt of electricity which is usually generated when water-logged clouds discharge electrons.

The earth is like a giant battery that needs to be restored of its lost electrical energy. When skies are cloudless, the negatively charged earth dissipates electrons into the positively charged upper atmosphere. This leakage is restored to the earth when thunderclouds pick up and store the electrons and then discharge them as lightning. A cloud can store as much as 100 million times that of the earth below. When this charge is "bolted out" as lightning, a bolt may have a charge of 3,750 million kilowatts which stretches from 1,000 to 9,000 feet in length.

The Odds: It is virtual certainty that a bolt of lightning will hit the earth or something on it. Each second, 100 bolts strike the earth. The point of impact is almost always open water or vegetation, especially trees, which are firmly "grounded" and therefore are natural lightning rods. In an average week, the odds are 1 in 2.6 that the Empire State Build-

ing will be struck. Each year the building attracts an average of 20 lightning bolts.

The odds of lightning hitting a human are far less, namely because there is a large contingent of people who have enough sense to come in out of the rain, though not nearly enough. Every once in a while, though, an unwitting individual gets hit by a lightning bolt. Most at risk are those living in the wild. In forested areas and jungles few records are kept. America, however, is a different matter. Odds of being injured by lightning are as follows.

On given any day	1 in 250 million
In any given week	1 in 35 million
In any given year	1 in 685,000
Over average lifetime	1 in 9,100

It should be noted that many lighting injuries are due to falling debris and not always from a direct strike.

Source: National Oceanic and Atmospheric Administration.

LIQUOR CONSUMPTION
Favorite Drinks

Definition: Sucking up the sauce.

No one likes to be accused of excessive drinking, and cities — in this regard—are no different than the people who populate them. Sadly, it is our nation's most socially volatile metros, D.C. and Miami, which must answer for the highest per-capita consumption of liquor in the nation.

The Odds: If an American tells you they have been drinking the odds are approximately 2 in 3 that the beverage was beer. The 1 in 3 drinkers who prefers the hard stuff is most likely to favor vodka, the choice of about 1 in 3 hard liquor drinkers. The odds are about 1 in 6 it will be cordials or liqueurs, the second most favored drink. Tequila, though among the eight favorites, is the least popular. Odds are 1 in 20 an American imbiber will favor tequila, usually in the form of a Margarita.

The following list represents the approximate odds that an average citizen of major cities will favor one of the of eight top selling distilled liquors.

Washington (Gin)	2 in 9
Miami (Vodka)	1 in 4
Tampa-St. Pete- . Clearwater (Vodka)	1 in 3
Atlanta (Gin)	1 in 5
Sacramento (Vodka)	1 in 4
Denver (Whiskey)	1 in 7
New York (Scotch)	1 in 5

Source: The Best and Worst of Everything.

Also See: Alcoholism

LITIGATION
Federal Cases

The Odds: A process whereby a defendant wins or loses his case, the outcome depending not so

much on whether or not he violated the law, but on who has the better attorney, the defendant or the plaintiff.

Some say the court system is overloaded and there is reason to believe it is not. The case loads of federal courts have almost doubled since 1970, when there were just under 150,000. Today, there are approximately 300,000 annually.

The Odds: Most civil cases are settled out of court, primarily due to the high cost of lengthy trials, which defendants and plaintiffs must bear. Of approximately 250,000 civil cases annually, 1 in 13 go to trial. Of those tried, 2 in 3 are decided by the presiding judge. It is the defendant's right to decide if he wants a jury trial, and 1 in 3 elect this option.

Criminal cases are entirely another matter. Of the approximately 50,000 annual cases commenced, 1 in 4 goes to trial. The other are either cases in which defendants decide to plea bargain and avoid court, or ones in which the prosecutor dismisses the case due to insufficient evidence. Criminal defendants are more likely to choose jury trials, though many lawyers try to convince them that juries are often harsher than judges. Despite the warnings, 1 in 3 criminal defendants choose jury trials.

Source: Office of the Clerk, Supreme Court of the United States.

Also See: Supreme Court.

LONGEVITY

Of Husbands and Wives

Definition: The relative length or duration of the lives of spouses.

The life expectancy in the twentieth century has improved dramatically. In the year 1900, the average person could except to live to age 50. Today, as the century comes to a close, life expectancy has increased 50 percent, to age 75, for those who are born in the 1990s.

The Odds: In any given couple, the odds are 7 to 3 that the wife will outlive the husband. Conversely, only 3 in 10 husbands will survive their wives. The odds show that the average wife will live an average of 15 years longer than her husband.

Female Superiority: More women than men beat the odds and succumb to fewer fatal diseases and accidents early in life. The odds are 4 to 1 against men living to the age of 85. Women's chances of making past 85, however, are twice that. More than 2 in 5 make it to the second half of their ninth decade. But will the female superiority last? Some researchers speculate that as differences between the lives men and women lead narrow, the gap in relative longevity will also narrow. Recent statistics suggest this may be true. However, the gap has been expanding since the 1920s and more statistics are needed before we will give odds on changes in relative longevity.

Source: Russel, Cheryl *100 Predictions For The Baby Boom*, Plenum Press, New York.

LOTTERIES

Definition: America's one-in-a-million shot at hitting the jackpot with a one-buck investment.

The rules are simple: a player picks a group of numbers from some larger field of numbers and if they match the random selection of the lottery, he wins, often large sums upwards of $1 million.

Smaller prizes are usually given to players who chose one or two incorrect numbers.

The Rollover: When no one wins the previous week's drawing, the prize money "rolls over" to the next week. The odds of guessing the numbers correctly remains the same despite the fact that thousands, maybe millions, more people are playing.

The Odds: There is a wide variation according to how many numbers are picked and from what the size of the field is. The following list represents the average odds in various lotteries in the U.S. and elsewhere:

Rhode Island
  Lottery   1 in 700,000
Iowa & West
  Virginia   1 in 600,000
Delaware   1 in 1.3 million
Massachusetts
  Tri-State 1 in 1.9 million
Oregon   1 in 2.8 million
Arizona &
  Missouri 1 in 3.3 million
Connecticut &
  Penn.   1 in 3.8 million
New Jersey &
  Oregon   1 in 5.2 million
Michigan &
  Ohio   1 in 7.1 million
South Aust-
  ralia   1 in 8.1 million
New York 1 in 12.3 million

California &
  Ontario   1 in 14.0 million
Western
  Canada   1 in 32.5 million
Sweden   1 in 6.7 million
Finland   1 in 15.4 million

Source: Clotfelter, Charles T. and Philip J. Cook, *Selling Hope; State Lotteries in America*, Harvard University Press, 1989.

LOTTERY "DOUBLE"

Definition: Hitting the big jackpot in a state lottery not once, but twice in a lifetime.

Life just isn't fair. A few of us never win the big lotto grand prize jackpot even *once* in our lives. Then we have to pick up the paper and read a story like that of Evelyn Marie Adams. Ms. Adams, a New Jersey woman, won her state's lottery *twice* within a four-month span.

The Odds: According to lottery officials, the odds against Ms. Adams were 17 *trillion* to one. Amazing, you say? Can't ever happen, you exclaim? Well, don't worry. Here come some pointy-headed Harvard professors to burst Ms. Adams's bubble.

According to Drs. Persi Diaconis and Frederick Mosteller, both of Harvard, the people who calculated that 17 trillion figure had it a little bit wrong. First of all, for a single lottery in which the odds of hitting the jackpot are a little more than 4 million to one, the odds of winning twice are indeed about 17 trillion to one. But that assumes that the player buys exactly one ticket for each of exactly two New Jersey state lotteries. Obviously, the more combinations you play, like Ms. Adams, the better your odds of winning.

Law of Large Numbers: It really shouldn't be that surprising that someone, somewhere should win twice. Statisticians like to talk about what they call "The Law of Truly Large Numbers," which, our Harvard professors say, states that "with a large enough sample, any outrageous thing is apt to happen." For instance, if something is a million to one shot to happen to someone today, chances are you'd expect 250 of these unlikely coincidences every day across America, where the population is 250 million. So it is with our poor Ms. Adams. Given the millions of people who buy lottery tickets in this country, it is decidedly not surprising that someone should win twice in a lifetime. Two statisticians from Purdue University even calculated the odds. With that large sample, a double lotto win somewhere in the country, they figure, is an *even bet* over a span of seven years. Over a four-month period, the odds are better than 30 to 1 — not out of the question by any means.

With those odds, we say to Ms. Adams, "Big Deal!"

Source: Journal of the American Statistical Association; New York Times.

LOTTERY, "INSTANT"
Scratch it Rich

Definition: 1) Money rushing down the stack pipe from a toilet bowl; 2) random-number game in which players scratch a thin substance from a ticket to reveal a three number combination which hopefully matches the winning numbers.

Depending on how players bet and how closely their number matches some other predetermined number, players may win a variety of predetermined prizes. Played in most states, the instant game is known by many names including: "The Instant Game", "Money Tree", "Scratch it Rich" and others.

The Odds: The chance of exactly matching 3 digits (the usual requirement to win) in a predetermined order is 1 in 1,000, which provides better than a 1,000-fold greater chance of winning than a full-blown lottery game. The payoff on a matching card is typically $500 which means the state is making $500 for each thousand tickets bought.

Box 6-Way Game: Requires matching three digits in any order. The odds are 1 in 167; the same for a number with two — 1 in 333. For "Front Pair", the odds of matching the first two digits in exact order are 1 in 100.

Back Pair: Requires matching the first two digits in exact order. The odds are 1 in 100.

Source: Clotfelter, Charles T. and Philip J. Cook, *Selling Hope: State Lotteries in America*, Harvard University Press, 1989.

LOW BIRTH WEIGHT

Definition: Neonatal birth weight of less than 2500 grams (5 lb., 8 oz.).

The Odds: Statistics show that 67.5 out of every 1,000 live births in 1985 fell into the category of low birth weight as defined above. The odds against such a delivery for the average woman are thus about 14 to 1. Unfortunately, low birth weight babies have been on the increase in recent years. The number of very low birth weight babies in the U.S. increased by 4 percent from 1981 to 1985, and another 2.7 percent from 1985 to 1987. The majority of underweight births are premature—52 percent of moderately and 93 percent of very low birth weight babies.

There is a persistent and troubling difference in risk between white and black babies in terms of low birth weight. A black infant is 2.2 times as likely as a white baby to suffer from low birth weight. Socioeconomic and health factors contributing to increased risk include unmarried motherhood, low educational level, lack of prenatal care, poor nutrition among mothers, and unwanted pregnancies.

The Risks: Research has shown that a proper intervention program for low birth weight infants, including home visits by therapists, attendance at child development centers, and parent group meetings, greatly enhances the odds of normal development. Odds of premature infants having an IQ score below 70 are 2.7 times greater for those who do not receive such treatment. Such intervention results in an average increase of 13.2 IQ points in moderately low birth weight infants and 6.6 points in very low birth weight infants.

Source: "Morbidity and Mortality Report," Centers for Disease Control, 1990, 39:137-152; "Low Birth Weight Infants: Can We Enhance Their Development?" *Journal of the American Medical Association*, June 13, 1990.

M m

MACHINERY ACCIDENTS

Fatalities

Definition: An unintentional or unexpected happening involving industrial or farm-related mechanical equipment which ends in the death of one or more human beings.

The Odds: One must be operating or be in close proximity to machinery to be involved in most machinery accidents. In the general population, the odds of being killed in a fatal machinery accident are less than 1 in 50,000 for men and about 1 in 1,000,000 for women. Fatal accidents involving farm machinery have increased since the 1930s when statistics were first taken. Farmers and their families have a 1 in 277,778 chance of being killed each year. Nonfarm machinery is less dangerous. The chances of falling off a crane or being smashed in a press are 1 in 344,827.

Age Relationships: The odds of farm accidents show two peaks. Children between the ages of one and five have a better than 1 in 100,000 chance of falling off or being caught in tractors and reapers. Likewise, the elderly are in danger. By age 70, farm accidents will be the cause of death for more than 1 in 25,000 senior citizens. The odds of dying in an accident with non-farm machinery show a much more conventional pattern. These odds peak at age 20 at which the odds of a fatality are 1 in 33,000.

Source: Baker, Susan P. et al, *The Injury Fact Book*, Lexington Books, 1984.

MALARIA

Definition: A disease caused by one of four protozoan species of the genus *Plasmodium* and characterized by fever, chills, headache, muscle pains and malaise.

Malaria is most commonly transmitted by the bite of an infected female Anopheles mosquito.

167

Among Americans, it is most commonly contracted during travel to sub-tropical or tropical regions of Africa, Asia, India, South America and the Caribbean. Once a great killer of those unaccustomed to tropical conditions, such as American workers on the Panama Canal and European inmates of South American penal colonies, malaria by the middle of this century had become preventable through the development of the anti-malarial drug chloroquine. Recently, however, several strains of malarial microorganisms have developed resistance to the drug, resulting in a threefold increase in malarial infection among American travelers since 1980. A new drug, mefloquine, is said to be highly effective to resistant forms of *Plasmodium* and has recently been approved by the FDA. Other anti-malarial drugs often have adverse side effects.

The Odds: From 1980 to 1988, 1,434 cases of malaria were reported among the approximately 8,900,000 Americans who traveled to Asia, South America and sub-Saharan Africa, making the odds against contracting the disease during tropical travel about 5,800 to 1. The greatest risk by far is in Africa, where odds of getting malaria are 660 to 1 for American travelers; in contrast, travelers to Asia, South America and the Caribbean face odds of only about 8,035 to 1.

According to the Centers for Disease Control, a number of factors are responsible for the greater risk in Africa. Most visitors to that continent spend a large portion of their time in rural areas, where malarial risk is greater. In addition, even in African cities, malaria is a threat. On the other hand, visitors to Asia and South America spend a greater portion of their time in urban regions, where malaria is extremely uncommon. Tourists who stay in air-conditioned hotels or homes, protected from insect bites, are much less likely to contract the disease than backpackers, adventure travelers, missionaries or Peace Corps volunteers.

The Centers for Disease Control advise all travelers to areas containing a malarial risk to receive the proper preventative shots and protect themselves against insect bites. Even with prescribed prophylaxis, though, malaria is not 100 percent preventable. It is, however, treatable, and is rarely fatal. Odds of dying of the disease, once contracted, are about 40 to 1 — but much lower if victims pursue immediate treatment.

Malaria in the U.S.: Malarial disease is not wholly unknown in America. Small outbreaks among migrant farmworkers in San Diego County, California, were reported in 1986, 1988 and 1989. Doctors suspect that immigrant workers from Mexico unwittingly may have brought with them mosquitoes carrying the disease.

The Centers for Disease Control maintain a Malaria Hotline to answer travelers' questions. The number is (404) 332-4555.

Source: Centers for Disease Control, "Morbidity and Mortality Weekly Report," 1990; 3:1-10 and 39.

MALE PREDOMINANCE

Where the Boys Are

Definition: The extent to which women are in the minority and a relative measure of the length a man will go to get his women.

With the exceptions of Israel, Ireland, Canada and Australia, every nation in the developed world has a minority of males. Worldwide, however, males account for 50.12% of the human population. The high concentration of males in Asia and the Middle East is the primary demographic compensation for the female majorities of the West. *The Odds:* In the Islamic nations of Bahrain, the United Arab Emirates and Kuwait, men outnumber women by a whopping 6 to 4. One explanation of this fact is the large number of male workers from Palestine, Egypt, Turkey and other nearby countries who, at least until recent events, have flocked to the oil-rich gulf states, while leaving their spouses and families at home.

The following list represents the proportions of males to females in the nations with the 10 highest ratio of men to women:

Bahrain	61 in 100
United Arab Emir.	60 in 100
Kuwait	59 in 100
Guam	57 in 100
Maldives	55 in 100
Pakistan	53 in 100
Jordan	53 in 100
Hong Kong	52 in 100
Solomon Islands	52 in 100
Taiwan	52 in 100

Source: The Best and Worst of Everything.

MANUFAC-TURING

Job Opportunities

Definition: The act of working on an assembly line or factory floor making various and sundry devices.

America still talks of itself as a great industrial nation, but such talk is colored mostly by nostalgia and wishful thinking. Though our overall global economic and financial decline is not so bad as the many prophets of doom would have us believe, the erosion of our traditional industrial base is self-evident. A city that bases most of its earning on the profits of its manufactures today may find itself in deep fiscal peril.

The Odds: The U.S. Census reports that of 85 million Americans who are on some sort of payroll, the odds are 2 in 9 that it will be at some form of manufacturing job. The odds are the highest that it will be in the electrical equipment field where 1 in 10 manufacturing jobs are found. The lowest employment in manufacturing is in the tobacco industry, which accounts for 1 in 431 manufacturing jobs.

Odds of finding a manufacturing job vary enormously from city to city. To compute the odds for finding employment, the book *The Best and Worst of Everything* was drawn on. The lists below represent the ratio of manufac-turing jobs to nonmanufacturing jobs in cities which are the most and least dependent on manufac-turers for employment opportunities:

MOST DEPENDENT CITIES

Kokomo, IN	63 in 100
Elkhart-Goshen, IN	61 in 100
Anderson, IN	58 in 100
Flint, MI	56 in 100
Hickory, NC	53 in 100
Danville, VA	51 in 100
Pascagoula, MS	51 in 100
Steubenville- Weirton, OH-WV	50 in 100
Anderson, SC	49 in 100
Rochester, NY	48 in 100

LEAST DEPENDENT CITIES

Anchorage	2 in 100
Santa Fe, NM	3 in 100
Bremerton, WA	3 in 100
Las Vegas, NV	4 in 100
Naples, FL	4 in 100
Grand Forks, ND	4 in 100
Honolulu, HI	4 in 100
Jacksonville, NC	4 in 100
Washington, DC	4 in 100
Tallahassee, FL	5 in 100

Source: Compiled research by editors.

Also See: Employment Opportunities.

MARIJUANA

American Cities

Definition: A situation in which a person answers all questions with

"Wow!", "Hey Man", "Ooh", "Wow, wow!" or "Do you have any chocolate, man?"

The purported adverse medical effects of marijuana and related THC derivatives are the subjects of innumerable technical and lay debates. There is little doubt, however, that these drugs can cause short term loss of memory, contribute to general malaise, and promote lung disease. Opponents also rail against the casual marijuana user's supposed easy slide into harder, more debilitating illegal substances. Whatever the case, many crimes and injuries often attend the use of pot.

The Odds: Below are the cities in which pot was most prevalent in emergency room trauma patients. The odds represent the ratio of marijuana related admissions in 1989 to the 105,850 drug related admissions in an average year.

Washington, D.C.	1 in 125
Chicago	1 in 132
Detroit	1 in 165
New York	1 in 172
Philadelphia	1 in 176
Los Angeles	1 in 231
Dallas	1 in 276
Atlanta	1 in 285
New Orleans	1 in 315
Denver	1 in 481

Source: "Overview of Selected Drug Trends," NIDA Drug Abuse Warning Network.

Also See: Drug Emergencies.

MARITAL FIDELITY

Definition: A vow taken by some 99 percent of couples at their wedding and forgotten by 48 in 100 men and 38 in 100 women.

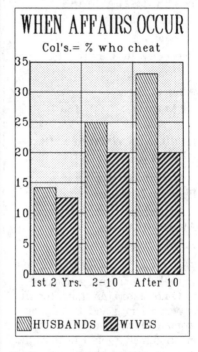

WHEN AFFAIRS OCCUR

Col's.= % who cheat

HUSBANDS WIVES

Estimates of unfaithfulness vary enormously, but there is no doubt that the rates of occurrence are high. *The Universal Almanac* reports 3 in 4 American married couples believe having extramarital sex is wrong and that 1 in 66 spouses are unfaithful at least once each year. The initial statistics in the definition portion of this entry are estimates from a *Playboy* Magazine poll which are considerably higher than most studies have shown.

The Odds: The following lists represents various ratios of unfaithfulness as reported by a study conducted by *American Couples*:

WIVES WITH AFFAIRS

Before 2 years
of Marriage   1 in 8
Between 2-10 years
of Marriage   1 in 5
After 10 Years
of Marriage   1 in 5.

HUSBANDS WITH AFFAIRS

Before 2 years
of Marriage   1 in 7
Between 2-10 years
of Marriage   1 in 4
After 10 Years
of Marriage   1 in 3

The Other Woman: Researcher Laurel Richardson, a sociologist at Ohio State University, reports between 1 in 5 and 1 in 3 single women have had affairs with married men. Only 1 in 10 of the women did not know the man was married. Among women who have affairs with married men, 1 in 10 would like to have him for a husband. Who eventually breaks the relationship? Some 7 in 10 affairs are called off by the man.

Source: Compiled research by editors.

Also See: Affairs and Money.

MARRIAGE

Definition: The state of being husband and wife and a prerequisite for getting divorced.

The Odds: Overall, the chances of marrying sometime in your lifetime are 3 in 4, the odds being greatest between the years 24 to 30 and decreasing significantly after the age of 35. For white, middle class, educated women under 38 years old, the odds of marrying are 2 in 3; for men in the same category, the chances are slightly better than 2 in 3. White women who are middle class and educated but over 35 have a less than 18 to 1 chance of marrying, while men fitting this category still have a 10 to 1 chance. Once a woman is hitched, according to an NBC poll, there's an even chance she'll be widowed by the time she's 56; 6 out of 7 widows never remarry.

Source: U.S. Census Bureau.

Also See: Divorce, Marriage Tips.

MARRIAGE TIPS

Definition: Pointers for finding someone to pop the question to.

Three out of 4 people marry sometime in their lives, the mid-twenties being the most common age to tie the knot. Research has shown that, despite the presumed down-side of wedlock, its benefits abound. Marriage adds almost ten years to a man's life and more than four years to a woman's.

Get Them While You're Young (and Beautiful): If you are a white, college-educated woman, you would be well advised to marry early, according to some experts. In a study conducted in 1986 by Yale University sociologist Neil G. Bennett, Columbia economist Dale E. Bloom and Yale doctoral candidate Patricia H. Craig, the academics found that women who fit that category had only a 1 in 5 likelihood of marriage at age 30 and about a 1 in 20 chance at age 35. Once a woman reaches 40, the researchers report, her chances of finally wedding plummet to about 1 in 100. The data, when released, caused such a stir that the researchers were forced to revise their information, dropping the category of "white, college-educated women" from their study entirely, but they did not retract their original findings. Researcher Bloom has said that the original study "was used to clobber many women over the head, and that was the furthest thing from our minds."

For Men Only: A 28-year-old man has a slightly better chance of getting married than does a woman of the same age — a little better than 2 to 1. The prospects for a man, however, don't drop as dramatically as he ages. For a man of 35, the odds of marrying are 10 to 1; not great, but still better than the 20 to 1 odds for a woman of the same age.

Happy Hunting Grounds: Where should a woman look for a husband? Authoritative reports reveal that you are unlikely to meet your mate at a bar, disco, or other singles hangout. College, work, church and through friends are the most common places and means of hooking up with Mr. or

Miss Right. Some occupations offer the woman willing to try them an ample supply of available men: fire fighting, trucking, mining and construction are all more than 98 percent male; secretarial and nursing jobs are predominantly female. On the other hand, if you're not adventurous enough to try a career field entirely dominated by the opposite sex, look into those in which the odds are still with you. You will still find about three men for every woman in advertising, marketing and computer science careers; there are about two women for every man in teaching, social work and physical therapy.

MASTERS DEGREES

Definition: Educational credentials conferred to those who complete the academic requirements for a degree which is one notch above a baccalaureate.

Each year some 300,000 Americans are awarded masters degrees in various areas of study. The choice to pursue such an advanced degree is dictated by the needs of the profession you are going into, and whether such a degree is either required or imperative for credibility in the profession. The top two subject areas fit these requirements respectively. The number one subject, education, requires a master's in order to attain rank in the teaching profession. In the number two subject, business and management, the M.B.A. has become the standard that many businesses require for today's marketplace.

The Odds: Among those who earn bachelor's degrees, approximately 1 in 7 will pursue the next step up the academic ladder, a master's. The following list represents the ten most popular master's degrees at U.S. colleges and universities and the proportions of them among masters degrees conferred:

Education	1 in 4
Business & Management	1 in 5
Engineering	1 in 14
Health Sciences	1 in 17
Public Affairs	1 in 18
Social Sciences	1 in 29
Visual & Performing Arts	1 in 35
Computer & Information Science	1 in 35
Psychology	1 in 37
Letters	1 in 49

Source: Digest of Educational Statistics.

Also See: Educational Attainment, Ivy League Scholars, Ph.D.s.

MEDICAL IMPLANTS

Definition: The replacement or enhancement of various parts of the body by artificial devices inserted into body cavities, tissues or organs.

Modern medicine has made it possible for over 6 million Americans to look and feel better. Diseases of the eye, bone and the cardiovascular system are the most common maladies which are treated by medical implantation.

The Odds: Approximately 1 in 40 Americans will have a medical problem treated by some form of implantation of an artificial device. The following list represents the proportions of Americans who undergo surgery involving various forms of medical implants:

Breast Implants	1 in 65
Artificial Eye Lens	1 in 100
Artificial Joints	1 in 156
Eardrum Tubes	1 in 250
Pacemakers	1 in 534
Dental Implants	1 in 909
Heart Valves	1 in 1,000

Some implant procedures are considered dangerous, especially breast implants. Implantation is generally regarded as safer than its alternative, transplantation of living tissues, which poses risks of rejection by the body's immune system.

Source: National Center for Health Statistics survey estimates.

MEMBERSHIP

Definition: The aggregate number of individuals who belong to in an organized group.

America is a nation of joiners. Approximately 3 in 5 Americans belong to some group other than their family or company. So it's not surprising that the largest association in the country is a driver's club, "Triple-A", which provides road service to millions of stranded auto passengers each year, giving jump-starts on those freezing winter days or tows to the local service station when the radiator overheats. AAA is primarily a service association; not so with the American Association of Retired Persons. As the nation ages, AARP increasingly is seen as a political force for the elderly, mobilizing against cuts in Social Security, Medicare, retirement benefits and other issues affecting the aged. Look for its numbers to swell in the coming decade, as well as its influence.

The Odds: The average American has a membership card for the listed groups in the following proportions:

American Automobile Association	1 in 10
American Assoc. of Retired Persons	1 in 9
YMCA of U.S.A.	1 in 18
National Geographic Society	1 in 24

National Right to Life Committee	1 in 36
National PTA	1 in 41
National Wildlife Federation	1 in 49
Natl. Committee to Preserve Soc. Sec. & Medicare	1 in 50
Four-H Program	1 in 52
Boy Scouts of America	1 in 52

Source: American Society of Association Executives.

MENTAL DISORDERS

And Heredity

Definition: Any of the various types of insanity or severe neurosis, including schizophrenia and depression.

The Odds: For each type of disorder the chances of being afflicted differs. In the case of schizophrenia the rate of occurrence is 3 in 500 individuals over each year and almost 1 in 100 over a lifetime. If a patient is suffering from schizophrenia, the odds are 1 in 10 he will commit suicide. Schizophrenia is often thought to be a genetic disorder which means the risk of suffering from schizophrenia is greater for those related to an affected person.

Below are the relative risks (the pun is intended) which those face based on having a family with a mental disorder:

Unaffected Parents	1 in 13
One Affected Parent	1 in 7
Twin (Identical)	1 in 2
Twin (Fraternal)	1 in 11
Child (One Parent Affected)	1 in 8
Child (Both Parents Affected)	2 in 5

For bipolar manic depression the odds are 1 in 200 each year, 7 in 1,000 over a lifetime. Each year 1 in 200 people will have a manic episode. For its opposite, depression, 1 in 20 will suffer each year. Almost 1 in 5 individuals will suffer depression during his or her lifetime. Of those suffering, 1 in 6 will commit suicide.

Obsessive compulsive disorders claim 1 in 100 individuals. Dementia is one of the most common disorders, especially among the elderly. Among those surpassing the age of 80, the odds are 1 in 5 of developing some form of debilitating dementia.

Source: Encyclopedia Britannica.

MENTAL HEALTH TREATMENT

Definition: A psychological condition in which an individual suffers anxiety, delusions, depression or other symptoms which interfere with normal brain function.

Until approximately the turn-of-the century, the innerworkings of the human mind were not studied. Those with impaired or abnormal brain functions were suspected to be "possessed by the devil," suffering from retardation or insane.

The Odds: It has been estimated that approximately 1 in 3 Americans suffers some form of mental illness at one time in his or her life. Almost 1 in 5 suffered in the last 6 months, and 1 in 16 has consulted a mental health professional in that time period. Incredibly, it has been reported that as many as 1 in 7 therapists has had sexual or erotic contact with these patients, certainly contributing to their anxiety level.

The following list represents the proportions of Americans who suffer from the most common mental health problems sometime in their lives, according to the National Institutes of Mental Health:

Alcohol Abuse	1 in 8
Phobias	1 in 9
Major Depression	1 in 16
Drug Dependency	1 in 16
Antisocial or Obsessive-compulsive Disorder	1 in 33
Panic Disorder or Mental Impairment	1 in 50
Schizophrenia	1 in 500

Also See: Mental Disorders.

Source: Compiled research by editors.

METEORITE DEVASTATION
Killer Rocks From Outer Space

Definition: Impact on the Earth from an asteroid sizable enough to wipe out life as we know it on the planet.

The threat of a devastating meteorite strike upon the Earth, once the stuff only for science fiction films and novels (such as the 1950s classic *When Worlds Collide*) has recently caught the attention of an increasing number of scientists, politicians and journalists. In an article on the subject in the June 18, 1991, edition of the *New York Times*, it was reported that in 1989, a half-mile wide asteroid missed striking the Earth by a mere six hours. A House of Representatives report concluded that had the rock struck the Earth, "it would have caused a disaster unprecedented in human history. The energy released would have been equivalent to more than 1,000 one-megaton bombs." NASA is researching the possibility of setting up an "asteroid shield," which would detect dangerous celestial bodies while they were still far off, allowing us to send out a rocket containing nuclear explosives that would give the offending space rock a gentle nudge out of the planet's path.

Such a system, according to H-Bomb guru Dr. Edward Teller, would cost less than $100 million to build. Asterophobes have enlisted noted space cadet J. Danforth Quayle (who once addressed a group of Mercury, Gemini and Apollo veterans as "fellow astronauts") to lobby on their behalf.

The Odds: Are we really that threatened by killer rocks from outer space? The discovery of some extremely large asteroid craters on Earth (too large to be ascertained from ground observation) has been made easier by the use of satellites. The largest of these yet discovered is a 124-mile-wide crater located in Ontario. The three-quarter-mile wide Meteor Crater in Arizona was created by a rock a mere 150 feet wide that struck the planet 50,000 years ago.

As recently as 1908, a meteor struck in remote Siberia with the impact of 12 megatons of TNT, leveling plant life for dozens of miles around. Scientists from the Planetary Science Institute, extrapolating from crater evidence here and on the moon, and from plots of asteroid paths, estimate that a cataclysmic asteroid strikes the Earth every 300,000 to 1,000,000 years. Given this, the estimated risk of death from asteroid impact for an American over a fifty year period is 1 in 6,000 (300,000 divided by 50) — more likely than dying in an airplane crash or a tornado! Should we fear this Omega asteroid more than airplanes? Should we all start wearing helmets?

With luck, cooler heads will prevail. Despite the specious reasoning that results in the frightful 1 in 6,000 figure, a look at the facts reveals that life on Earth does not vanish every 300,000 years, or even every million years. Perhaps the best way to establish the odds is to look at the fossil record. Many scientists now agree that the extinction of the dinosaurs was caused by a major celestial catastrophe some 60 million years ago — most probably, an asteroid strike. No other fossil records point to another major catastrophe since that time.

So, we could estimate from the facts that a truly devastating meteor strikes not once every 300,000 years, but once every 60 million, giving the odds of life as we know it being wiped out in a fifty-year time span as 1 in 1,200,000. Even this reasoning is flawed, however, since the evidence does not suggest that these meteors strike in any regular 60-million-year pattern. In any event, the odds of an American dying from a catastrophic meteor that wipes out human life on Earth are much less than 1 in 6,000. So don't worry. The sky is not falling.

Source: New York Times.

MISSING IN ACTION

Viet Nam MIAs

Definition: A military combatant who fails to return from hostile action or whose whereabouts is unaccounted-for in a war zone after fatalities are recorded and identified. [common term "MIA"]

The U.S. military regards MIAs as unfinished business and does not easily give up for dead its unaccounted-for military men and women. During the war in Southeast Asia, 8.7 million men served their country. Officially 47,382 lost their lives, but another 2,273 were listed as missing in action as of the end of 1991.

The Odds: For those in the military during the war, the odds of becoming missing in action could now be calculated as 1 in 3,827. Actual troops engaged in combat can only be estimated, due to the military's policy of classifying much of its information. Estimates range from just over 1 million actual combatants to as high as 1.5 million. Given these figures, the odds of a combatant becoming missing in action range from 1 in 440 to 1 in 660. This is about two to three times less than the odds of dying from a battle related injury, which are approximately 1 in 180. If MIAs are counted as "war casualties," as perhaps they should be, 1 in 9 casualties are MIAs.

Rumors run rampant that some MIAs are still being held prisoner. The Pentagon reports 1,509 live sightings of suspected MIAs. The list below represents the official explanation for these sightings.

"Accounted For"	7 in 10 *
Distorted Reports	1 in 5
Fabrications	1 in 4
Under investigation	1 in 15

*i.e. missionaries or POWs returned at end of war

Source: U.S. Department of Defense.

Also See: War Casualties

MILITARY ENLISTMENTS

Where You May Serve

Definition: The fighting men and women in the U.S. Armed Forces.

Though the U.S. Selective Services Administration requires all men to "register for the draft", military conscription is no longer in practice. An all-volunteer military will most likely be the rule, unless the U.S. is faced with a sudden emergency which its 5.3 million troops cannot handle.

The Odds: Almost 1 in 37 American adults is in the active or inactive military services. Of them, 2 in 5 are on active duty and the remainder are in the active or inactive reserves. Among the active military forces, 1 in 11 persons is female, 1 in 5 is black and 1 in 24 are Hispanic.

Where will you serve? Those who are considering joining up will want to know that the odds are 3 to 1 that you will be stationed in the United States. The odds that you will serve elsewhere are 1 to 5 for Europe, and 1 to 14 for Asia and the Pacific.

The minions of our peacetime Army—and of its somewhat-civilianized sub-chapters, the National Guard and the Coast Guard—are scattered equitably throughout our great and broad land. In greatest numbers, they have followed the sun—to populous land-rich states like California and Texas, and to sun bleached U.S. utopias like Hawaii and Florida.

The following list represents the proportions of military personnel in the ten states with the most troops:

California	1 in 10
Texas	1 in 15
Virginia	1 in 20
North Carolina	1 in 22
Florida	1 in 28
Georgia	1 in 34
Hawaii	1 in 47
South Carolina	1 in 48
Washington	1 in 48
Colorado	1 in 49

Source: U.S. Census Bureau.

Also See: Military Casualties, Women in Uniform.

MILITARY CASUALTIES

Losses in Action

Definition: Injuries sustained from the enemy's weapons, friendly fire, or an accident during the course of a war.

According to military historian John Keegan, writing in *The Face of Battle*, a number of reasons account for the sharp decrease in death rates. First, the last century has seen a quantum leap in the ability to treat the wounded, made possible by medical advances and by the helicopter, which has given armies the ability to pull wounded men from the battlefield, sometimes in the middle of a fire fight, and transport them to a field hospital within a matter of minutes. In addition, hygiene practices in armies, almost nonexistent in the Civil War, have improved markedly.

The Odds: Of the 8,744,000 Americans who served in Southeast Asia, total battle deaths came to 47,382, or about 1 out of every 184 who served. This represents a dramatic decrease in lethality from the Civil War, in which 1 of every 16 who served died in battle. The odds of dying from a non-battle cause in Vietnam were even more remote — about 1 in 817, compared to *1 in 10* in the Civil War. So the modern soldier is relatively much safer than his past counterpart. And you'll want to hope the U.S. keeps picking tiny opponents to flex its muscles. Of the American troops who saw action in Grenada in 1983 and Panama in 1989, only 1 out of 800 were killed. In the War in the Persian Gulf in 1991, approximately 1 in 3,300 troops died while serving.

IMPROVING THE ODDS

Volunteer: If there is a reasonable chance that you are going to get drafted, don't wait for your papers; go to your local recruiter and sign up. There are two main advantages to volunteering, in the event that the country does mobilize:

You're Safest in the Sky and on the Sea: You can pick the branch of service in which you will serve. The most dangerous branch of service is the Marine Corps. In World War II, the odds of a leatherneck dying in battle were 1 in 35, compared to 1 in 48 for an Army soldier (including the Army Air Corps) and 1 in 113 for a sailor; in Vietnam, 1 in 61 Marines died in battle, compared to 1 in 140 Army soldiers. The Navy and Air Force are the safest branches: odds of dying in battle in Vietnam were 1 in 1,024 for those in the Air Force and 1 in 1,146 for sailors. In the War in the Persian Gulf the odds of being killed in battle were a much more acceptable 1 in 2,667.

Behind the Lines: Volunteers also usually are given a choice of the job they'd like to do. And the sheer number of non-combat troops that a modern army needs means that there are plenty of relatively safe jobs for a volunteer, including such areas as logistics, supply, administration, command and communication staff and maintenance.

Then Again: In a large-scale conflict such as one in recent one in the Middle East, military historian Keegan says that the command, communication and support troops behind the lines may actually be in even greater danger than front-line combatants. In a conflict between two technologically advanced opponents, the key to victory will rest in large part on the ability to disrupt the chain of command and communication. So staff positions will be no hiding place from danger.

Source: Original research by editors.

Also See: Friendly Fire.

MILITARY SERVICE

Definition: A time in life, usually among young males, to serve your country by being a member of its armed forces.

Even with the depletion of manpower from the War in the Persian Gulf (an estimated 100,000 Iraqis lost their lives), the Iraqi Army, as of this writing, remains a potent power in terms of sheer numbers. Moreover, with the relief of tensions between NATO and the Soviet Union, significant cuts are expected in both U.S. and Soviet forces, such as the initial 25 percent cut in American military personnel proposed by the Pentagon.

The Odds: In countries such as Iraq, North Korea or others which have military conscription (mandatory service) the probability that physically fit males will serve is 100 percent. In the U.S., however, where military service is strictly on a volunteer basis, the proportions of the population who serve voluntarily in one year are as high as some nations where military service is required.

The following list represents the countries with the largest military personnel and the proportions of the population who are active-duty military personnel, including paramilitary forces:

Iraq	1 in 21
North Korea	1 in 25
Vietnam	1 in 54
Turkey	1 in 64
Soviet Union	1 in 66
South Korea	1 in 71
France	1 in 96
United States	1 in 110
Pakistan	1 in 198
Brazil	1 in 277
China	1 in 320
India	1 in 568

Source: U.S. Arms Control and Disarmament Agency, *World Military Expenditures and Arms Transfers,* annual.

Also See: Military Personnel.

MISS AMERICA

Definition: A much sought-after title conferred by a panel of judges on an unmarried woman deemed to be talented, beautiful, and personable; conventionally prefixed to the name of the winner of a beauty pageant in which one representative of each of the 50 states participates.

The Odds: "Well, ah do declahr." How many times have the judges of the Miss America contest heard those cuddly little words from a Southern belle who was just informed that she is the prettiest single woman in the U.S.? If you are like the rest of the population, you probably would answer, "So what else is new?", believing that all Southerners like to perpetuate that the idea that their women are the best looking in the country. However, in the overall view of the Miss America pageant since its beginning in 1921 (for a total of 61 pageants — none were held in 1922, 1928-32, 1935 and 1950), only one in 5 winners were from Dixie, about on a par with those farmers daughters from the Midwest (1 in 6) and the Plains (1 in 6). That's far behind the beauties from the East, who have captured 18 Miss America titles, for odds of about 1 in 3. The worst showing has been by babes from the West, with only 1 title in 7.

Source: The World Almanac.

MOB BOSSES
Getting Away with Big Time Crime

Definition: Little men who look like your grandpa, but will have you erased over a $100 dispute.

If it wasn't for the American media's fascination with crime, most of us would think names like Gotti and Capone were high fashion designer brands. Newspapermen and Hollywood producers know that names can mean a lot. Thanks to the romantic stories in the press and on the screen, "Bugsy", "Big Tuna", and "Fat Tony" have captured our hearts, while blowing the heads off their enemies.

Once a mobster gets high enough in a crime family, he is "hot copy" (pressworthy) in the eyes of news directors and editors. The Feds and the cops always want to catch the fish wrapped up in the most newspapers, and they are quite successful at it. The biggest media play on the mob may have been in 1986 when *Fortune* Magazine ran a list of the top 50 Mafia bosses, the "Fortune 50." According to the magazine, they are among the wealthiest men in America. But do they get away with it?

Above: Tony Accardo, "Big Tuna", 70 years in the business — never spent the night in jail.

The Odds: In 1986, less than 1 in 2 of the infamous "50" were free — 27 of the 50 were in jail and 1 in 8 (6 mobsters) were out on bail. The following list represents the disposition of these big fish by 1991, five years later:

In Prison	1 in 2
Retired	1 in 5
Still Pursuing Crime	1 in 6
Dead	1 in 8
On Bail	1 in 16
On the Lam	1 in 50

So, does big time crime pay? Indeed, if you don't mind being the richest man in prison . . . or the cemetery.

Source: The Associated Press.

MOBILE HOMES

Definition: Transportable houses including trailers and single family homes designed to be readily detached from their foundations in order to move to a different location.

With skyrocketing property taxes, unworkably high mortgage rates and the drastic costs of construction, mobile homes have become an increasingly popular alternative to conventional housing. In the rugged, open regions of the West, nearly 1 in 5 permanent residential structures is mobile.

No one knows for sure why mobile residences are always placed squarely in the path of tornadoes.

The Odds: In the U.S., 1 in 15 housing units are mobile homes or trailers. The following list represents the proportions of mobile homes in the ten states with the highest ratios:

Wyoming	1 in 5
Montana	1 in 7
New Mexico	1 in 8
Arizona	1 in 8
Nevada	1 in 8
Alaska	1 in 9
West Virginia	1 in 9
Idaho	1 in 10

South Carolina	1 in 10
North Carolina	1 in 10

Source: U.S. Census Bureau, American Housing Survey for the United States.

MONEY YEARS

The Richest Generations

Definition: The period in life when you'll have the most dough.

Disposable cash per individual rises steadily with age, until you reach your fifth or sixth decade in the fast lane. By that time, you may be ready for retirement, but you are likely to have over $14,000 of discretionary income and approximately $100,000 in net equity in your home. Youngsters 15 to 24, on the other hand, have a mere $7,790 to kick around on in the average year. More than an allowance perhaps, but less than a fortune.

The Odds: In 1963, almost 1 in 5 Americans (19 percent) were over age 65. This age group had a disproportional share of the nation's wealth, 26 percent. By 1986, this age group grew slightly to 21 percent of the population, but then owned 33 percent of the nation's wealth.

In 1963, those under 35 also represented about 1 in 5 Americans (18 percent) and had 6 percent of the nation's wealth. By 1986, when the baby boomers were grown and represented almost 1 in 4 Americans (23 percent), these youngsters still had only 6 percent of the nation's wealth, no gain whatsoever.

The reason the older generation has more wealth is due to the fact that they have equity in their homes. In the age group 25 to 34, only 1 in 7 Americans owned homes. At age 45 to 54, approximately 9 in 20 Americans are homeowners; by age 55, 8 in 10 Americans are. An incredible 17 in 20 homeowners over age 65 own their homes outright. The impact of having a home which was purchased at the lower prices of the fifties and sixties is dramatic. Lower mortgage payments and increased equity a mean higher economic status.

Below is a ranking of the richest years in a person's life, as judged by the amount of discretionary money available to an individual in a household:

1. 55-59	$14,580
2. 45-49	$14,450
3. 60-64	$14,360

4. 50-54	$13,550
5. 65-69	$12,920
6. 35-39	$12,400
7. 30-34	$10,920
8. 25-29	$9,130
9. 15-24	$7,790

Source: U.S. Bureau of the Census.

MONTE CARLO

"Breaking the Bank"

Definition: Winning big in the poshest gambling venue in the world.

Warren Weaver, in his book *Lady Luck*, describes an event at Monte Carlo which he has heard authentically reported, but for which he could not find any hard evidence. As the story goes, at a particular gaming house in that swank gambling paradise, a certain roulette wheel came up "even" 28 straight times. Just what are the chances?

The Odds: Let's calculate the odds of coming up with 28 straight evens. At Monte Carlo, the roulette wheel holds 18 even and 18 odd numbers, plus 0, which is ruled neither odd nor even. Thus the odds of a particular ball coming up even is 18/37 (that extra zero, of course, is where the house gets its advantage). Since each spin of the wheel is independent of the previous one, the probability of even coming up 28 straight times is 18/37 multiplied by itself 28

times, or about 578 million to 1! Anyone want to make a wager?

However, it shouldn't be so surprising that *at some time* over the course of the century, even such a long shot as 578 million to 1 should come in at Monte Carlo. As Weaver reports, each roulette table at Monte Carlo averages about 500 "coups" a day, with 3 spins per coup—giving about 1,500 chances at even per table per day, or 550,000 spins per year. Since the odds of a particular string of 28 evens coming up is 578 million to one, it's about even money that such a string would come up in 1,000 years of play on a single wheel (578 million divided by 550,000).

This means that with only ten wheels working, it's even money that a string of 28 evens will come up at some point in first century of play, which is the streak that Weaver reports. But, figuring out *when* that streak will hit, that's a gamble!

The following list represents the odds for selected long strings of evens in roulette, on a wheel with 37 numbers:

2	1 in 4.2
5	1 in 37
8	1 in 319
10	1 in 1350
15	1 in 50,000
20	1 in 1.8 million
25	1 in 67 million
28	1 in 578 million
50	1 in 4.4 quadrillion

100	1 in 19 with 30 zeros

Source: Warren Weaver, *Lady Luck: The Theory of Probability,* Anchor Books, Garden City, NY.

THE MONTY HALL PROBLEM

Definition: Picking the door that yields the grand prize, rather than the one with a goat.

Okay. You've made it to the final round of that fabulous game show, *Let's Make a Deal.* You've endured the humiliation of dressing up as a water fowl on national television. You've screamed you're way into the attention of the host, Monty Hall. You've correctly chosen the package of Mennen deodorant over the Turtle Wax, Arm & Hammer Baking Soda and Pine Sol as the product that costs exactly $1.57, successfully resisting the temptation to take Monty's offer of $800 to call it quits. You've won a complete outdoor patio set and now you're in the final grand prize round.

You are now presented with three doors. Behind one of the doors is a car; behind the other two are goats. You select door number 2. Monty reveals door number 3, which contains a goat. He then offers you the opportunity to switch to door number 1. Should you switch?

Here is a scenario that has caused an earthquake throughout the normally serene world of mathematical academia since Marilyn vos Savant, the person with the world record IQ, posed the problem in Parade magazine. After vos Savant published her response – that the odds of winning are better if you switch – she received thousands of letters, many from mathematicians and scientists challenging her conclusion. Common sense, the detractors say, tells you that at the outset of the game, your odds are 1 in 3 of picking the winner. Since one of the doors has revealed a goat, the odds that each of the other doors is the winner is now even. There is no advantage in switching from one to the other.

The Odds: But probability and common sense don't always agree. The fact is, the odds on your door haven't changed they're still 1 in 3. So, since there is only one other door left, the odds on it are 2 in 3. You've got only a 33 percent chance of winning if you stay, but if you switch to the other door, you increase your chances to 66 percent.

To fully understand the situation, some rules for the game have to be explained. Monty knows which door contains the prize. He knows which door you've picked. He always reveals one of the doors with the goat, but not the door you've picked. And he always offers you the chance to switch.

Instead of going through an elaborate mathematical explanation on why you should switch, consider the fact that Monty is more bound by what he knows about what is behind the doors than one might think. He must reveal a goat, no matter what door you've picked. This is the crucial psychological fact that increases the odds for switching.

Source: New York Times.

MOONLIGHTING

Definition: Keeping the bill collector at bay by taking a second job to supplement income from the first.

The Odds: One in 16 Americans is likely to need and find extra income from a second job. Who are they, these under-earners who struggle just to stay even? The odds of the necessity of moonlighting have been increasing for all income groups. Men, whose odds of taking a second job are 1 in 15, are slightly more likely to moonlight than women whose odds of taking a second job are 1 in 17. On the other hand, whites, whose odds of taking a second job are slightly greater than 1 in 15, are much more likely to moonlight than blacks, whose odds of taking a second job are 1 in 23. Why are so many doing it? The odds are almost even that moonlighters of all groups are working extra jobs just to up with daily living expenses and to pay off debt. The usual causes of the upswing in moon-

lighting are cost pressures from rising housing prices and the ballooning credit card debt of the American people.

Source: Future Vision, The 189 Most Important Trends of the 1990s, Sourcebooks Trade, 1991

MORTGAGES

Can You Qualify?

Definition: The chief reason Americans are always broke at the beginning of each month.

One of the most common concerns of young marrieds is will they ever save enough money to buy a home. Once the money is in the bank, however, what's the next, and probably biggest, worry? Will you qualify for a loan.

The Odds: Most people do qualify, some 8 in 10. Though banks claim the decision whether to make the mortgage loan is based on financial data, racial bias is suspected to come into play when the loan committee reviews applications. Whether or not it is, there are considerable variations along color lines and national origins.

REJECTION RATES

Whites	1 in 7
Blacks	1 in 3
Hispanics	1 in 5

Statistics for Asians are not part of the above research; however in a survey in Chicago, which has a more-or-less typical mix of American born and foreign born Asians, the rejection rate for this group was 1 in 10, lower than the three largest groups shown above.

Bankers claim these variations are due to differences in income among ethnic and racial groups. When low-income whites are compared to upper income blacks, however, the whites were rejected in ratios of 1 to 7 and blacks were rejected 1 to 5. In other words, the rates are quite close, considering the opposite income poles. Is this for purely racial reasons? If asked, odds are that bankers will tell you it is due to individual credit histories.

Source: Federal Reserve Board, 1991 study of lending institutions.

MOTHERHOOD

American as Apple Pie?

Definition: The state in which a woman has given birth to a child.

What is more American than your mom or her apple pie?

Apple pie may be very American, but the proclivity of American women to be a mom is *uniquely* American. That is, moms in America are much rarer than elsewhere. Aside from Europe, where fertility and birth rates are the lowest, the women of the U.S. have far fewer children than those in other countries. The

average American woman will have 1.9 children versus 3.3 as a world average. Fertility rates are highest in Africa where women have an average of 5.1 children, and are lowest in Western Europe where they are 1.6.

The Odds: Approximately 8 in 10 women around the world will become moms. In America, the overall odds that an average woman will have a baby are only 6 in 10. This rate is consistently getting lower. In 1976, for example, 65 percent of American women could be expected to have children. By 1988, only 62 percent would procreate. Among women 18 to 44 years old, 1 in 16 will give birth during a 12-month period.

The list below represents the proportions of American women in various categories who will have a child in a year:

Blacks	94 in 1,000
Hispanics	87 in 1,000
Whites	66 in 1,000

The following list represents the odds that a first birth will take place during various age periods in a women's life:

Under 20	1 in 4
20-24	1 in 3
25-29	1 in 4
30-34	1 in 8
35 +	1 in 25

Source: The National Center for Health Statistics.

Also See: Birth'n Babies, Teen Pregnancies.

MOTOR OIL

Definition: The black slimy gook which is drained from the crank case of your car when you get an oil change.

What happens to the liquid junk that oozes from your engine every 3,000-5,000 miles when you get it changed? You might be surprised to know that the mechanics save it, sell it and it is a multimillion dollar industry involving 1.4 billion gallons of the murky mess. Most of it is somehow burned for heat and it releases 600,000 pounds of poisonous lead in the air. The gray, hazy smoke which results is responsible for more airborne lead pollution than any other source, even gasoline with lead, the now-banned fuel which automobiles used prior to 1970.

The Odds: What is the probability that your discarded oil will contribute to lead pollution of the environment? The following list represents the proportions of old motor oil that will be used far various purposes:

For Heat	1 in 2
Refined & Reused	1 in 20
Dumped in	
Land Fills	1 in 3
Other Industrial	
Uses	1 in 33

Source: Study conducted by the Sierra Club, the Hazardous Waste Treatment Council, the Izaak Walton League of America and the Natural Resources Defense Council.

Also See: Pollution.

MOVIE ACTORS

Definition: A person who, on occasion, acts in motion pictures, but who more often makes up the long lines at Hollywood unemployment offices.

The Odds: All right. So you have graduated from drama school, paid your dues by starting out in Hollywood as a carpenter, grip, or production assistant, and somehow surmounted the Catch-

22 of the Screen Actors Guild, which says you must appear in a Union film to become a member of the Guild, but Union films rarely give roles to persons who are not already members of the Guild. What are your chances of landing a part in a feature film, work that may last for three days if you are a "bit" player, or only from four to six weeks if you are a good supporting player? The answer explains why even name actors often find it hard to land a role. The Screen Actors Guild has 70,000 members who compete for an average of 24 roles in the production of only 300 films a year, making the odds of landing one of these parts 1 in 10. Bear in mind, however, that against this grim statistic of 1 in 10, many non-Union companies make films today in locations scattered around the country, and Guild members cannot work in these films. Additionally, job growth among actors is expected to increase 23 percent through the mid-1990s, although role seekers will still outnumber the available roles by a large margin.

Source: A Guide to Putting Yourself in the Movies, James Orr.

MULTIPLE BIRTHS

Definition: The cause for the malady SIBSOP (simultaneous insanity, bankruptcy and sleeplessness of parents).

It's a Boy! It's a Boy! It's a Boy!

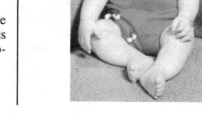

You think you've got trouble with your kid. Some parents of newborns have troubles and troubles, while others have troubles, troubles and troubles, and others can have ...

Multiple births are on the rise. Medical science believes the reason is that women today are having children at an older age. Once a woman is past the age of thirty, she is more likely to have more than one egg in the womb during ovulation and is therefore more prone to fertilize more than one egg, hence giving birth to more than one child.

The Odds: Approximately 1 in 100 pregnancies involve either the splitting of an egg or multiple eggs being fertilized. The following list represents various multiple birth situations and the odds of occurrence.

Twins	1 in 90
Triplets	1 in 9,000
Siamese Twins	1 in 100,000
Quadruplets	1 in 900,000
Quintuplets	1 in 85 mil.

Because high multiple births such as quadruplets and quintuplets often result in low birth weights or underdevelopment, the risk is high that all the children will not survive infancy. Siamese twins are also risky because of the need for a surgical procedure to separate them. Frequently, such surgery is successful.

Source: Compiled research by editors.

MURDER

Definition: The most permanent damage possible that can be inflicted on the victim of a crime.

The Odds: In the U.S., the odds that you will "die by the sword" – be murdered by any means – is a frightening 1 in 99 shot. In any given year, however, it is a more reassuring 1 in 12,000 shot. Violence-prone criminals would be well advised to know that the odds a violent crime will result in a murder are an astonishing 1 in 75.

Source: Compiled research by editors.

Also See: Crime; Killers; Murder Scenes, U.S.; Murder Abroad; Murder Methods; Police Homicides.

MURDER ABROAD

Definition: The act of bumping off someone outside the United States.

Human nature is universal, and violence is an inevitable feature of any society. Acts of violence, however, do not occur in a vacuum. Climate certainly has an effect. The murder capitals below all lie within the tropics or in hot, arid semi-deserts – so much for paradise. Political, ideological and economic strife also serve as undeniable provocations to homicide.

The Odds: In the U.S., approximately 1 in 12,000 people are murdered annually. In foreign countries with the 10 highest murder rates, the odds of the big M are between 17 and one-and-half times greater.

The following list represents the odds that an average person will be hit in the nations with the 10 highest murder rates:

Lesotho	1 in 710
Bahamas	1 in 4,370
Guyana	1 in 4,502
Lebanon	1 in 4,919
Netherlands Antilles	1 in 8,019
Iraq	1 in 8,375
Sri Lanka	1 in 8,389
Cyprus	1 in 9,001
Trinidad/Tobago	1 in 9,606
Jamaica	1 in 9,756

Certainly the only thing more murderous than these countries is spelling them.

Source: Interpol International Crime Statistics.

Also See: Crime, Killers, Marriage.

MURDEROUS JOBS

Homicides on the Job

Definition: Getting to heaven before you get home from work.

Do you know someone who has a killer of a job? If you know a cabbie, you do. Taxi drivers face the greatest danger of being murdered on the job of any worker. As with most other occupations high on the murder list, taxi-driver murders usually occur in the midst of an armed robbery. Why are cabbies are so prone? An isolated, mobile crime spot, a solitary captive victim normally looking the other way, easy access to cash, and 24-hour availability. A good scene for a murder!

The Gainesville Rule: Convenience store clerks are the second most numerous homicide victims on the job. Indeed, of the 310 men on death row in Florida, 1 in 10 are there for a convenience store homicide. Some cities, such as Gainesville, Florida, now require convenience stores to keep at least two employees on the job during night-time hours, to discourage potential robberies. Legislators and convenience store employees are also calling for bullet-proof glass and even for armed guards on duty.

The Odds: The following list represents the odds of being killed at the most murderous jobs in one year:

Taxi Driver	1 in 28,986
Convenience Store Clerk	1 in 45,455
Trucker Gas Station	1 in 61,729

Attendant	1 in 76,923
Retail Sales Clerk	1 in 112,360
Restaurant/	
Bar Worker	1 in 138,889

Source: National Institute for Occupational Health and Safety.

Also See: Murder, Job Deaths.

MURDER METHODS

Where There's a Will...

Definition: Creative ways people criminally kill each other.

If you are stopped on the street by a stranger with a canister who pleads, "give to the criminally insane or I'll kill you!", do what he says, especially if times are bad. Though the odds favor he will snuff you out with a gun, when the economy is especially poor, murders by gun increase, while other methods remain relatively the same.

The Odds: During periods in which the U.S. economy is humming along, about 3 in 5 murder victims (58 percent) die from gun shots. When the economy is the pits, almost 2 in 3 murder victims (65 percent) are fatally shot.

Since you are more likely to die as a result of murder (a 1 in 99 shot) than as a victim of many diseases, it is nice to know what you might expect at the moment of truth. Bludgeoning? Strangulation? Not much to look forward to. A gunshot, on the other hand, is not so bad compared to the others you might face. No one knows for sure which is the best way to die in a murder because there are no known cases in which a victim was murdered twice by different means, nor are there any recorded cases of anyone relating details about dying at the hand of murder.

The following list represents America's favorite murder techniques and a decade average of the odds murder victims will face gun, knives or other instruments of destruction in their final moments:

FAVORITE WAYS TO KILL EACH OTHER

Gunshots	3 in 5
Cutting/Stabbing	1 in 5
Bludgeoning	1 in 16
Strangulation	1 in 2
Arson	1 in 70
Other	1 in 25

What are some of the "others"? Favorites include running someone over with a car, pushing someone in front of one, poisoning, pushing someone down stairs, throwing them over railings and other creative ways to spoil someone's whole day.

Source: F.B.I. Uniform Crime Reports.

Also See: Killers on the Loose, Murders, Murder Scenes,

MURDER SCENES

U.S. Murder Capitals

Definition: The cities in which you are most likely to get criminally snuffed out.

Drug deals go bad. Kids shoot each other over perceived slights — basketball jackets or maybe the expensive shoes they couldn't afford. Not surprisingly, our nation's capital, with its tremendous economic problems, is also the country's murder capital. Among big cities, Pitttsburgh is the safest with a lowly 4.6 murders per 100,000 people. Interestingly, although New York leads the nation every year in the total number of murders it logs on its streets, it ranks only thirteenth in per capita murders.

The Odds: Getting murdered is approximately a 1 in 12,000 shot. In the nation's largest cities the odds are more than 4 times greater than elsewhere. In the murder capital of the nation, Washington D.C., the odds are nearly twice what they are in other crime-ridden urban centers and 7 times greater than in the total U.S.

Following are the top cities in murders per-capita and the odds the average citizen will get plugged, stabbed, poisoned, bludgeoned to death or take a fatal hit of any kind in one year.

GOOD PLACES TO BE HIT

Washington, D.C.	1 in 1,681
Detroit	1 in 1,727
Atlanta	1 in 2,047
Denver	1 in 2,304
New Orleans	1 in 2,358
Dallas	1 in 2,778
Newark	1 in 2,788
St. Louis	1 in 3,040
Baltimore	1 in 3,268
Oakland	1 in 3,279
Kansas City	1 in 3,344
Memphis	1 in 3,846
New York City	1 in 3,876

Coincidentally, the odds of being killed in the Big Apple or other major cities are about the same as those faced by soldiers who served in the War in the Persian Gulf, except in the nation's capital where you are three times more likely to be killed than one of Norman Schwarzkopf's troops were. (See Military Casualties.)

Source: U.S. Federal Bureau of Investigation, *Crime in the United States*, annual.

Also See: Murder; Murder Scenes, International; Murder Weapons.

MURDER VICTIMS

Definition: The guy on the wrong end of the gun or knife.

The most likely souls to do us mortal harm, the F.B.I. says, are acquaintances, but not friends. Does this mean you should befriend more of your acquaintances? Not really. Spouses and lovers are more likely to bump you off than your friends. In fact, these loved ones are just as probable to kill you as a stranger. Combined, spouses and lovers account for 13.8 percent of all murders of their victims, while strangers account for only 13.1 percent.

The Odds: Women should note that no matter how mad their husband may be at them, their friends are twice as likely to kill them. The facts also reveal that, if you are murdered, the chances of it being at the hand of a friend or wife average about 1 in 5. Sadly, roughly 1 in 30 victims goes at the hands of his or her own child. Incidences of parents killing a child are very uncommon, though even the best parents have had reasonable provocation, so they say.

The following list represents the most common relationship of murderers to their victims and the proportions involved in homicides:

Acquaintance	3 in 10
Unknown Relationship	1 in 4
Stranger	1 in 8
Friend	1 in 21
Wife	1 in 25
Girlfriend	1 in 38
Husband	1 in 42
Other Family	1 in 43
Son	1 in 63
Daughter	1 in 72

Source: F.B.I. Uniform Crime Reports.

Also See: Killers on the Loose, Murders, Murder Abroad, Murder Methods, Murder Scenes, Police Homicides.

N n

NATIVE AMERICANS

Definition: Descendants of the original inhabitants of the United States, primarily Indians and Native Alaskans (Eskimos and Aleuts).

Millions of Americans, especially those who are descendants of the early Anglo-Saxon immigrants claim some "Indian blood." The Federal Government, however, recognizes only approximately 1.5 million Americans as Indians and 64,000 as Native Alaskans. According to other estimates, there are almost 2 million Native Americans.

The Odds: Estimates of Indian populations vary due to the fact that only 1 in 4 now live on reservations. Almost 2 in 3 now live in urban areas. Most current estimates indicate about 1 in 125 Americans (1.96 million) are Indians or Native Alaskans.

WHERE THEY LIVE

Alaska	1 in 31
Western States	1 in 2
Southern States	1 in 4
Midwestern States	1 in 6
Northeastern States	1 in 166

Native Americans suffer a plethora of social and health problems which is far greater than those of other Americans. More than 1 in 8 are unemployed and in some tribes, 3 in 4 are overweight. The rate of tuberculosis among Native Americans is 5 times higher than the national average and diabetes rates are two and one-half times higher. Alcoholism and cirrhosis of the liver is also two and one-half times higher.

Infant mortality is one of the few health plagues which Native Americans have conquered. Before 1960, 1 in 66 infants would die shortly after birth. Today the rate is virtually the same as other Americans, about 1 in 100. The rate, however, for sudden infant death syndrome is 50 percent higher among Indians than the general population. Perhaps the most dramatic gap in the health statistics for Native Americans is that 1 in 3 will die before reaching age 45. This compares to 1 in 9 among the general population.

Source: U.S. Public Health Service.

Also See: Indians.

NEWS SOURCES

Definition: The pages and spots on the dial which Americans turn to get the scoop on Liz's new loves, Yeltsin's new headaches, Trump's new disasters and . . .

Mass communications is now almost a worldwide phenomenon. In America, news reporters have been elevated to high status and TV news-land is a subculture followed by millions with enthusiasm. The combined readership of all newspapers in the U.S. is over 100 million and over 90 million people have television sets.

The Odds: Many radio listeners admit to changing stations when the news is reported. Though America has 3 major newsweekly magazines, their combined circulation is just 8 million in a country of 250 million. Odds are most Americans get their news from the papers and TV as shown below.

Late TV News	2 in 5
Daily paper	3 in 5
Sunday paper	2 in 3

Though no official data exists, odds are overwhelmingly evident that much of the news is culled by consumers from three sources—taverns, beauty parlors, and at work during breaks.

Source: Statistical Abstracts of the U.S.

NOSTALGIA
TV's Golden Age

Definition: The means by which Americans over age 40 amused themselves with a new toy—a television set.

Ask someone what they remember best about the fifties. Odds are they will either tell you about the family car or the hours logged in front of the TV with the whole family mesmerized in unison. What's on the list of their fondest memories? The list is notable for its preponderance of the now extinct variety show, as well as the prime-time quiz show.

Today's TV generation is, in fact, made up of the children of yesterday's TV generation. So, in the name of mutual understanding—and in attempt to bridge the generation gap with a single span—here are the golden hits of Ma and Pa's couch-potato past and the odds it is indelibly etched in their memory.

The Odds: The following list represents the proportions of the fifties viewing audiences who watched the top 10 shows of the decade at the time it was regularly aired:

Arthur Godfrey's Talent Scouts	1 in 3
I Love Lucy	3 in 10
You Bet Your Life	3 in 10
Dragnet	1 in 4
Jack Benny Show	1 in 5
Arthur Godfrey and Friends	1 in 5
Gunsmoke	1 in 6
Red Skelton Show	1 in 7
December Bride	1 in 7
I've Got a Secret	1 in 8

Source: A.C. Nielsen.

O o

OCCUPATIONAL WISH LISTS

Definition: The things working men and women would rather be doing to earn their daily bread.

In 1988, *The Jobs Rated Almanac* examined 250 jobs. The research indicated that many of the so-called "most desirable" jobs were the pits. Actors, football players, ballerinas and models, received some of the lowest scores in desirability.

More recently in 1990, Americans confessed what professions they would rather be in other than the ones in which they are presently employed. The top choices were as follows:

AMONG MEN

Athlete	1 in 2
Business Leader	2 in 5
Musician	1 in 4

AMONG WOMEN

Singer	1 in 3
Author	1 in 3
Doctor	1 in 4

Source: Liebeman Research Inc., mail poll for *Sports Illustrated*.

OIL CONSUMPTION

Definition: The act of either using oil as an energy source, or drinking it, but especially using it as an energy source.

Few people who are still alive drink crude oil. Not only is it poison but it is said to taste awful. It is suggested that readers do not challenge this assertion. Those who do are likely to croak.

The Odds: What happens to a barrel of oil once it is pumped from the ground? Depending on world conditions at the time, both economic and geo-political, most barrels are consumed within one year, however somewhere between 1 in 10 and 1 in 20 barrels go into some sort of reserve tanks for use during an oil shortage. The odds are 1 in 2 that a barrel of oil used in America is from a foreign source.

The list below represents the odds of a barrel of oil being eventually consumed for the following purposes.

Transportation	2 in 3
Industrial Production	1 in 5
Heating Buildings	1 in 13
Electrical Generation	1 in 25
As a Beverage* (estimate)	1 in 1 billion

Highly unrecommended by culinary experts and doctors.

Source: Interior Department.

Also See: Energy Sources.

ORGAN DONORS

Then and Now

Definition: 1) an individual who contributes funds to a church so that the choir will have a musical accompaniment 2) an individual who consents to having his vital organs removed after death for the purpose of transplanting them into the body of another individual.

Information regarding donating pipe or electrical organs to churches is not well documented. Those who donate their hearts, livers and other vital body parts, however, is carefully monitored. Estimates of Americans who have consented to donate their organs upon their death are 67 million.

The Odds: Approximately 1 in 4 Americans have signed consent decrees to donate their organs under the terms of the Uniform Anatomical Gift Act or similar laws. This relatively high rate is a result of making it easier to get a consent form in front of an individual. Today many states put the consent agreement in printed form on the back of state driver's licenses.

One of the greatest benefits of this "make it easy" policy has been to make it more possible for minorities to obtain organs. Due to the need to match tissues from donors to recipients as closely as possible, an over or under representation of racial types can mean danger. Blacks, in particular, have been under-represented among donors. The Howard University Transplant Center points out that blacks are 20 times more likely than whites to suffer kidney disease, and nearly 1 in 3 dialysis patents are black. The Center's public awareness policy has significantly increased the rate of blacks who donate their organs as evidence shows on the list below which is based on data from a 1991 Gallup Poll.

SIGNED DONOR CARDS

RACE	1985	1991
Blacks	1 in 16	1 in 4
Whites	1 in 5	3 in 10

**WILLING TO DONATE
RELATIVE'S ORGAN**

RACE	1985	1991
Blacks	1 in 2	7 in 10
Whites	7 in 10	4 in 5

Source: The New York Times
November 6 , 1991.

Also See: Organ Sharing, Transplants.

ORGAN SHARING

Supply and Demand

Definition: Not two people at the keyboard of an organ, but rather the demand for replacement parts for chronically ill people.

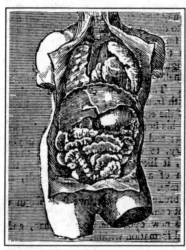

Have a heart. That old cliche means something different to a heart patient in need of a new ticker. He would say, "Have a heart?" and hope and pray to get an affirmative answer.

Though various organs can be transplanted, the most common ones actually implanted in the chronically ill are kidneys, hearts, livers and corneas. Though transplants are relatively successful treatments today, the biggest risk patients face is finding some one to give them one. Humans have two kidneys, but only one heart and one liver. This circumstance of the anatomy means that a kidney patient can, and often does, get a needed replacement from a relative, usually a sibling. Nonetheless, kidneys are the hardest organs to get, simply because the demand is so high.

The Odds: Roughly speaking, about 1 in 2,000 people will want and need new organs in their lifetime but only about 1 in 2 of them will get them. With 19,000 kidneys in demand, only about 9,400 people will get one, hence the odds are slightly less than 2 to 1. It's a pretty good bet however that a patient who has been diagnosed as needing a heart transplant will get one. Last year, 2,228 patients needed a new heart and 2,012 got one, therefore the chances of getting a heart can be calculated at 9 in 10. Liver demands, like most organ needs, often require a wait of 1 to 2 years. In 1990, 2,547 patients got new livers and, at mid year in 1991, 1,577 were in need of one, hence the odds are favorable that they will get one.

Next to just finding an available organ, the biggest risk factor in transplants is the compatibility of the donor organ with the recipient. Tissue from unrelated donors — almost invariably the source except in kidney transplants — often do not match well. With the supply not ample, and patients getting nearer death as they wait, most take what they can get. Livers and hearts last 5 years or more. Kidneys have been known to have amazing lasting power, sometimes serving the recipient into old age.

Source: United Network for Organ Sharing.

Also See: Organ Donors, Transplants.

P p

PALESTINIAN REFUGEES

Definition: A group of displaced Arabs who trace their roots to the ancient land once called Palestine, a former nation which was split up by a U.N. mandate in 1949.

The largest portions of their land was given to Jews in order to form their own nation. Jordan was also given a large portion of land in the Palestinian region.

The more than 5 million Palestinians are spread throughout the Middle East. They have vowed to get their land back, at any cost, and have focused their hostilities toward Israel, which now has the most developed portion which was once occupied and ruled by Palestinians.

The majority of Palestinian refugees now live in parts of ancient Palestine which are now under Israeli or Jordanian rule. Though Jordan has been sympathetic to the Palestinian cause, so far they have not consented to giving up land. The Israelis have fiercely fought doing the same.

The Odds: No one knows how the Palestinian question can be resolved. The following list, however, may hint at some parts of the keys to the solution. The list represents the proportions of Palestinians living in the Middle East. Giving them their own government and nation in a location with the highest ratios is likely to be the solution.

WHERE PALESTINIANS LIVE

Jordan	1 in 3
West Bank	1 in 5
Israel	1 in 8
Gaza Strip	1 in 8
Lebanon	1 in 16
Syria	1 in 17
Other Middle Eastern Nations	1 in 11

Source: Institute for Palestine Studies.

PAPER, RECYCLED

Definition: Old newspapers which, by the miracles of technology, are turned into old newspapers again.

The U.S. is the largest per capita consumer of paper in the world, and decries the fate of the forests which feed that hunger for paper. But there is a way to lessen the effects of such a voracity on the world's woodlands – recycling.

The Odds: The U.S. currently recycles about 1 in 4 pounds of paper of its annual paper consumption. But, as the list below shows, that's a far cry from the leaders in the recycling arena. Tiny Hong Kong, with its limited natural resources and waste disposal opportunities, recycles fully two- thirds of all its waste paper. Clearly, the U.S. has a long way to go before overcoming the pervasive attitude of the disposable society; the first faltering steps are now being made through increased environmental awareness. The countries that recycle the least and the ratio of poundage recycled to new milled paper are: Nigeria (1 in 50), Malaysia (1 in 33), Iceland (1 in 20), and Sri Lanka (1 in 11).

The following list represents the ratio of paper poundage to new milled paper in the nations which lead the world in paper recycling:

Hong Kong	2 in 3
Kenya	11 in 20
Greece	1 in 2
Japan	1 in 2
Finland	9 in 20
Netherlands	9 in 20
Taiwan	9 in 20
Portugal	9 in 20
Kuwait	9 in 20
Switzerland	9 in 20
Panama	9 in 20
Mexico	2 in 5
Spain	2 in 5
Austria	2 in 5
Germany	2 in 5
Sweden	2 in 5

Source: "Materials Recycling: The Virtue of Necessity," World Watch Institute, Washington.

PAROLEES

Definition: Criminal offenders who must keep their noses clean without benefit of tissues or bars of soap.

As jails become more and more overcrowded, many states have no other recourse to alleviate the problem than to ease the process of parole, freeing criminals before their full sentence in order to free up prison space for new batches of convicts. This can create problems of recidivism; in addition, respect for the criminal justice system is lessened on the part of both the convict and the public in general; finally, many in the public wonder if the courts and the prison systems are taking their role seriously.

The Odds: The odds that a criminal will not serve out his sentences in the U.S. are excellent. The average prison sentence is 36 months, yet the average offender is released on parole in 16 months. Of those released from prison, however, 8 in 10 will return at least once. A dismal 9 in 20 will return a third time and 1 in 5 will go back 6 times or more. Indeed, George Bush was on the mark in the 1988 Presidential campaign with an ad that depicted the prison system as a revolving door.

The following list represents the ten states where the door revolves the fastest and the odds that a random man or woman on the street is a parolee:

District of Columbia	1 in 126
Texas	1 in 175
Pennsylvania	1 in 206
Washington	1 in 236
New Jersey	1 in 371
Tennessee	1 in 389
Georgia	1 in 411
Maryland	1 in 423
Louisiana	1 in 434

Source: "Probation and Parole," U.S. Department of Justice.

PAVED ROADS

Global Occurrences

Definition: Highways, byways and thoroughfares covered by concrete, asphalt, dead bugs and squashed animals.

In addition to industrialization and technical advancement, a major indicator of the level of country's development is its transportation system. Not surprisingly, the United States, where the car is king, enjoys the most extensive road system in the world—four times as much roadway as the Soviet Union, the largest country in the world. And we have the Cold War to thank for it.

Our interstate highway system was built, at least in part, with military preparedness in mind; passenger and commercial travel wasn't the only, or even the most important, reason for the construction of our elaborate and efficient systems of interstate roadways. But even more telling of a country's development is how much of its road network is paved: for instance, Brazil has the second longest road network, but a mere 1 in 13 miles of the road system in that country is paved, whereas 9 in 10 in the U.S. are hard-topped, as are virtually all the roads in Western Europe.

The following list represents the proportions of paved roads to dirt roads in the ten countries with the most roadways:

NATION	MILES PAVED	ODDS
U.S.	6,242,200	9 in 10
Brazil	75,000	1 in 13
U.S.S.R	1,549,000	N/A
Japan	1,098,900	2 in 3
Australia	853,000	1 in 2
Germany	539,500	99 in 100
U.K.	352,300	98 in 100
Poland	340,200	6 in 10
Spain	318,000	2 in 3
Italy	301,600	Near all

Source: World Road Statistics, International Road Federation, Geneva.

PH.D. DEGREES

Definition: The highest level of educational achievement, a doctorate.

The Ph.D. degree is the most difficult to actually attain because of the length of time in school required – the wait for many doctoral students can last more than ten years! As can be expected, the most Ph.D.s are to be found in the field of education, because it is the logical extension of the field itself.

The numbers of Ph.D.s awarded is quite small, approximately 30,000 each year. This compares to 1 million baccalaureate, or bachelors degrees and 300,000 masters degrees. In a wry comment on wisdom through increasing education, the Ph.D. in business and management is ranked 10th, dropping from the 1 and 2 spots it occupies for the B.A. and Masters.

The Odds: The following list represents the top ten areas of study in which doctorate degrees are awarded annually and the proportions of Ph.D. degrees they represent:

Education	1 in 4
Engineering	1 in 8
Physical Sciences	1 in 8
Life Sciences	1 in 9
Psychology	1 in 10
Social Sciences	1 in 10
Theology	1 in 24
Health Sciences	1 in 24
Letters	1 in 26
Business & Mng't.	1 in 27

Source: Digest of Educational Statistics.

Also See: Ivy League Scholars, Masters Degrees.

P.I.D. IN WOMEN

Pelvic Inflammatory Disease

Definition: Swelling in the pelvic area of females which causes chronic pain and often results in infections and various medical complications.

Infertility and death is often the result of this little-known disease which affects some one million women each year. The illness is especially dangerous because many women may have PID and be unaware of it. The epidemic cost $4.2 billion in 1990 and by the end of the decade, given no inflation, the spread of the disease will increase the cost to $10 billion.

The Odds: Each year as many as 1 in 100 women will experience some form of PID. The most dangerous form of the disease is "silent" PID which is mostly suffered by women who have been infected with the venereal diseases gonorrhea and chlamydia. With no symptoms, the silent suffers will learn years later that their reproductive organs have been damaged severely. Those who are "fortunate" enough to have the symptoms will seek treatment and 1 in 5 of them will have to be hospitalized.

Long term complications will be suffered by 1 in 4 women with the disease. They will experience chronic pain in the pelvic area. Some may be afflicted with infertility and ectopic pregnancy, an affliction in which a fertilized egg becomes implanted in the fallopian tube or elsewhere outside the uterus. Ectopic pregnancies can, and often do, cause fatalities in pregnant women.

Source: Journal of the American Medical Association report by Dr. A. Eugene Washington and colleagues at the University of California at the San Francisco Center for Health Policy Studies. Analysis assisted by the Federal Center for Disease Control and the National Center for Health Statistics, Hyattville, MD.

PILOTS

Flying Under the Influence

Definition: The state in which the mouth of the operator of your airplane looks more like cotton than the clouds below.

The Federal Aviation Administration (FAA) requires that pilots submit medical disclosure forms on which any reported incidences of driving while under the influence of alcohol (DUI) is cited. Of the 670,000 pilots who are registered with the FAA, some 70 percent have not submitted their records as of September, 1991. Time is flying. Can it be the fly boys are too high remember?

The Odds: Among those who have gotten their medical histories to the FAA, the odds of them having been convicted of a DUI offense is 1 in 36. Of the 47,000 pilots licensed to fly passenger aircraft, some 400 have been convicted of alcohol-related driving incidents. Therefore, the odds that one will be piloting you through the skies is a frightening 1 in 117, and it is likely to be higher during the holiday season when pilots attend parties like all of us do.

Below is a list which represents the odds that a pilot of a major airline has been convicted of a DUI offense which has been reported to the FAA:

Northwestern	1 in 77
Continental	1 in 129
Southwest	1 in 138
U.S. Air	1 in 139
Delta	1 in 163
United	1 in 165
American	1 in 167
TWA	1 in 170

Source: Federal Aviation Administration, 1991.

Also See: Air Crashes, Travel.

PIZZA PIES

Definition: Next to burgers, the primary fuel that powers America's teenagers.

The old adage that a man's stomach is the way to his heart has been turned around. Today, most teen-age boys know that nothing impresses a girl more than the right pizza. But what is the right pizza? This seemingly trivial question is more important than most grownups think.

The Odds: Pizza parlors are perhaps the most competitive businesses in America. Even for those who prefer to pig out at home, pizza wins over all other munchables—among telephone orders for food to-go, pizza accounts for 17 in 20 phone orders. Wherever your prefer to fill your face, the most popular pizza always wins, though. The following list represents the most popular types of pizza pies and the proportions served in America:

Thin Crust	1 in 2
Thick Crust	1 in 4
Pan Pizza	1 in 5
Stuffed	1 in 50

But what do you put on top of it to really impress a girl nowadays? Masters and Johnson, we need some help here!

Source: National Restaurant Association (1990 figures).

PLASTIC SURGERY

Definition: When neither Revlon, Avon nor Miss Clairol can help; the solution of last resort.

The most popular facial plastic surgery continues to be the venerable nose job, nearly 100,000 a year. In this procedure, bone and cartilage are reconstructed and excess is removed from the nose to achieve a new shape. In the fifties, reconstructive nose surgery consisted mainly of a uniform, stylized nose with a turned-up, ski-jump angle and a highly sculpted tip, but the trend has changed.

The New Look: Through the magic of computer imagery, a plastic surgeon can individualize the nose-job, giving the patient a wider bridge, a stronger, fuller nose, a gently refined tip. Some patients even choose, ironically, to make the nose longer. Other elective procedures that are growing in popularity include mentoplasty, or chin implants (often in conjunction with a face-lift and rhinoplasty to improve the profile), blepharoplasty, or eyelid surgery, which eliminates fat and excess skin around the eye to remove bags and pouches, and dermabrasion, or face sanding, in which wire brushes gently scrape the face, removing the outer layer of skin, smoothing its texture and removing superficial scars and age lines.

Procedures that have declined in popularity over the past several years include eyebrow surgery, hair transplants and surgery on birthmarks.

The Odds: Of the over 2 million plastic surgery procedures performed annually, 6 in 10 are to repair damages from accidents or injuries and to correct birth defects. Among patients, 1 in 8 were men. The following list represents the 10 most popular procedures and the proportions of the U.S. population who elect to have them in one year:

Nose Surgery	1 in 2,500
Head/Neck Tumors	1 in 3,500
Head/Neck Trauma	1 in 5,800
Injectable Fillers (Zyderm)	1 in 6,000
Head/Neck Reconstructive	1 in 6,100
Eyelid Surgery	1 in 6,600
Scar Revision	1 in 8,300
Facial Fractures	1 in 9,600
Face-lift	1 in 11,900
Face Sanding	1 in 16,700

Source: American Academy of Facial Plastic and Reconstructive Surgery.

PLAYBOY PLAYMATES

Definition: A naked female Pollyanna pictured in the center fold of *Playboy* magazine who loves her father, brother, country and being in the buff.

New York's iconoclastic *Spy* magazine recently took it upon itself to analyze the 160 Playboy Playmate data sheets from July 1977 to September 1990 to see what really makes a Playmate.

The average All-American playmate, *Spy* found, is 5'6" tall, weighs 113 lbs. and stacks out at 35-23-34.

The Odds: Of the 160 Playmates during the aforementioned period, 1 in 8 had first names that begin with K. Racially, 1 in 32 were African-American, 1 in 40 were Asian-American, 19 in 20 were white and 6 in 10 were blonds. But these women are not just figures on a data sheet (or an air-brushed centerfold). They have hopes, dreams, desires – in a word, *ambitions*. Better than 1 in 4 of all Playmates hope to become actresses some day – but even they should know that Hollywood just is not big enough for all those pairs of . . . well, you know what. Only 1 in 80 actually went on to become famous actresses, like the late Dorothy Stratten and Julie McCullough, of *Growing Pains*. Appearances in ZZ-Top and other music videos don't count.

Below are the odds that playmates aspire to the following goals.

Acting	2 in 9
Happiness	6 in 10
Modeling	1 in 7
Success	1 in 8
Travel	1 in 11
Personal Growth	1 in 13
Help Others	1 in 15
Lasting Relation/ Marriage	1 in 15
Family	1 in 16
Live Life to the Fullest	1 in 16

Source: *Spy* magazine.

Also See: Playmate Turn-ons and Turn-offs

PLAYMATES

Turn-ons — Turn-offs

Definition: That which gets every honey of a bunny either ready to GO! — or ready to go.

Want to know what really turns a girl on? Forget those "How to Make a Woman Love You" books and tapes. Here is everything you need to know, according to *Spy* magazine's previously mentioned survey.

Your best bet is to pick her up in your car with your dog, turn on the stereo, drive to the beach (in your clothes), pick some flowers (naturally somewhat hard to do on the beach), watch the sunset, then do some dancing in the rain. Whatever you do, don't rudely light up a cigarette, be jealous of her old boyfriends (or the guys ogling her on the beach), and don't get stuck in traffic.

The Odds: If you are on a date with a playmate, and really want to score some brownie points, tell her you love the following (even if you don't). The odds that you can score points are as follows.

Music	1 in 5
Cars	2 in 11
Animals	1 in 6
Beach and Ocean	1 in 7
Clothes	2 in 15
Flowers	1 in 9
Sun and Sunset	2 in 19
Outdoors/ Nature	1 in 10
Dancing	1 in 11
Thunder Storms	1 in 11

Turn-offs: Odds are that the following will turn-off even the most eager of the bunny bunch.

Tobacco/smoke	1 in 7
Rudeness or Pushiness	1 in 7
Jealousy	1 in 8
Traffic	1 in 10
Waiting	1 in 10
Pessimism	1 in 11
Phoniness	1 in 15

Egomania	1 in 16
Lying	1 in 16
Waking up Early	1 in 16

Source: *Spy* magazine.

Also See: Playmates.

PLOWBOYS

Definition: Men (and some women) who plow the fields and have a proclivity to pick their teeth with hay — and bacon and beans from a breakfast menu.

While many third-world farmers still use ox-drawn plows or even simple sticks to cultivate their land, farmers in the advanced nations have long since abandoned muscle power in favor of the tractor.

The Odds: The most agriculturally mechanized country in the world is the United States, with more than 4.6 million tractors in use, or about 1 in 5 of all the farm tractors in the world. About the only developed countries that don't have a large proportion of tractors are tourist-rich island nations or oil-rich Gulf states.

The following list represents the ratio of tractors to citizens in the most mechanized agricultural nations:

TOP TEN IN TRACTORS

Germany	1 to 38
Canada	1 to 40
Poland	1 to 46
Italy	1 to 48
United States	1 to 53
Spain	1 to 64
Japan	1 to 72
U.S.S.R.	1 to 106
Brazil	1 to 201
China	1 to 1,301

Source: Food and Agriculture Organization Production Yearbook.

Also See: Women in Agriculture.

POKER HANDS
The Opening Deal

Definition: The turn of five cards on which some bet their lives and family farms.

Though some bet substantial portions of their pay on state lotteries where odds are millions to one, it is doubtful that these same people would make a similar wager on being dealt four aces on the opening hand of a poker round. Ironically, the odds of that happening are almost exactly 1,000 times greater than winning a lottery jackpot.

The following list represents possible opening poker hands and the odds that you will be dealt them:

Royal Flush	649,739 to 1
Other Straight Flush	72,192 to 1
Four of a Kind	4,164 to 1
Full House	693 to 1
Flush	508 to 1
Straight	254 to 1
Three of a Kind	46 to 1
Two Pairs	20 to 1
One Pair	4 to 3
No Matches	2 to1

Source: The efficacy of mathematics.

Also See: Craps, Lotteries, Monte Carlo.

POLICE EMERGENCY

911 Emergency Calls

Definition: A citizen's call for help on a special phone number (911) which is reserved for emergency reports.

A significant feature of the 911 reporting system is that usually calls are not screened to insure an actual emergency is taking place. Many police "emergencies," therefore, are the most mundane or trivial routine matters ranging from illegally parked vehicles to dog and cat bites. In Chicago alone, 2.7 million 911 reports had to be answered each year, yet less than 10,000 crimes are actually reported.

The Odds: Between 3 and 7 percent of all 911 calls prove to be true emergencies. Given these estimates and averaging them, the odds that a 911 call is a true emergency is 1 in 20. Let's hope that policemen do not always think "the little boy who cried wolf" is on the phone. Chicago alone sports some 2.6 million such callers.

Source: The Chicago Tribune, October 10, 1991.

POLICE HOMICIDES

Definition: Acts of violence in which a law officer is killed in the line of duty.

Police work, according to the *Jobs Rated Almanac,* is the third most hazardous occupation. In 1989, police officers affected over 14 million arrests. Over 600,000 of these arrests were for violent crimes.

The Odds: The odds that an arrest was listed as a violent crime were 1 in 20. Odds that an arrested individual was a suspect in a murder were 1 in 641.

The odds in an average year that the murder victim will be a police officer is 1 in 49. Each year approximately 380,000 police officers are assaulted. The odds an officer will be murdered in an assault is 1 in 2,533, about the same as a soldier being killed in a battle (See Military Casualties).

Source: Compiled research by editors.

Also See: Crime, Murders, Murder Weapons, Murder Scenes, Murders Abroad.

POOR FOLKS
Dens of Urban Poverty

Definition: Urban places in America in which the populace earns an average of less than $3,000 per family member.

Poverty is commonplace in America, and its symptoms are seldom scarce in our great cities. Our images of urban poverty center around the inner sectors of our largest cities. In actuality, urban poverty is most concentrated in our small and mid-sized metropolitan areas. The most poverty-stricken towns are those along the border with Mexico, where a large number of poor immigrants from south of the Rio Grande have settled, at least for the moment. The regions that know poverty the least are primarily in the upper Midwest.

The Odds: The following lists represent the ten poorest and ten richest metropolitan areas in the country out of the top 275, and the odds that an average citizen in them will be living below the poverty level:

TOP TEN POOR CITIES

McAllen-Edinburg-Mission, TX	35 in 100
Brownsville-Harlingen, TX	32 in 100
Gainesville, FL	23 in 100
Pine Bluff, AR	22 in 100
Las Cruces, NM	23 in 100
Bryan-College Station TX	22 in 100
El Paso, TX	22 in 100
Florence, SC	21 in 100
Tallahassee, FL	21 in 100

LEAST POVERTY

Sheboygan, WI	5 in 100
Casper, WY	6 in 100
Appleton-Oshkosh-Neenah, WI	6 in 100
Rochester, MN	7 in 100
Cedar Rapids, IA	7 in 100
Minneapolis-St. Paul	7 in 100
Reno	7 in 100
York, PA	7 in 100
Manchester-Nashua, NH	7 in 100
Janesville-Beloit, WI	7 in 100

Source: U.S. Census Bureau.

Also See: Poverty and Homelessness.

POST-TRAUMATIC STRESS DISORDER

Definition: The recurrence of symptoms related to re-experiencing traumatic events, especially when the recurrence is to a debilitating degree. Post-traumatic stress disorder is said to be particularly prevalent in veterans of the Vietnam War.

We've all seen the movies and the TV news footage, read the books or the news accounts of the psycho Vietnam vet whose troubling experiences in Southeast Asia lead him to pack up his M-16 and wipe out a school yard full of kids. From *The Deer Hunter* to *Rambo*, Vietnam has been viewed socially and culturally as a different war, and its veterans as different from those of previous wars.

When the GIs came back from the "Good War" against Hitler, they were met with parades, hugs and kisses. But the country's treatment of the Vietnam vet was a resounding, and well-documented indifference, even animosity, a relic of the war that nobody wanted, and that the country didn't try to win.

Symptoms: Physicians and psychologists have determined a number of symptoms related to post-traumatic stress disorder. These include:

POST-TRAUMATIC STRESS DISORDER

Re-experience: Repeated nightmares, dreams or painful memories about military experiences: the feeling of reliving a disturbing military experience.

Increased Arousal: Trouble falling to sleep or sleeping too much; trouble concentrating; irritability, short temper, explosions of anger or aggressive behavior; jumpiness or feeling of having to be on guard at all times.

Avoidance: Avoidance of activities that might remind the vet of things that happened in the military; loss of interest in daily activities; feeling of distance from people, even close relatives or friends; feeling that life is not meaningful.

The Twin Study: One recent study looked at a group of more than 2,000 sets of twins who served in the military during the Vietnam era. The researchers interviewed each veteran as to whether he served in Southeast Asia, whether he served in a combat role, and the degree of combat exposure. The latter was measured by 18 specific factors, such as receiving incoming fire, serving as a "tunnel rat," checking enemy base camps and being in a patrol that was ambushed. Interviewees were asked to comment on whether, and if so how frequently, they have experienced the various symptoms of PTSD within a six-month period.

The Odds: According to the results of the twin study, the odds are about 1 in 6 that a soldier who served in Southeast Asia during the Vietnam war still exhibits symptoms of Post-Traumatic Stress Disorder, compared to about 1 in 20 among those in the military at that time who did not serve in Southeast Asia. Those who saw a high level of combat, moreover, were twelve times more likely to suffer nightmares, eight times more likely to feel as if a disturbing experience were recurring, thirteen times more likely to avoid activities reminiscent of the military, four times as likely to be startled or jumpy, and twice as likely to have trouble sleeping, trouble concentrating and to anger.

Overall, those who served in Southeast Asia are 4.5 times more likely to suffer from Post-Traumatic Stress Disorder as those who didn't serve in the theater, and those who saw a high level of combat are *nine* times as likely to suffer as those who did not serve in Southeast Asia. Of the three million soldiers who served in Southeast Asia, then, approximately 500,000 suffer to a greater or lesser degree from PTSD, with the odds greatly increasing depending on the actual amount of combat experienced. Nearly twenty years after the end of that divisive war, veterans are still plagued by the horrors of Vietnam.

Source: "A Twin Study of the Effects of the Vietnam War on

Posttraumatic Stress Disorder," Dr. Jack Goldberg et al, *Journal of the American Medical Association*, March 2, 1990.

Also See: Military Casualties, Vietnam War.

POVERTY
In the Land of Plenty

Definition: "Poverty is a state of mind, unlike *broke*, which is merely a financial condition" — Anonymous.

Ask any poor person and they will tell you poverty sucks. Who are these have-nots in the land of plenty? Officially, the "poverty line" is defined as an income of $12,674 or less for a family of four. According to Federal Government statistics, most of the nation's poor are white, 20,785,000 of them. There are about half as many blacks, 9,302,000, and just somewhat less than half as many Hispanics, 5,430,000, who make up the 35.4 million poor in the U.S.

The Odds: 1 in 7 Americans suffer the affliction of poverty. Contrary to the public perception of immigrants, recent immigrants from Asia and Africa have fared reasonably well in America.

Below are some of the most relevant odds on poverty.

Among Whites	1 in 10
Among Blacks	1 in 3
Among Hispanics	1 in 4
Newly Poor Americans (last 12 months)	1 in 5,890
Homeless (all U.S.)	1 in 340
Homeless Children	1 in 2,500
Can't Afford Health Insurance	1 in 7
Denied Care for Lack of Funds	1 in 25
Don't Seek Care for Lack of Funds	1 in 18

Source: U.S. Bureau of the Census (1989 figures).

Also See: Poverty, Worldwide.

PREJUDICE

Definition: A state of mind in which you have convinced yourself that those from different ancestral backgrounds don't hold a

candle to you and your high standards of fairness and intelligence.

The Odds: Hate is not dead in America. It is a very subtle, yet real phenomena. Below is a list of the odds that you will find prejudicial feelings about various groups in the hearts and minds of the average American. They have responded to the question: "who would you not want to move in your neighborhood?"

Catholics	1 in 33
Protestants	1 in 20
Jews	1 in 20
Blacks	1 in 9
Hispanics	1 in 6
Vietnamese	1 in 6
Unmarried Couples	1 in 4
Religious Fundamentalists	1 in 2
Religious Sects & Cults	2 in 3

The lesson to be learned from these revelations is an especially poignant one for black Protestants contemplating cohabitation with Jewish women from Central America who have converted to Catholicism and become leaders in the "Jews for Jesus" cult. It's a cinch that everyone will hate you, probably even your mother.

Improving the Odds: It is suggested that all Vietnamese tell their neighbors they are black. Blacks should represent their ancestry as Jewish. Jews would do well to claim they are Puerto Ricans and Mexicans should never cohabitate or join religious sects. Given the odds of who can be expected to hate whom, these suggestion almost guarantee a kinder more gentler America, if you don't mind sharing it with a bunch of liars, that is. So, for the sake of your country, be patriotic and lie like hell about your race and religion. Like Quaker Oats for breakfast, "it's the right thing to do."

Source: The Gallup Organization

PRESIDENTIAL ELECTIONS

Voter Turnouts

Definition: The rate at which U.S. voters go to the polls to cast their ballots for the lesser of the two evils.

The newly freed minions of Eastern Europe look to the United States as their democratic ideal. But, truth be told, voters are fickle in this country. Sometimes they are penetrating in their analysis and their desire to grapple with central issues. At other times they vote to follow fashion, on an impulse or out of habit. Other times, they don't vote at all.

The Odds: U.S. voters are much less likely than the Soviet electorate to cast ballots for the top political office. In the Soviet Union, over 9 in 10 voters go to the polls to elect the General

Chairman of the Communist Party. In the U.S., voter turnout for the highest office in the land attracts only 1 in 2 voters.

The following list represents the ten states with the highest voter turnout in the last presidential election and the proportions who cast ballots in them:

Minnesota	66.33 in 100
Montana	62.41 in 100
Maine	62.15 in 100
Wisconsin	61.98 in 100
North Dakota	61.54 in 100
South Dakota	61.54 in 100
Utah	60.02 in 100
Iowa	59.27 in 100
Oregon	58.59 in 100
Massachusetts	58.06 in 100

Source: Committee for the Study of the American Electorate.

PRISON ESCAPES

Definition: A way to leave the pen a little ahead of schedule and without the restrictive rules mandated by the parole board.

Our courts and prisons are crowded to the bursting point. Some convicts, therefore, take it upon themselves to relieve conditions. Prison escapes represent the return of desperate, dangerous, corrosive elements to real communities. The overcrowding and underbudgeting of the American correctional system contributes to the alarming incidence of prison escapism.

The Odds: The list below represents the states where the prisons are the leakiest and the proportions of inmates who escaped. (For comparison check out the relatively secure Federal Prisons System listed last):

Michigan	1 in 8
Florida	1 in 24
California	1 in 33
North Carolina	1 in 40
Federal Bureau of Prisons	1 in 229

Source: Population Density in State Prisons, Dept. of Justice.

Also See: Divorce, Parolees.

PROPERTY RECOVERY

Stolen Loot

Definition: Getting your stuff back after it's been ripped off.

What's the cure for the sinking feeling you get when you find out you've been robbed? Believe it or not, there is some solace for victims. The cops are on the job better than you might expect. A great deal of stolen property is recovered by the police and eventually it is returned to the rightful owner.

Each year in the U.S., over $12 billion of property is stolen, more than half of which, based on its value, are automobiles. Over $1 billion dollars of jewelry is stolen and nearly $700 million in currency or notes is ripped off. Nearly 2 in 3 arrests for property crimes (66.5 percent) involve juveniles. Total arrests for property crimes number over one million and about 85 percent of those arrested are males. Do so many arrests mean you will get your stolen property back?

The Odds: Based on dollar value, odds are almost 2 in 5 that you will recover your property. In 1988, 38.6 percent of all stolen goods which were reported to the police were recovered, based on value. Odds are best that your automobile will be recovered. Over 66 percent of stolen cars are eventually recovered. Amazingly, the odds are better that stolen money will be recovered than televisions, stereos or jewelry.

The following list represents the odds that various types of merchandise will be recovered:

Motor Vehicles	2 in 3
Consumable Goods	1 in 4
Livestock	1 in 5
Clothing and Fur	1 in 9
Firearms	1 in 10
Household goods	1 in 14
Office Equipment	1 in 16
Currency and Notes	1 in 18
Jewelry & Precious Metals	1 in 20
TVs and Stereos	1 in 21
Misc. Goods	1 in 11

Source: FBI Uniform Crime Report, Crimes in the United States (1989).

Also See: Juvenile Delinquency.

"PROP 48"

Definition: Proposition 48, an NCAA rule which requires that you must be somewhat intelligent if you wish to play college football, shoot hoops or any other pursuit in which some of the dumbest individuals have overcome their own stupidity.

Proposition 48 sets a minimum score of 700 for ACT (Academic Achievement Tests) as the floor at which an athlete can be eligible to compete in the NCAA

(National Collegiate Athletic Association).

The Odds: Among college freshmen 1 in 15 fail to make the grade.

Source: NCAA.

PROSTITUTION

Definition: Love for sale, the world's oldest profession.

Despite the AIDS epidemic, there are still a large number of men who provide a market for women who engage in prostitution. If arrests are a reflection of the activity in the profession, prostitution in the U.S. is declining by 11 percent.

Fees charged by prostitutes vary in a range as broad as the barter of a few dollars worth of crack cocaine to several thousand dollars charged by the "classiest" of the lot. Most prostitutes who service away-from-home businessmen in their hotels charge between $50 and $100 dollars.

The Odds: In 1988, nearly 90,000 Americans were arrested for prostitution or "commercial vice," the act of soliciting for prostitution. By 1989, just over 83,000 were arrested. Averaging these years reveals that about 1 in 2,250 women and 1 in 4,800 men are arrested yearly for crimes involving some kind of prostitution offenses.

Among those arrested for prostitution-related offenses, 1 in 3 were men. Only 1 in 51 men were under the age of 18. Among women, who account for 2 in 3 prostitution related arrests, 1 in 82 were under the age of 18.

In the late 1980s, 1 in 3 men admitted to having had sex with a prostitute. Meeting men in bars is the most common way female prostitutes obtain clients. Another common way some prostitutes solicit customers is through classified ads. According to sex researchers Masters and Johnson, women who run ads for sexual solicitation, (for either fun or money) receive an average of 49 calls per ad. Men who advertise average 15 calls.

Source: Department of Justice, Federal Bureau of Investigation; Uniform Crime Reports for the United States, 1990.

Also See: Crime, Intercourse.

PSYCHIATRIC CARE

Definition: The treatment of mental disorders by trained psychotherapists.

Not very long ago, one had to brave major social taboos to seek psychiatric care. In this era, however, psychotherapy has become downright routine. Each year some 50 million Americans suffer from some form of mental illness and approximately 10 million Americans are under professional care to treat or cure symptoms.

The Odds: A National Institute of Mental Health survey of 17,000 Americans revealed that between 3 and 4 in 10 individuals have suffered from a mental health problem. The most common form is alcohol abuse which affects 1 in 8 Americans. Over 1 in 9 suffer phobias, 1 in 16 suffers major depressions and 1 in 50 suffers from a panic disorder associated with mental impairment.

Treatment for mental health disorders tends to be very regional. The following list represents the ratio of individuals in the population to the number of visits to mental health professionals in the ten cities with the most mental health problems:

District of Columbia	1.4 to 1
New York	1.3 to 1
Connecticut	9 to 10
Colorado	7 to 8
Utah	7 to 8
New Hampshire	3 to 4
Virginia	7 to 10
Massachusetts	3 to 5
Arizona	3 to 5

Some might consider it reason for concern that the city of our national leaders, where the vital decisions of our day are made, leads the nation in sessions on the couch. But it is no surprise that New York appears near the top of the list. Most people know that you've got to be crazy to live in New York in the first place.

Source: Mutual of Omaha Company.

Also See: Mental Disorders, Mental Health Treatment.

PUBLIC AID

Definition: A variety of social measures which are provided for by various branches of the government for people who cannot meet minimum financial standards.

The Odds: Almost 1 in 3 Americans will rely on government relief in their lifetime for a variety of maladies ranging from natural disasters to lost jobs. At any given time in the U.S., 1 in 10 Americans receives some form of public assistance. Most aid is given in the form of payments directly to the economically afflicted Americans in the following ways and proportions.

Social Security (all payments)	1 in 6
Social Security (retirees)	1 in 9
Survivors and Dependents	1 in 25
Disability	1 in 83
Food Stamps	1 in 13
Unemployment Benefits	1 in 20

It is a commonly held misconception that the majority of Americans receiving welfare and other public assistance are denizens of the inner city. In actuality, public aid is very much a rural phenomena, with nearly 1 in 5 persons receiving some form of assistance in the troubled, agrarian South.

The following list represents the ten states with the highest incidence of public aid recipients and the ratios of their populace who receive it:

Mississippi	1 in 5
Louisiana	1 in 6
California	1 in 11
Michigan	1 in 11
West Virginia	1 in 12
New York	1 in 13
Ohio	1 in 13
Wisconsin	1 in 13
Illinois	1 in 14
Kentucky	1 in 14

Source: U.S. Census Bureau.

Also See: Poverty.

PUBLICITY

Definition: Getting your name before the public, usually by a mention or story in the mass media.

The Odds: Nearly three-quarters of all Americans are mentioned in the media at least one time in their life. One in every 4 are on television at least once. The odds of a politician or a career entertainer getting publicity are virtually 100 percent.

A search of the periodicals in the Magazine Database, a full-text, on-line service offering articles from 86 magazines for the period from 1986 to 1991 revealed the odds of getting stories in the media are highest among entertainers, more so than national politicians. Those entertainers listed below received the most mentions in magazines ranging from *The Atlantic* and *Cosmopolitan* to *Playboy* and *Working Woman*. The score at right is the overall number of articles in the database in which the celebrity is mentioned.

1.	Madonna	383
2.	Woody Allen	281
3.	Michael Jackson	256
4.	Jane Fonda	221
5.	Paul Simon	197
6.	Bruce Springsteen	186
7.	Frank Sinatra	181
8.	Bill Cosby	171
9.	Johnny Carson	169
10.	Eddie Murphy	148

Five of the top ten celebrities were musicians (after *Who's That Girl?* Madonna can no longer be considered an actress), while three were movie stars and two were television personalities. Other celebrities scoring high include Sting with 164 mentions, Cher (146), Jack Nicholson (143) and Steven Spielberg (141).

Some of the celebrities who have dropped a bit from the public eye include Tony Curtis (18), William Shatner (15), Gene Wilder (9), and the lowly Liza Minelli (4). In order to be truly pop-culturally literate, you'd better bone up on *Vogue, Manhattan* and *Thriller,* but you can safely plead ignorance to *Rent-a-Cop*.

Why are some of the juiciest celebrity stories about those who have passed on? Maybe late celebrities get so much outlandish press because according to American law it is impossible to slander a dead person. The odds then that a sleazy story about the deceased will produce a law suit are virtually zero. The courage of reporters who write slimy stories about Elvis and Marilyn Monroe is understandably enormous.

The following list represents the top ten deceased celebrities you can count on reading about:

1.	Elvis Presley	362
2.	John Wayne	168
3.	Laurence Olivier	157
4.	Marilyn Monroe	156
5.	John Lennon	126
6.	Charlie Chaplin	103
7.	Fred Astaire	97
8.	Cary Grant	81
9.	Orson Welles	79
10.	Humph. Bogart	70

Others who scored high include James Dean (69), who trails Bogie by only one point for the last spot in the list, Gary Cooper (67), and, in a surprise, Frank Capra (52), the director of that ubiquitous Christmas classic *It's a Wonderful Life*. Capra outscored such highly regarded directors as Alfred Hitchcock and John Ford.

Source: The Best and Worst of Everything.

PUNKS WITH ARMS

Definition: Disagreeable school kids who are as likely to shoot you as look at you, and at the slightest provocation.

In the five year period 1986-1990, hundreds of students severely wounded or terrorized classmates or school employees. Six school employees and 65 students were killed, 201 were injured and 242 were held hostage.

Gambold High, Indianapolis: A uniformed security officer stands beside a row of 10 wooden chairs. Nine buses unload and the students enter the gym where the security officer ushers 560 students through metal detectors. Cardboard boxes await the daily contraband. What happened to "dear old golden rule days?"

The Pez gun has been replace by the hand gun, that's what has happened. *USA Today* has estimated that 135,000 guns are brought into the nation's schools each day. As many as 2 million teenagers in the U.S. carry guns, knives, razors and clubs and many of these arms are brought to school right along with notebooks and lunch boxes.

The Odds: Approximately 1 in 5 teenagers are armed and 1 in 5 of them sometimes pack guns according a survey of 11,631 students. The following list represents the proportions of high school students who carried a gun, knife or club in the last 30 days.

MALE STUDENTS

Whites	1 in 4
Blacks	2 in 5
Hispanics	2 in 5

FEMALE STUDENTS

Whites	1 in 19
Blacks	1 in 6
Hispanics	1 in 8

Next time a smart aleck kid gets your dander up, it might be wise to back off. Many are armed and dangerous as hell.

Source: 1990 Centers for Disease Control poll of 11,631 students, grades 9-12.

R r

RADIO EVANGELISM

Holy Tuning

Definition: Zapping the airwaves with 50,000 kilowatts of heavenly power while pitching like the devil for donations.

Although the trial of Jim and Tammy, and the tribulations of Jimmy Swaggart, have dealt a serious blow to American televangelism, fundamentalist Christianity remains an extremely vital national force. While ratings and revenues for televised religious programming have suffered a general decline, listenership and proceeds for radio-based ecclesiastical fare are on the upswing.

The Odds: The following list represents the cities with the greatest odds of getting listeners who tune into the heavens. Figures were derived from market shares, that is, the proportions of listeners whose dials are set on stations which are broadcasting evangelistic programs.

TOP TEN MARKETS

Shreveport, La.	13 in 100
Jacksonville, Fl	10 in 100
Huntington, W. Va.	7.1 in 100
Lancaster, Penn.	6.6 in 100
Birmingham, Ala	6.4 in 100
Memphis, Tenn.	5.7 in 100
Eugene, Ore.	5.6 in 100
Greensboro, N.C	5.5 in 100
Billings, N.D.	5.2 in 100
Fresno, Calif.	4.9 in 100

Source: American Radio Magazine.

Also See: Religious Beliefs, Religious Practices.

RAPE, FORCIBLE

Definition: A criminal act in which the victim, usually a woman, is physically forced to commit a sexual act.

According to most state criminal laws, forcible rape is punishable with a severity second only to murder. Many convicted rapists, however, receive sentences exceeding those of murders.

HIGH RISK U.S. CITIES

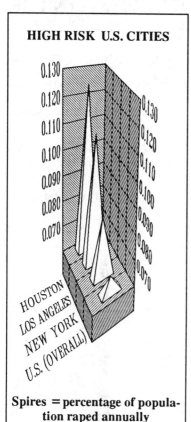

Spires = percentage of population raped annually

The Odds: Compiled crime reports fail to indicate the gender of victims, though arrest reports list the gender of the accused. Assuming the victims are women, the odds of getting raped in the U.S. in one year are approximately 1 in 1,500. In the four largest cities the odds of

women getting raped in 1991 are as follows:

New York	1 in 1,200
Los Angeles	1 in 900
Houston	1 in 800
Philadelphia	1 in 1,800

In the U.S., approximately 1 in 65,000 women and 1 in 4,000 men is arrested for rape. Some 1 in 15 accused rapists is a woman. Among men arrested for rape, 1 in 6 is under the age of 18.

Source: FBI Uniform Crime Report.

REAL ESTATE INVESTING

Top U.S. Cities

Definition: Plunking down your nest egg in an investment property and praying like hell the punks

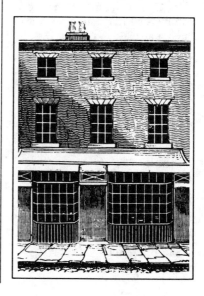

and winos won't take a shine to the neighborhood.

Looking for someplace to put your money? Try West Coast real estate. In a survey of leading economists and professionals in the real estate industry, five West Coast metropolitan areas—Los Angeles, Seattle, Orange County, San Francisco and San Diego—came out on top in expected investment performance. Such optimism among real estate professionals is further indication that the economic might of the country is shifting from its traditional centers in the big Northern cities.

The Odds: Metros in the Northeast are not expected to fare as well. According to majority opinion, the odds are 1 in 5 that real estate firms will be less active in the coming years. Nearly 1 in 3 respondents named New York City as the most overpriced commercial real estate market in the country.

The list below represents a ranking of the top 10 picks of real estate professionals surveyed.

TOP TEN CITIES
1. Los Angeles
2. Atlanta
3. Seattle
4. Washington
5. Chicago
6. Orange County
7. Dallas-Ft. Worth
8. San Francisco
9. San Diego

10. Orlando

Source: Ernst & Young.

RECESSION OF 1990-92

Jobless Woes

Definition: The downturn in the economy which was preceeded by eight years of exceptional growth.

The old adage is that a recession is when someone else loses his

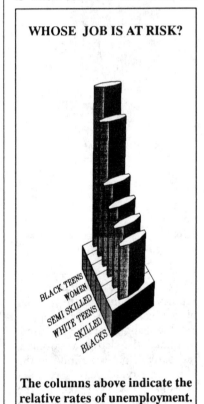

WHOSE JOB IS AT RISK?

BLACK TEENS
WOMEN
SEMI SKILLED
WHITE TEENS
SKILLED
BLACKS

The columns above indicate the relative rates of unemployment.

job, and a depression is when you lose your job. Definitions are not the only thing that clouds the economic picture. Labor statistics can be equally as misleading. For example, how many people are "out of work?" That depends on how many are defined as "working." Are the employed just those who work 40 hours weekly? Or are they part-time workers, or occasion workers too?

The Odds: A reasonable estimate is that 1 in 2 people choose to work, hence the labor pool in America is about 125 million. According to the U.S. Department of labor, 1991 closed with 8.5 million "unemployed," or almost 1 in 15 people. This translates to an unemployment rate of 6.8 percent, but that may be misleading. By early 1992, the figure soared to close to 8 percent.

There are also a large number of recession victims which official unemployment rates do not take into account, namely, the under-employed, discouraged workers and those who work only part-time because they cannot find a full-time job. Adding these workers to those officially designated as unemployed brings the total to almost 16 million in 1991, or almost 1 in 8, who is out of work in one way or another. Among these "out of work," 1 in 4 are employed part-time due to economic reasons. Almost 1 in 9 is a discouraged worker, that is, one who is no longer counted as unemployed because he or she has given up obtaining a job.

The list below represents various ratios of those who are officially on the unemployment roles, presumedly due to the recession:

Skilled-Workers	1 in 7
Semi-skilled Workers	1 in 5
Women	1 in 3
Whites	1 in 16
Blacks	1 in 8
White Teens	1 in 6
Black Teens	2 in 5
Under Age 25	1 in 8

Source: U.S. Department of Labor.

Also See: Homelessness, Poor Folks, Poverty, Public Aid, Worries.

RECIDIVISM

Definition: The rate at which criminals will return to prison.

Most first-time offenders for minor nonviolent crimes will not be sentenced to prison or jail. For most of those sentenced to prison, crime is a way of life. The odds that a prisoner will return are better than 3 in 5. The odds of reconviction for a similar crime are almost 1 in 2. The odds of going to jail for it, however, are only 2 in 5.

Source: U.S. Department of Justice.

Also See: Sentencing.

RECREATION EXPENDITURES

Definition: The money people spend to forget about their jobs, their mortgages, their unmowed lawns and all else which interferes with a little fun now and then.

WHERE'S JOE?

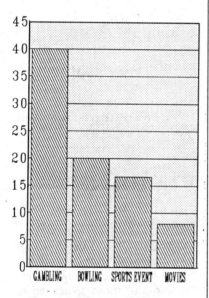

The colums represent outside-the-home activities and their proportion of recreation expenses in the U.S.

The beach is free, sex is free (hopefully), but just about everything else costs money. Where is it spent in America?

The Odds: In 1990, $62.8 billion was spent on the most popular types of recreational activities. The list below represents the ratio of dollars expended on them:

Gambling	2 in 5
Books	1 in 4
Records, Tapes & CDs	1 in 10
Movie Tickets	1 in 13
Video Tape Rentals	1 in 23
Bowling	1 in 25
Pro Sports	1 in 33

Source: Christiansen/Cummings Associates of New York CIty, for *Gaming and Wagering Business Magazine. The Statistical Abstract, 1991.*

Also See: Gambling Expenditures.

RE-ELECTION

Definition: The action in which an office-holding politician must defeat a challenging candidate who most likely has an infinitely better record of telling the truth to the electorate.

The Odds: A challenger's chances are 49 to 1 against defeating an incumbent Congressperson. Among representatives seeking re-election in 1986 and 1988, a full 98 percent were returned to Congress. Among successful opponents, more than 85 percent received at least 65 percent of the vote. In the future, the remap of federal districts based upon the 1990 census will doubtlessly improve chances for challengers, since incumbents will have to run in districts with newly drawn lines and possibly changed demographics. However, political action committees, whose contributions have so much to do with the incumbent's high odds of winning, will doubtlessly continue making gifts to those already in office rather than those merely seeking it from the outside.

Source: The New York Times, February 2, 1990.

RELIGIOUS BELIEFS

Definition: Convictions which individuals hold regarding God, worship, morals and all that pertains to spirituality and the supernatural.

Who is religious in America? The demographics will surprise you. According to the book *The Day America told the Truth,* 95 percent of those who espouse a religion are under the age of 65. Approximately 1 in 4 is a college graduate and 2 in 3 have attended college. Among religious people, 1 in 7 describes himself as "very religious."

The Odds: The list below represents the beliefs of Americans that the following phenomena exist.

God	19 in 20
Satan	11 in 20
Heaven	42 in 50
Afterlife	2 in 3
Ghosts	9 in 20
Magical Powers	3 in 10
Witchcraft	19 in 50
Black Magic	12 in 50
Voodoo	1 in 50

Source: Compiled research by editors.

Also See: Religious Practices, Religious Affiliations.

RELIGIOUS PRACTICES

Definition: What an individual actually does in his religious life, rather than what he says he does, or is supposed to do.

Though the various religions call their places of worship by many different names — churches, temples, mosques, and others — the word "church" is used to mean any place of worship regardless of the specific religion.

The Odds: What is a good Christian, Jew or Muslim supposed to do according to his religion? All the following, of course, but these are the odds they actually do them:

Daily Bible Reading 1 in 10

Go to Church   2 in 5

Went to Church
  as Child   29 in 50

Pray Daily   57 in 100

Belong to Church   7 in 10

Admit Women
  to Ministry   1 in 12

Amen!

Source: Compiled research by editors.

Also See: Religious Beliefs, Religious Affiliations, Jews.

REMARRIAGE

Marital Status of Brides and Grooms

Definition: The previous marital history of the woman in white and the man dressed like a penguin.

The Odds: Approximately 1 in 100 people in the U.S. will get married in any given year. Approximately 1 in 9 of them is a marriage comprised of at least one partner who has been divorced.

The list below represents the ratio and previous marital status of marriage partners in 1988 (the latest available statistics) in marriages in which at least one partner was previously married.

Divorced Men to Never-Married Women: 10.7 in 100

Divorced Women to Never-Married Men: 10.9 in 100

Before 1988, a higher percentage of never-married women were wedding divorcees. In the nineties, the trend will reverse and a higher percentage of divorced women will tie the knot with never-married men. The reason for the reversal is that men are getting married later in life now. The explanation may also be associated with the phenomena of the baby boom generation. Since most men prefer to marry younger women, the lower birth rates of the sixties and seventies, will translate to fewer younger women for male baby boomers to marry. They will therefore turn to older women who have a greater chance of having been married previously.

Source: The National Center for Health Statistics.

Also See: Marriages.

RESEARCH AND DEVELOPMENT

Definition: Money spent by many businesses to discover new things no one needs, but will probably buy if they spend enough bucks on advertising.

The Odds: The U.S. has 949,000 scientists and engineers, double the number of Japan. Research and development (R & D) expenditures are highest among the world's industrial giants, but how the funds are proportioned has almost no parity, as evidenced by the ratios of R & D expenditures and gross national product, which are as follows:

TOTAL R & D

Germany	$2.80 in $100
Japan	$3.00 in $100
U.S.	$2.00 in $100

FOR DEFENSE: The ratio of R & D for defense related expenditures versus others costs is as follows.

Germany	$1.00 in $8.00
Japan	$1.00 in $16.00
U.S.	$2.00 in $3.00

Source: The Chicago Tribune, October 13, 1991.

RESTAURANTS

Definition: A retail establishment which cooks, sells and serves food on its premises.

Most people regard restaurants as more than just a place to eat. Dining in them is one of America's favorite leisure activities. How many people go to them and how often?

The Odds: Below is a list which reflects America's eating out habits.

Daily	1 in 2
Once a Week	1 in 3
Chinese Food	1 in 8.5
McDonalds	1 in 15
McDonalds everyday	1 in 20
Kids eating Burgers (daily)	1 in 19

Source: Compiled research by editors.

RETIREES AND BANKRUPTCY

Who Pays the Doctor Bills?

Definition: The possibility that your money will run out before you do.

The Odds: Will you live to retirement age? More than 8 in 10 Americans will make it to age 65 or older. There is a downside to longevity, though. Odds are that the average person will have annual medical health care costs over $8,000 (in 1991 dollars) after age 65, if he is good health. If home care is required, the costs will average $15,000. If nursing-home care is required, the tab jumps to $77,000.

When will your money run out: Many working people incorrectly believe that Medicare and Medigap insurance will cover their old age health costs. They will have a sad awakening.

The following list which was released by Northwestern National Life Insurance Co. represents the age at which the average American's money will run out at various ages and the average annual cost of health care when retired:

AVERAGE HEALTH CARE

AGE NOW	AGE BROKE	CARE COST
25	75	$9,652
35	80	$8,132
45	89	$6,521
55	90	$4,878
65	90 +	$3,360

NURSING HOME CARE

AGE NOW	AGE BROKE	CARE COST
25	71	$18,432
35	72	$15,885
45	73	$13,472
55	74	$10,701
65	78	$7,840

The Cure: What to do? Make sure that your present health insurance, if you have it, will cover you during your retirement years. Just slightly better than 1 in 2 Americans expect their company's insurance will cover retirement health care, but only 1 in 3 companies offers such coverage. Only 1 in 3 such policies covers retirement for employees under age 65 and 2 in 5 offer coverage for those younger than 65. Just slightly less than 3 in 10 companies lessened retire coverage. Only 1 in 100 companies dropped health care for current retirees. In each such case, the companies went bankrupt . . . before the retirees did.

Source: USA Today, November 14, 1991.

Also See: Longevity, Retirement.

RETIREES

Where Are All The Old Folks?

Definition: Individuals who built our country, raised our children, fought our wars and are rewarded with retirement payments which average $600 per month.

The aging of the American population is a widely reported phenomenon. The high rates of public pensioners in many locales are clear warnings of the difficult times ahead. Not surprisingly, the nine top cities for social security recipients are in the retirement havens of Florida, while the cities with the lowest numbers of social security recipients are college towns—Iowa City, Champaign and Provo.

The Odds: The lists below represents the cities with the greatest and least percentages of Social Security recipients.

TOP TEN CITIES

Sarasota, FL	37 in 100
Bradenton, FL	30 in 100
Fort Myers-	
Cape Coral, FL	28 in 100
Daytona Beach, FL	28 in 100
West Palm Beach	

Boca Raton-	
Delray Beach, FL	26 in 100
Ocala, FL	26 in 100
Tampa-St. Pete.-	
Clearwater, FL	25 in 100
Fort Pierce, FL	24 in 100
Naples, FL	22 in 100
Scranton-	
Wilkes-Barre, PA	22 in 100

FEWEST RETIREES

Bryan-College	
Station, TX	7.9 in 100
Houston-	
Galveston, TX	8.0 in 100
Fayetteville, NC	8.3 in 100
Midland, TX	8.3 in 100
Casper, WY	8.4 in 100
Odessa, TX	8.5 in 100
Provo-Orem, UT	8.8 in 100
Iowa City, IA	8.9 in 100
Lawton, OK	9.0 in 100
Champaign-	
Urbana, IL	9.1 in 100

Source: U.S. Bureau of the Census.

Also See: Longevity, Retirement.

RIGHT-WINGERS

In Congress

Definition: The tally among Congresspersons who vote to ban abortions, keep guns in the hands of criminals, money away from the needy and therefore vote on most social issues as if they lived on one of the moons of Jupiter.

Although the Democratic party still controls the House of Representatives, the conservative block of voters in the House and Senate still swing a mighty bat. Now characterized by the superannuated likes of Jesse Helms and Strom Thurmond, the younger members of this set still get together to stop abortion, tear the guts out of the NEA and go on buying sprees for the military. Compiled by the American Conservative Union (ACU), these statistics represent the percentage of times each representative voted with the ACU position on 25 selected votes in 1989. Failure to vote did not lower scores. Intriguing names in this right-wing pantheon include new-comer Ileana Ros-Lehtinen from Florida, the first Cuban-American to serve in Congress.

The Odds: Expressed in percent of voting record in accord with the ACU position.

THE HOUSE

The following Congressmen voted with the ACU 100 percent of the time:

Wally Herger, California

William E. Dannemeyer, California

Ileana Ros-Lehtinen, Florida

Phillip Crane, Illinois

John Hiler, Indiana

Gene Taylor, Mississippi

Clarence Miller, Ohio

John Kasich, Ohio

Don Ritter, Pennsylvania

An additional 22 Representatives voted with the ACU 96 percent of the time.

THE SENATE

The following Senators voted with the ACU 100 percent of the time:

William Armstrong, Colorado
Jesse Helms, North Carolina
Malcom Wallop, Wyoming

The following Senators voted with the ACU 96 percent of the time:

Connie Mack, Florida
Steve Symms, Idaho
Trent Lott, Mississippi
Gordon Humphrey, New Hampshire
Don Nickles, Oklahoma
Strom Thurmond, South Carolina
Phil Gramm, Texas
Jake Garn, Utah

Source: 1990 Congressional Quarterly Almanac.

ROBBERY

Definition: 1) A bill from your lawyer; 2) the cost of emergency road service; 3) the act of forcibly taking property.

Robbery is the fastest growing violent crime in America, up 9 percent in 1991. By comparison, rapes increased 4 percent, aggravated assaults rose 2 percent and property crimes rose 1 percent.

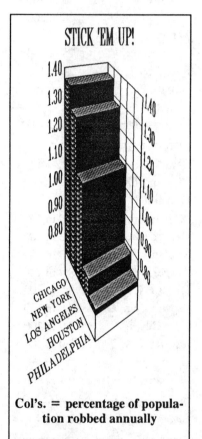

STICK 'EM UP!

CHICAGO
NEW YORK
LOS ANGELES
HOUSTON
PHILADELPHIA

Col's. = percentage of population robbed annually

The Odds: In the U.S., approximately 1 in 500 people are robbed each year. Some 1 in 12,000 women and 1 in 1,200 men are arrested for robbery. Unlike some crimes which are more uniformly spread throughout the nation, the odds of being robbed in the nation's largest cities are 1 in 90, approximately six times higher than the national average. The list below represents the odds of being robbed in 1991 in the nation's five largest cities, based on reports for the first six months of 1991.

New York	1 in 78
Los Angeles	1 in 92
Chicago	1 in 73
Houston	1 in 128
Philadelphia	1 in 138

Source: FBI Uniform Crime Report.

Also See: Stolen Property.

RHYTHM METHOD

Definition: The attempt to control pregnancy by adapting sexual practices to a woman's naturally fertile and infertile periods.

The Odds: Since a woman can become pregnant at only certain times each month, a few days before and a few days after ovulation, which usually occurs in the middle of the menstrual cycle, a calendar method, a temperature method, and a mucous method are often used by couples to track these fertile or infertile days. In all three methods, says Better Homes and Gardens' *Woman's Health and Medical Guide*, a woman's infertile days usually are from day 1 of menstruation to day 9 after, and from day 18 through menstruation again. The calendar method for measuring this is considered the least effective, with the odds 1 in 5 against pregnancy, principally because so few women have regular menstrual cycles. Temperature and mucous odds vary widely, due to the inconvenience for the woman in obtaining them, and, again, because menstrual cycles often change monthly, but generally they are 1 in 20 to 1 in 30 against pregnancy. The Columbia University *Complete Home Medical Guide* recommends a combination of these methods, while the *Woman's Health and Medical Guide* promises a great deal of accuracy by using all three methods. Among groups offering information on natural family planning, the Columbia book mentions The Natural Family Planning Development Program, Seton Hall University, South Orange, New Jersey, 07079.

Source: Compiled research by editors.

Also See: Birth Control Effectiveness, Contraceptive Methods.

S s

SAD

Seasonal Affective Disorder

Definition: A mental disorder which is marked by symptoms of depression or moodiness when the duration of daylight is affected by the change of seasons.

Millions become depressed as summer fades into fall and winter. The condition is not brought on by the cold. Doctors are finding that it is related to the amount of light one experiences. A remarkable new treatment has been developed. The victim of SAD merely sits in front of a highly luminous light box for a prescribed period of time. The exact medical effect is thought to be that light stops production of melatonin, a hormone produced by the pineal gland, which is generally considered to be associated with depression.

The Odds: In the United States, 1 in 25 people is a victims of SAD. Women outnumber men victims by 7 to 2, a circumstance scientists believe to be caused by gender-related hormonal differences. Other variations are found. Those who live closer to the equator, where seasonal differences in light are more minimized, have a lower rate of affliction to SAD. Studies have shown at as many as 1 in 10 residents of New Hampshire suffers, while in Florida, 1 in 67 is a victim.

Dr. Norman E. Rosen, a chief psychiatric researcher at the National Institute of Mental Health has developed a test for the public. If you experience more than 3 of the 7 symptoms listed below, you may be a SAD case and would do well to check with a qualified psychiatrist.

1. Needing more sleep

2. Eating more

3. Gaining weight

4. Losing energy

5. Socializing less

6. Feeling less cheerful

7. Having difficulties coping with life as a result of these changes.

Source: Parade Magazine, November 3, 1991.

SEAT BELT USAGE

Definition: The relative incidence of those who buckle up their automobile safety belts rather than depending on the efficacy of prayer.

Ever see what happens to a human head in a head-on auto collision at 30 miles per hour? At fifty? Ever see a squashed watermelon? At 30 miles per hour, an automobile involved in a head-on comes to a full stop in about a tenth of a second. Passengers who are not belted continue until they hit something—the steering wheel, the windshield or some just keep on going to meet up with a telephone pole. Each year, about 50,000 Americans are killed on the roads, and almost two million more are injured.

Can seat belts save your life in these collisions? You bet . . . whether you use them or not. It is estimated that 1 in 10 automobile accident victims is alive today because he or she was wearing a seat belt. This translates to about 5,000 people per year. Another way to think of it is that in the 1990s there will be enough people saved by their seat belts to fill up Yankee Stadium.

The Odds: If only 1 in 10 lives is saved by seat belts, are those who are not involved in an accident wasting their effort? Those foolish enough to think they are may take comfort in knowing there are many fellow fools around who use their belts. Ten years ago, just over 1 in 9 people used their seat belt. Public service advertisements steadily increased usage to today's rate which is 3 in 5 overall.

Rates of usage vary enormously and tend to be influenced by the perceived danger in the roadway traveled. In Rhode Island, for example, just over 1 in 4 uses a belt. In Hawaii, 17 in 20 buckle up. In the 20 largest cities in the U.S., slightly greater than 1 in 2 uses a belt.

Source: National Highway Safety Administration.

Also See: Automobile Accidents, Fatalities.

SEGREGATION
In Major U.S. Cities

Definition: A phenomenon in which various races and ethnic minorities are separated into homogenous neighborhoods within large American cities.

The three largest metropolitan areas in the U.S. are also the three most segregated, with Chicago topping the list as the most segregated city in the country. A simple drive through any racially beleaguered city will show how entrenched the racial divisions are: at one point you'll be driving through a neighborhood where all the faces are of one color. But cross a dividing line such as a major street, a railroad overpass or a public park, and suddenly the racial make-up is radically different. In a hyper-segregated city, such boundaries are not just geographic but psychological, and politicians and social reformers in Chicago and other cities have been learning just how hard it is to erase those psychological boundaries that divide the races in the United States.

The Odds: In the 47 largest metropolitan areas in the U.S. in which blacks make up at least 20 percent of the population, 2 in 3 will be highly segregated. In the metropolitan areas where Hispanics make up at least 20 percent of the population, only 2 in 33 cities (New York and Los Angeles) are highly segregated. Only one American city, San Francisco, has 20 percent or more Asians. Asian Americans, for the most part, are not highly segregated in America.

The list below represents the 10 most segregated U.S. cities as ranked by the book *The Best and Worst of Everything*:

1. Chicago
2. New York
3. Los Angeles-Long Beach
4. Milwaukee
5. Cleveland
6. Gary-Hammond, IN
7. Paterson-Clifton-Passaic, NJ
8. Philadelphia
9. Newark
10. Detroit

Source: Douglas S. Massey and Nancy A. Denton, "Hyper-segregation in U.S. Metropolitan Areas," *Demography*, August, 1989.

Also See: Integration.

SENATE VOTES
The Liberals

Definition: Theballots cast for the proverbial "little guy" in America who, collectively, has demonstrated he will elect even a snake, if he will put some money in his pocket.

When they run for office they make a lot of speeches about care for the down-trodden, national health insurance, funding education and cutting the defense budget. When they are in the Senate, they vote for these things. If the 1988 Pres-idential campaign proved one thing, it was that the nation was not yet ready for a bow-tied, flop-eared, slow-talking liberal from farm country to lead it. But the people of Illinois are, sending ultra-liberal Paul Simon back to the Senate in 1990 after his unsuc-cessful bid for the Democratic Presidential nomination in 1988.

The Odds: Some Senators vote liberal 100 percent of the time including Paul Simon (Illinois) and Patrick Leahy (Vermont).

Others are bent toward liberal is-sues, but cannot necessarily be counted on to bolster liberal causes. With data compiled by the liberal interest group Americans for Democratic Action, the list below represents the odds that a senator can be expected to vote in accordance with the ADA position on 20 selected votes during the 101st Congress.

Tim Wirth
(Colorado)   95 in 100
Tom Harkin (Iowa)   95 in 100
John Kerry
(Massachusetts)   95 in 100
Howard Metzenbaum
(Ohio)   95 in 100
Brock Adams
(Washington)   95 in 100
Herb Kohl
(Wisconsin)   95 in 100
Dale Bumpers
(Arkansas)   9 in 10
Joseph Biden
(Delaware)   9 in 10
Barbara Mikulski
(Maryland)   9 in 10

Source: Congressional Quarterly Almanac.

SENATORS

Re-election Prospects

The U.S. Senate has often been called a millionaire's club and a men's club. Both are still fairly apt nicknames. Many in the upper house are still wealthy, and while the following ranking shows that Nancy Kassebaum of Kansas is one of the country's most popular elected officials, a total of 8 women lost their 1990 bids to enter the senate. Among winners, the one with the smallest margin of victory was Bill Bradley of New Jersey.

The Odds: Some Senators' chances of being re-elected are iffy, to say the least. Bradley, the former New York Knicks basketball star, a man who is regarded as one of the great minds of the Senate, received just 51 percent of the vote as compared with his challenger Christine Todd Whitman's 49 percent.

The following list of the Senates top vote getters represents the relative chances of being re-elected, provided of course their general performance and voting record do not change substantially:

David L. Boren
(Oklahoma)   83 in 100
John W. Warner
(Virginia)   82 in 100
Nancy Kassebaum
(Kansas)   74 in 100
Pete V. Domenici
(New Mexico)   73 in 100
Max Baucus
(Montana)   70 in 100
Al Gore
(Tennesee)   70 in 100
John D. Rockefeller IV
(West Virginia)   69 in 100
Ted Stevens
Arkansas   67 in 100

Robert C. Smith
(New Hampshire)   67 in 100
Strom Thurmond
(South Carolina)   66 in 100

Source: Congressional Quarterly.

SENATE ATTENDANCE

Definition: Being present at a U.S. Senate session while the rest of the nation is working.

While it might be fun to blame all our nation's troubles on absentee Senators who vote when they please and spend most of their time on yachts with pin-up girls in their laps, the fact is that attendance in the Senate is extraordinarily high.

The Odds: A study of 310 votes showed a 98 percent participation rate in the 101st Congress. The odds are better than 9 in 10 that the average Senator will be present when the Senate is in session. The lowest odds was scored by Al Gore of Tennessee, whose odds in 101st Congress was 89 in 100. Gore, it should be noted, was called away by an illness in the family.

The following list represents Senators who you can almost count on being present when the Senate is in session—they have 100 percent attendance records:

Robert Byrd (West Virginia)
John Chaffee, (Rhode Island)
William Cohen (Maine)

Kent Conrad (North Dakota)
Alan Dixon (Illinois)
Slade Gorton (Washington)
Charles Grassley (Iowa)
Howell Heflin (Alabama)
Earnest Hollings (South Carolina)
J. Bennett Johnston (Louisiana)
John Kerry (Massachusetts)
Bob Kerrey (Nebraska)
Joseph Lieberman (Connecticut)
Mitch McConnell (Kentucky)
George Mitchell (Maine)
Larry Pressler (South Dakota)
Charles Robb (Virginia)
Richard Shelby (Alabama)
Arlen Specter (Pennsylvania)
Strom Thurmond (South Carolina)

Source: 1990 Congressional Quarterly Almanac.

SENILITY

Definition: Deterioration of one's short-term memory or alertness, commonly attributed to old age, but also caused by disease.

The Odds: Here is a myth that needs to be destroyed: Anybody over the age of 65 who happens to show some memory lapse or who is not as sharp as he should be is on the road to senility. Not so, say experts in gerontology, whose studies show that only a small number of older people will ever become senile, and that most older people retain their brain and motor skills throughout their lives, give or take some natural slowing down which in turn provides wisdom. The ability of the mind to grasp and retain facts, and to reason, are affected by many factors, among them anxiety and depression over the loss of a loved one, heart disease, or alcoholism, all of which can affect younger persons as well as the elderly. Truly debilitating senility, which may ultimately cause irreversible brain damage, actually is very rare. While the normal aging process does bring some brain cell loss, most people function very well without those cells. So, the odds of a person 65 or older becoming senile are 1 in 10, and of those, 1 in 5 will find the condition reversible if it is properly diagnosed and treated.

Source: Better Homes and Gardens *Woman's Health and Medical Guide.*

SENIOR CITIZENS

Definition: The grandmas, grandpas and golden oldsters in their retirement years.

Though Florida leads the nation in senior citizens with nearly 18 percent of its population past the minimum retirement age, most seniors choose to stay at home to luxuriate in the time they've earned. Florida is followed, not by Arizona, Nevada and California on the list of most senior states, but by such humdrum commonwealths as Pennsylvania, Iowa and Rhode Island.

The Odds: The following list represents the ten states with the highest ratios of population 65 years and older:

Florida	1 in 6
Pennsylvania	1 in 7
Iowa	1 in 7
Rhode Island	1 in 7
Arkansas	1 in 7
West Virginia	1 in 7
South Dakota	1 in 7

Missouri	1 in 7
Nebraska	1 in 7
Oregon	1 in 7

Source: U.S. Bureau of the Census.

Also See: Elderly, Retirement.

SENIOR LONELY HEARTS

Around the World

Definition: Those who grow older and wiser with no mate to share the benefits of their increased wisdom and experience.

In some nations the elderly are venerated and catered to in their last years. The situation in this nation has been very different. In the U.S., where almost 1 in 3 seniors live alone, our treatment of the elderly has lately bordered on neglect. And the problem will become even worse as the baby-boom generation ages. But the U.S. is not the country where the largest percentage of seniors are living alone. This neglect is widespread throughout the industrialized world.

The Odds: The following list represents the odds that a person will grow old alone in the nations with the highest and lowest rates of senior citizens living alone:

THE TEN HIGHEST ODDS

Sweden	40 in 100
Norway	40 in 100
Germany	38.9 in 100
Denmark	38.3 in 100
Finland	32.9 in 100
France	32.6 in 100
Czechoslovakia	32.4 in 100
Belgium	31.9 in 100
Netherlands	31.3 in 100
Austria	30.9 in 100

THE TEN LOWEST ODDS

Fiji	1 in 50
Korea	1 in 45
Singapore	1 in 43
Philippines	1 in 33
China	1 in 29
Colombia	1 in 20
Mexico	1 in 16
Malaysia	1 in 19
Costa Rica	1 in 14
Indonesia	1 in 14

Source: U.S. Census Bureau.

SENTENCING

Definition: Carrying out a punishment for a crime in which the guilty party is required to 1) pay a fine; 2) go on probation; 3) do community service; 4) go to prison or jail; 5) be executed.

An incredible 1 in 200 Americans has been incarcerated at least once. Among young blacks, the figure is 1 in 7. Those convicted of lesser crimes go to county or city jails and are sentenced to an average of 9 months. In the U.S., prison sentences average 4 years and 10 months. In state prisons the average sentence is 6 years and 10 months. Average sentences for drug traffickers are 22 months, less than that for aggravated assault or robbery.

The Odds: The odds of actually going to jail vary enormously from state to state. Odds are also dependent on the intensity of public opinion at the time a crime is being prosecuted. The average American is likely never to spend even one day incarcerated. Overall odds of incarceration are as follows.

Americans	1 in 200
Youths	1 in 1,226
Women	1 in 4,483

Below are the odds that you will go to the slammer if convicted of various crimes:

FELONY CONVICTIONS

To Prison	23 in 50
To Jail	1 in 5
Nonincarceration	1 in 50

DRUG CONVICTIONS

To Prison	1 in 3
To Jail	1 in 4
To Probation	1 in 3

MURDER

To Jail	1 in 50
To Prison	9 in 10
To Death	1 in 50

Ironically, although many Americans claim that authorities are soft on crime, the statistics do not confirm it. Any softness which may exist is in the release policy of prisoners. The odds that they will be released early are 7 in 10.

Source: Compiled research by editors.

Also See: Mob Bosses, Murder, Prison Escapes, Recidivism, White Collar Crime.

SEX DISCRIMINATION
Breaking the Glass Ceiling

Definition: Breaking through or avoiding the artificial, discriminatory barrier to promotion, which prevents promising women executives from entering the very highest levels of business.

The Odds: Though women are now entering the work force in almost the same proportions as men, only 1 in 20 senior management positions is held by a woman. Among the largest 1,000 firms, this number is approximately 1 in 33. In the case of CEOs (Chief Executive Officers) the proportion is 3 in 500 at the largest companies listed by *Fortune* Magazine in their annual "500 Issue.".

Becoming a woman manager is not the rule. Though women have not reached the very highest levels of management, the odds are 3 in 10 that a woman entering the work-force will end up in a managerial or professional job. Women now earn more college degrees than men. As early as 1975, they were earning 75 percent as many college degrees as men. Despite the improved odds that a college education brings, women have not been admitted to the managerial club en masse.

Source: Future Vision, The 189 Most Important Trends of the 1990s, Sourcebooks Trade, 1991.

SEXUAL ABUSE

Among Children

Definition: An incident in which a minor is violated in a sexual or erotic way, frequently by a parent.

The numbers and ratios of individuals who have been the victim of sexual abuse are hard to pin down. Most victims suppress these incidents. In a study done in Colorado, 1 in 2 victims of sexual abuse maintained that they did not recall the incidents until age 30 or beyond.

The Odds: Sexual abuse is very common. Estimates by various experts range from 1 in 3 women and 1 in 5 men to 1 in 4 women and 1 in 6 men. Dr. Thomas Roesler, clinical director are of Adult Survivors maintains abuse rates are as high as 1 in 4 females and 1 in 8 males.

Those unfortunates who suffer sexual abuse report the following circumstances in which it occurred:

By Parent or Step Parent	2 in 5
Penetrated (any form)	8 in 10
Physically Abused	6 in 10

Source: The Chicago Tribune, October 13, 1991.

Also See: Abuse by Family.

SEXUAL HARASSMENT

Definition: "[Behavior or remarks] in the workplace which interfere with work performance or create an intimidating, hostile or offensive working environment." – Section VII of the 1964 Civil Rights Act.

The most prevalent forms of sexual harassment are offensive sexual remarks rather than unwanted touching or physical contact. Women Employed, a national advocacy group, estimates 45 percent of women at work have been victims of sexual harassment. The American Women's Association of Female Doctors and Medical Students estimates harassment of women to be 27 percent. There are no substantial numbers of men who report sexual harassment.

The Odds: Given the estimates above, the odds of a woman experiencing some sort of sexual harassment are 1 in 3. Incredibly, the odds that a man will be reported in any way for sexual harassment are 1 in 10. Odds that he will be officially reported to be in violation of Section VII of the 1964 Civil Rights Act are 1 in 10,700. It has been speculated that many women fear repercussions of some sort if they formalize a complaint.

Source: The Chicago Tribune, October 10, 1991.

SHARK ATTACK

Definition: Assault on the human body by a fish of the order *Squaliformes,* whose main intent is to turn you into lunchmeat.

The Odds: Although there are more than several dozen different species of sharks in the world — totaling millions lurking in the oceans — the odds of being attacked by one is estimated to be an astronomical several million to one, far greater than the odds of being struck by lightening.

The greatest hazard zone is between latitudes 43°N and 43°S. In the tropics, shark attacks occur year-round, but in temperate regions, they are most likely to occur in the summer months, when the ocean temperature is between 60° and 70°. Most attacks occur among bathers during daylight hours in water less than 1 meter deep and about 100 meters from shore. Sharks go for the juiciest morsels: most injuries are to the buttocks and lower limbs, followed by the forearms and hands. If you are attacked, your odds of surviving are slim: Mortality rates for shark attacks have been estimated as high as 70%; hemorrhage and shock are the biggest killers among victims.

Source: Compiled research by editors.

SHOWER SHARING
Average Wait

Definition: The singer's favorite location to croon a tune, especially when someone is waiting at the bathroom door to get his turn.

The Odds: How much time do people spend in the shower on average? Odds are a shower will last 10 minutes. Coast Molding, Inc., of San Diego sees the practice as a terrible waste of water. Three minutes, they say is plenty of time to wash behind your ears and in other places in need of a cleansing. The company has invented a device similar to an egg timer which will shut off the water after the sand has measured exactly 3 minutes. If you want a longer shower, they say, just turn the timer over and the water returns. What's the point? The average family can save 20,000 gallons of water a year. How much more dirt their bodies will accumulate is unknown.

Source: New York Times News Service.

SINGLES

Definition: Those who sleep alone, but get the most sex; keep the most company, but are the loneliest; have the most disposable income, but are the most broke.

Sometimes the single life swings, at cool bars, in fast cars, with easy acquaintances. Other times, the solo life is lonely, flat, boring and depressing. Like everything else in life, the decision to remain or return to being single is a double-edged sword.

The Odds: In America there are 180 million people over the age of 18. Odds are 2 in 5 they have no present marriage partner. Among singles 48 in 100 are men; 52 in 100 are women.

AMONG MEN	
Never Married	30 in 100
Estranged	3 in 100
Widowed	3 in 100
Divorced	8 in 100
AMONG WOMEN	
Never Married	20 in 100
Estranged	4 in 100
Widowed	13 in 100
Divorced	10 in 100

Source: U.S. Bureau of the Census/Living Arrangements, 1990.

Also See: Dating, Divorce, Estrangement, Marriage, Single Mingles, Widows.

SINGLES MINGLES

Best Cities to Meet

Definition: The process in which unmarried people undress each other with their eyes, frequently culminating in undressing them with their front teeth.

The list below represents the top ten cities in the country, in terms of sheer numbers, for meeting single people and the odds an average citizen will be single.

New York	1 in 7

Los Angeles	1 in 4
Chicago	1 in 5
Philadelphia	1 in 4
Detroit	1 in 3
Boston	1 in 10
Washington, D.C.	2 in 3
Houston	1 in 6
Minneapolis-St. Paul	1 in 10
Atlanta	1 in 11

Source: Sales and Marketing Magazine, Survey of Buying.

Also See: Dating, Divorce, Estrangement, Marriage, Singles.

SKIN CANCER

Definition: A largely preventable skin disorder mostly caused by over-exposure to the sun, with fair-skinned white people with blue eyes most susceptible, and most common in the southern and southwestern U.S.

The Odds: That beautiful, blue-eyed blonde parading her great tan along the beach may be heading for the cemetery, if statistics on this rapidly increasing illness are to be believed. Although the odds each year against an adult being diagnosed with skin cancer are 1 in 460 at the present time, this figure is expected to be sliced in half in the next ten years. Most of these skin cancers are of the non-melanoma type, however, and are easily cured because they do not spread through the body. The most dangerous type of skin cancer, which often proves fatal, is called malignant melanoma, which does spread through the body. Here the odds each year on an adult being diagnosed with the disease are 1 in 6,805, and of dying of the disease 1 in 22,407. Thus the odds of dying from a malignant melanoma once diagnosed are 1 in 3. Remember, any mole developing on the body is suspect and should be looked at by a doctor. Women especially should be keenly aware that the sites on their bodies most susceptible to skin cancer are the lower legs, the arms, and the head.

Source: Columbia University College of Physicians, *Complete Home Medical Guide*; American Medical Association, *Family Medical Guide*; *Woman's Health and Medical Guide*.

Also See: Cancer.

SLUMMING IT
World Nations

Definition: Living in a loathsome, self-perpetuating den of poverty, despair and crime.

In many sectors of the third world, 60 percent or more of the urban population makes its home in squalid, underbuilt, over-populated ghettos.

The Odds: The following list represents the odds that an average citizen of the poorest cities in world will reside in a slum:

TEN SLUMMIEST CITIES

Addis Ababa, Ethiopia	9 in 10
Yaounde, Cameroon	9 in 10
Douala, Cameroon	9 in 10
Buenaventura, Colombia	8 in 10
Mogadiscio, Somalia	3 in 4
Ibadan, Nigeria	3 in 4
Lome, Togo	3 in 4
Santo Domingo, Dom. Rep.	7 in 10
Casablanca, Morocco	7 in 10
Nairobi, Kenya	7 in 10

Source: Advertising Age.

Also See: Poverty.

SMALL TOWN VIOLENCE

Definition: A disruption in the relative peace and quiet of cities

with populations between 25,000 and 50,000.

The Odds: America has a reputation for violence; however, rates of violent crimes vary enormously with the relative size of cities. In major metropolitan areas, odds of being the victim of a violent crime in one year are about 1 in 60. In the suburbs, the odds fall to about 1 in 1,000. In small towns, however, the odds drop to about 1 in 2,000.

LOWEST ODDS

Biloxi, MS	1 in 2,900
State College, PA	1 in 2,779
Minot, ND	1 in 2,526
Stow, OH	1 in 2,300
Waukesha, WI	1 in 1,750
Menomonee Falls, WI	1 in 1,740

Source: Bureau of the Census population figures and the F.B.I.'s Uniform Crime Reports for 1989.

SMOKING

Definition: The inhalation of tobacco smoke for the purpose of giving you a mild nicotine buzz and lung cancer, all at the same time and for the modest cost of about 12 cents a smoke.

At the supermarket what is the most common grocery item? A carton of Marlboros. It is no wonder at all. There are 55 million Americans who suck cigarettes. Each day, Marlboro sells 368 million of the little white suckers to other suckers. Cigarette marketing is no small segment of the economy. In the U.S., somewhat more than $500 million is spent annually on advertising by cigarette companies.

Though the practice of smoking in America is tapering off, elsewhere on the globe, the practice is thriving. Even today, as America wises up to the dangers of smoke, each day the following number of cigarettes are sold in the U.S.: 1,562,739,726. Yes, you probably read the numbers correctly, that is 1.52 billion ciggies—*every day*. Each year over $50 billion is spent on purchasing cigarettes.

The Odds: Nearly 40 percent of all Americans give smoking a try, but 71 percent of all smokers try to quit at one time or another. Approximately 1 in 3 will give up the habit. Following is a closer look at specific groups of American smokers.

Smoke Cigarettes	1 in 4.5
Marlboros Smokers	1 in 4.2
Kids who Smoke	1 in 16
Starting Smoking	1 in 2.6
Die of Smoke-Related Ills	1 in 3
Try to quit	7 in 10
Try to Quit Using Nicorette Gum	1 in 46

Source: On an Average Day, Tom Heymann.

SMOKING, PASSIVE

Definition: Exposure to other people's tobacco smoke, also called sidestream smoking; a term that came into general use in the early 1980s following studies of the problem.

The Odds: Nothing is more disgusting for a non-smoker than to come home from a night out reeking of other people's tobacco smoke. But the danger from passive smoke is not just to clothing—it is also to the health of the non-smoker. Here is the fulcrum of the anti-smoking crusade in America, upon which, in part, businesses, health groups, irate housewives, angry restaurant diners, and the U.S. government have built their cases against smoking in public places. Sidestream smoke, they say, causes cancer in greater proportion than that suffered by the smokers themselves, due to chemical changes in the smoke that is exhaled. Studies show that the risk of cancer doubled in non-smoking women (principally housewives) whose husbands smoked 20 or more cigarettes at home each day. Based on those studies, and interpolating for other environmental factors (offices, restaurants, public places), the odds of dying from cancer (principally lung cancer) from sidestream smoke is 1 in 40,000. Although this danger is less than that from alcohol-related murders and accidental deaths, such statistics, in hard numbers, mean that more than 6,000 innocent non-smokers are killed every year in the U.S. by the noxious habits of their fellow men and women.

Source: World Almanac and Book of Facts; American Cancer Society, *Facts and Figures on Smoking*.

SOUTHEASTERN SNOW BIRDS

Before The Ice Melts

Definition: Americans escaping the harsh winters of home who head south for sun and fun.

Want to see some tourists? Try anywhere from South Carolina south to Florida, and from Georgia west to New Orleans. There you will see hoards, with cameras strung around their necks and arms greasy from suntan oil. Where do all these tourists come from? From the snowiest places in America, of course. The following list represents the cities which have the most snow to escape from:

TOP TEN IN SNOW

1. Sault St. Marie, Michigan	114.9
2. Juneau, Alaska	99.9
3. Buffalo	92.3
4. Burlington, Vermont	77.9
5. Portland, Maine	71.5
6. Albany,	65.5
7. Concord, New Hampshire	64.3
8. Denver	60.3
9. Great Falls, Montana	58.3
10. Salt Lake City	58.2

The Odds: If you were to stop and ask a typical Southeastern Snowbird what part of the country he is from, odds are he will answer according the proportions shown on following lists:

The West	1 in 5
The Midwest	1 in 6
Great Lakes	1 in 9
The Northeast	1 in 9
The Southeast	1 in 3

Source: U.S. Travel Data Center.

SOVIET FARMS

Peasant Owned Production

Definition: A miracle of eastern European farm technology

whereby wheat is planted on Soviet soil and it grows in Kansas.

Some 60 years ago Josef Stalin confiscated millions of individually owned farms, *kulaks*, plots which owned more than 3 cows. The owners were promptly sent to Siberia and their land was merged into collectives. Stalin was poised to prove that the new Soviet Union would revolutionize agriculture. Within several years, over 10 million people starved to death.

Back to the boards again, Soviet officials loosed up a bit under Gorbachev and allowed 1 in each 33 acres of farm land to be privately owned. After counting their chickens and apples, they were surprised to find that this tiny minority of privately owned plots produced up to 30 percent of the nation's agricultural output.

They could have saved the experiment and just read the report by the Rural Development Institute, which consistently showed that U.S. and Canadian farms outproduce those in the Soviet Union by 10 to 1. Though North America has better growing conditions, the institute calculated that even after adjusting for them, North American farms outproduce Soviet farms by 2 to 1.

The Odds: Somewhat less that 1 in 100 Soviet farms is privately owned. The following list compiled by *Economy and Life*, a Soviet publication, represents the proportions of total farmland which is peasant owned in the eight principle growing regions of the Soviet Union:

Georgia	1 in 192
Russia	1 in 555
Uzbekistan	1 in 2,500
Kazakhstan	1 in 714
Ukraine	1 in 10,000
Byelorussia	1 in 3,333
Kirghizia	1 in 526
Azerbaijan	1 in 2,500

In the four remaining Soviet republics, Tajikistan, Moldavia, Armenia and Turkmenistan there are virtually no privately owned farms.

Source: Compiled research by editors.

SPEECH DISORDER

Definition: A medical or psychological condition which impairs speaking ability in children and adults.

The Odds: Some 1 in 20 Americans suffers from some form of speech disorder, approximately two-and-half million Americans. This includes 10 million with speech disorders, 9 million Americans with hearing impairments of handicapping magnitude and the 2 million who suffer from neurological problems which impair speech. Among children, disorders of articulation are most frequent. In the future, the victims of other handicaps are gradually beginning to see people with speech disorders as normal productive individuals with as much or more to offer as the rest of society. The following list breaks down the odds of the various kinds of speech disorders occuring in Americans:

Functional	
Articulatory	1 in 33
Stuttering	1 in 142
Voice	1 in 500
Cleft Palate	1 in 1,000
Cerebral Palsy	1 in 500
Retarded	
Development	1 in 333
Impaired Hearing	
(with speech	
defect)	1 in 200

Source: Encyclopedia Britannica.

SPEECHWRITER

Definition: A person who writes speeches for someone who does not stand a ghost of a chance of sounding articulate by himself.

The Odds: Here is a job with a fast-growing future for the 1990s, and usually a free-lance job at that. With the proliferation of seminars on every conceivable subject, the growing lecture circuit, the call upon CEOs to reveal their secrets, and, of course, the creeping illiteracy of today's politicos and newsmakers, the call is out: HELP! As one of the mushrooming horde of aspirants answering the call, it is important to keep in mind the odds on keeping your listeners awake while the speaker reads the message you wrote for him. A recent speechwriting survey found that the odds of a business executive falling asleep at least once in any given year during somebody's speech are 8 in 10. (But, having to sit through a year-long speech, can you blame them?) So, to all you budding pundits and speechifyers out there: keep it short, keep it vivid, and make sure you provide plenty of bang for the bucks you are paid to ghostwrite.

Source: Chicago Reader.

STROKE

Definition: A sudden reduction of blood flow to the brain, caused by a clot or a piece of fatty plaque in a blood vessel, or by a cerebral hemorrhage induced by high blood pressure or the rupture of a weakened blood vessel to the brain.

The Odds: Although stroke is the third leading cause of death among Americans in the 55-74 age group (following heart disease and cancer), the mortality from this dread affliction has declined more than 50 percent since 1970, as high blood pressure controls have been improved. Nevertheless, it still is one of the scourges of growing old for both men and women, with men suffering a one-third higher rate than women. Death or physical impairment are the results of a stroke, the extent and type of which depends on which side of the brain it occurs on. If it occurs on the left side of the brain, paralysis of the right side of the body may result. In the right side of the brain, a stroke may paralyze the left side of the body and result in difficulties in eating and dressing. One in 3 strokes is fatal; another 1 in 3 causes permanent damage; and the remaining third leave no lasting effect. To minimize the probabilities of ever having a stroke, fight excessive weight gain, do not smoke, reduce your fat intake, and, if you have diabetes, have it monitored regularly by your doctor.

Source: The Merck Manual; American Medical Association, *Family Medical Guide*; Columbia University College of Physicians and Surgeons, *Complete Home Medical Guide.*

Also See: Heart Disease.

STUDY HABITS
High School Students

Definition: 1) The steady (sic) habit of doing less homework than your mother thinks you should.

No one does enough homework to please his parents or teachers, but according to a recent report, most kids do enough to please themselves which makes for a very low threshold for satisfaction.

The Odds: It is only a 9 in 25 bet that the average high school student will study more than one hour each day. Odds are 1 in 5 a high schooler will spend over 11 hours each week hitting the books. If you think these odds are bad, the odds are even worse when high school students are asked how much more they *plan* to study than they currently do. Almost 8 in 10 say they will work about as hard as they currently do. Odds are only 1 in 5 that a student plans to work harder. Oh, the bored (sic) of education needs revitalizing!

Source: Who's Who Among American High School Students.

Also See: Educational Attainment.

255

SUBURBAN FLIGHT

Where it's Worth the Drive?

Definition: A refuge from the hassles of the city where home-owners commute two hours daily to work, pay the highest taxes, fight with the school board, mow the lawn, rake the leaves, shovel the snow, fix the plumbing, and otherwise enjoy the more relaxed life of suburbia.

Ah, suburbia, how our tired, un-washed souls long for thee! How thou hast supplanted the city of yore, with greener lawns, wider driveways, safer schools and the most boring malls. Cry not for Metropolis, O car commuter, or thou shalt miss the gathering of yon P.T.A.

The Odds: The following are the metropolitan areas with the big-gest suburban populations. Fig-ures shown represent the per-centage of individuals in a metropolitan area who live in suburbia, rather than within the city limits.

TOP TEN SUBURBAN METROS

New York	60 in 100
Los Angeles	75 in 100
Chicago	36 in 100
San Francisco	88 in 100
Philadelphia	53 in 100
Detroit	68 in 100
Washington, D.C.	83 in 100
Boston	64 in 100
Atlanta	92 in 100
St. Louis	82 in 100

Source: Sales and Marketing Magazine, Survey of Buying Power.

SUBURBAN VIOLENCE

Definition: Incidents in which citizens of satellite communities of major cities get creamed by an attacker, just like their far-off neighbors in the ghettos of the urban jungle.

The affluent folks of Wilmette, Il-linois, a suburb of Chicago along the northern shore of Lake Michigan, enjoy a relatively crime free environment. But on occasion these sleepy towns are rocked by hideous crimes that reveal the dark underside of sub-urban life. In 1988, in the neigh-boring town of Winnetka, a troubled young woman named Laurie Dann went on a shooting spree at a local elementary school, killing one student and wounding several others before she finally took her own life. Such shooting rampages seemingly al-ways occur in quiet, peaceful suburban communities — San Ysidro, Stockton, Winnetka. Per-haps some of the tensions that result in such a high number of murder in major cities are lying just below the surface of sylvan suburbs, exploding all the more violently for their suppression.

256

The Odds: In the nearby urban jungles, the odds of being the victim of a violent crime are 1 in 61 in one year. In the safer, more affluent suburbs, the odds drop to between 1 in 1,000 to almost 1 in 5,000. In an "average" better suburb the odds are about 1 in 2,000

LOWEST CRIME RATES

Wilmette, IL	1 in 4,871
Ridgewood, NJ	1 in 3,601
Rockville, MD	1 in 3,983
Upper Arlington, OH	1 in 3560
Northbrook, IL	1 in 2,361
Wheaton,IL	1 in 1,664
Garfield, NJ	1 in 1,789
Winona, MN	1 in 3,200
Strongsville, OH	1 in 1,786
Nutley, NJ	1 in 1,706
Kirkwood, MO	1 in 1,555

Source: Bureau of the Census population figures and the F.B.I.'s Uniform Crime Reports for 1989.

SUICIDE

Definition: The act of taking one's own life, an event usually taking place during times of great desperation or severe mental depression.

Suicide is the eighth leading cause of death in the U.S., accounting for over 30,000 deaths annually. Every 20 minutes a successful suicide is committed. The most common method is death by a handgun followed, in decreasing order of frequency, by drug overdoses, cutting and stabbing, jumping from high places, inhaling poisonous gas, hanging and drowning. Each year, there are more people who are killed by their own hand than by criminals and more die from suicide than from liver disease, atherosclerosis, kidney disease and homicide.

The Odds: In the U.S., 1 in 67 people dies as a result of suicide. Each year, 1 in 580 Americans will attempt suicide and slightly greater than 1 in 14 will be successful. Women account for 1 in 5 successful suicides. Many doctors believe official suicide rates are estimated too low. It is suspected that many suicides are covered up to save the deceased's families from embarrassment.

Officially, 1 in 7,900 individuals will commit suicide each year. The highest incidences in the U.S. are in the Western states and the lowest are in the Northeast. The following list represents the ratio of suicides to the population during an average year in the states with the highest and lowest rates:

HIGHEST STATES

Nevada	1 in 3,900
Arizona	1 in 4,900
New Mexico	1 in 5,000
Montana	1 in 5,100
Alaska	1 in 5,600

LOWEST STATES

New York	1 in 14,300
New Jersey	1 in 12,200

Connecticut	1 in 10,500
Massachusetts	1 in 10,100
Hawaii	1 in 9,800

Source: National Center for Health Statistics.

Also See: Suicides, at any age.

SUICIDE
Age Relationships

Definition: The age at which individuals are most prone to deliberately kill themselves.

Suicide among children is relatively low; however, once the teen years are reached, the odds that individuals will kill themselves increase dramatically with age. Though teen suicide is a widely publicized phenomenon, the odds are far greater among the elderly.

The Odds: The National Institute of Health reported in 1991 that people 80 to 84 years of age are twice as likely as young adults to kill themselves. White men 80 to 84, have the highest rate, 71.9 per 100,000 versus the national average of 12.4 per 100,000. This alarming statistic translates to odds that elderly white men are six times more prone to suicide than the young.

The following list, which is compiled from data from the National Center of Health Statistics, represents suicide rates in 1991 in various age groups:

All Ages	1 in 7,874
0-4	NA
5-14	1 in 142,857
15-24	1 in 7,751
25-34	1 in 6,494
35-44	1 in 6,667
45-54	1 in 6,289
55-64	1 in 2,024
65-74	1 in 5,155
75-84	1 in 3,876
85 and older	1 in 4,525

Source: Compiled research by editors.

Also See: Suicides.

SUPREME COURT
Case Appeals

Definition: The highest court in the land, composed of 9 members, "Justices", whose primary job is to decide cases which have worked their way up through the lower state and federal courts.

It is rare that the Supreme Court is the court of original jurisdiction. It is given that status only in cases involving the following: 1) states against states; 2) the U.S. against a foreign nation; 3) citizens of one state against another state; 4) foreign ambassadors.

Cases other than those previously mentioned must either work their way through the lower U.S. courts or come directly from state supreme courts.

The Odds: Each year approximately 300,000 cases are commenced in U.S. District courts. Of them, 1 in 8 are appealed to the next highest court, the U.S. Court of Appeals. Once a case moves to this level, it is disposed of in an average of 10 months. Of these approximately 40,000 cases which are up for appeal, 1 in 7 is then appealed to the U.S. Supreme Court, if the defendant can show cause that an issue was not properly resolved. Of these cases, 1 in 30 are argued annually before the justices and 1 in 38 will be answered by signed opinions.

The aforementioned process of climbing up the ladder of the U.S. court system translates to approximately 1 in 50 federal cases reaching the Supreme Court dockets, and only 1 in 1,800 being resolved by this highest of courts.

Source: Office of the Clerk of the Supreme Court of the United States.

Also See: Litigation, Federal.

T t

TALK SHOWS

Where's that Dial?

Definition: Television programs in which the average American learns about socially relevant issues, especially the lesbian nun issue, the cat coat fad, doggy psychiatry, and mother and daughter strip acts.

THE TOP TALKERS

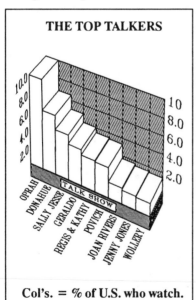

Col's. = % of U.S. who watch.

Did Bette Midler have an orgasm when she did it in the bathroom with Geraldo? Was Bette on top or Geraldo? What does Oprah look like naked? Is Maury Povich really Phil Donahue in heavy make-up? If these questions keep you up at night, odds are you are a talk show junkie.

The Odds: Approximately 1 in 3 Americans tunes into TV talk shows. With the stiff competition each day, what are the odds that an average American will have his dial tuned to some of the biggest shows? The list below is based on "gross rating points," media measurements in which each point represents 921,000 TV households watching. If each point is thought of as 1 percent of the somewhat more than 90 million households with TV sets, the odds are as follows:

Oprah Winfrey	1 in 10
Phil Donahue	1 in 15
Sally Jessy Raphael	1 in 20
Geraldo Rivera	1 in 24
Regis and Kathy Lee	1 in 29
Maury Povich	1 in 30

Joan Rivers	1 in 59
Jenny Jones	1 in 67
Chuck Woolery	1 in 71

Source: USA Today.

TEEN-AGE USA
Where are those darn Kids?

Definition: Places in the U.S. where the phone lines are jammed, the radios are blaring and the streets are packed.

Some say that adolescence is a very difficult time; for Mom and Pop, at least, that is certainly true. On the other hand, George Bernard Shaw said youth is wasted on the young, but so are some of the nation's most scenic states—the Wild West—where youths spend their idle hours chatting on the phones and spinning CDs indoors.

The Odds: The classic U.S. teenager (a youth 14 to 17 years of age) is declining. In 1970, 1 in 13 Americans was a teenager. By 1990, only 1 in 19 Americans was a teenager. Many older Americans who have seen several generations progress from childhood to adolescence have observed that "teen-age behavior" is displayed at younger and younger ages in successive generations. Today's child of 5 or 6 is not too dissimilar to the potato chip-munching, gum-chewing, sass-backing teenager of yesteryear.

Given this, the following list is offered which represents the teenagers and honorary teenagers in the ten states with the highest ratios of population under 18 years of age:

TOP 10 IN STATES WITH KIDS UP TO AGE 17

Utah	37.3 in 100
Alaska	32.0 in 100
Idaho	30.3 in 100
New Mexico	29.8 in 100
Mississippi	29.8 in 100
Texas	29.6 in 100
Louisiana	29.4 in 100
Wyoming	29.4 in 100
Georgia	28.0 in 100
South Dakota	27.6 in 100

Source: U.S. Bureau of the Census.

TEEN DRINKING

Definition: The imbibing of alcoholic beverages by youths.

The Surgeon General of the United States is currently putting pressure on the alcoholic beverage industry to ban aiming advertising at youths. There is good reason to do so. Some 8 in 10 high school students consume alcoholic beverages compared to only 1 in 5 who use cocaine. Some 3 in 4 people in prisons in the U.S. got there because of alcohol or drug related problems.

The Odds: At least 1 in 20 people in the U.S. will become an alcoholic. During the formative years, however, the odds that a youngster will fall prey to alcohol are far greater. According to government surveys, 2 in 5 teens drink weekly and greater than 1 in 4 are classified as alcoholics during their teen-age years. The following list represents drinking habits of Americans between the ages of 12 and 17.

USE ALCOHOL

Past Month	1 in 4
Past Year	2 in 5
During Lifetime	1 in 2

LEVELS OF USE

Tried Alcohol	1 in 2
Binge	
(5 or more drinks)	1 in 4
Current User	1 in 4

WHY THEY DRINK

When Upset	2 in 5
To Get High	1 in 4
When Bored	1 in 4
Other Reasons	1 in 11

Source: National Council on Alcoholism and Drug Dependence, Surgeon General Survey.

Also See: Alcoholism

TEEN PREGNANCY

An American Epidemic

Definition: The state in which a woman conceives a child while still in her teens.

Teen-age pregnancy is a burden on our social system. Young mothers, ill-prepared for the responsibilities of parenthood, make increased demands, both for themselves and their infants, on the nation's already thinly-stretched safety net. One more teen mother most often means one more underprivileged youth without a high school diploma, unemployable.

The Odds: Somewhat more than 1 in 4 women becoms pregnant before reaching age 20. According to *The Universal Almanac*, almost 1 in 2 girls between ages 15 and 19 has lost her virginity; 1 in 4 become pregnant. Considering that a poll by the U.S. Department of Health and Human Services showed that better than 1 in 2 young women practices no form of birth control, this statistic is not surprising.

Among teen-age boys, 6 in 10 are sexually active. On average, boys in this age group who are sexually active will spend at least six months with no sexual partner; however, during their teen years, they will average 2.66 episodes of sexual intercourse each month.

According to the U.S. Census Bureau figures, if you were to stand on a street corner in various cities and pick out teen-age girls among the crowds, the odds are as follows that one will be pregnant at that given moment:

TOP TEN MAJOR CITIES

Newark, NJ	1 in 39
Baltimore, MD	1 in 42
St. Louis, MO	1 in 46
Shreveport, LA	1 in 47
Atlanta, GA	1 in 48
Detroit, MI	1 in 49
Louisville KY	1 in 51
Cleveland, OH	1 in 51
Fort Worth, TX	1 in 52
Cincinnati, OH	1 in 52

BOTTOM TEN MAJOR CITIES

San Francisco, CA	1 in 123
Anchorage, AK	1 in 120
Arlington, TX	1 in 115
Seattle, WA	1 in 112
Virginia Beach, VA	1 in 108
San Diego, CA	1 in 104
Anaheim, CA	1 in 99
St. Paul, MN	1 in 94
Portland, OR	1 in 93
Minneapolis, MN	1 in 91

Source: Compiled research by editors.

Also See: Birth'n Babies, Birth Control, Motherhood.

TELEVISION

Definition: A box in which Peter Jennings lives with Connie Chung.

"Don't go home without it," could just as well be the slogan of the National Association of Broadcasters, rather than American Express which has a similar motto. Few Americans do go to a home without a television. America has less than 5 percent of the world's population, yet it has three-quarters of the world's 700 million television sets.

The Odds: In the slightly less than 100 million households in American, television is entrenched as follows.

Have TV	49 in 50
Have 2 or more TVs	3 in 10
Have color TV	19 in 20
Have cable TV	6 in 10
Have VCR	7 in 10
Watch the late news	4 in 10
Watch daytime TV	4 in 10
Read while watching	3 in 10
Eat while watching	1 in 5
Do housework	1 in 6
Do nothing but watch	1 in 4
Appeared on TV (men)	1 in 4
Appeared on TV (women)	1 in 5

Source: International Television & Video Almanac.

Also See: News Sources; Television, Kiddy TV.

TELEVISION

Kiddy Programs

Definition: Thirty to 60 minutes of blood, and guts, cereal and toy commercials, .88 bags of potato chips and 1.1 spilled Cokes on the sofa.

Kids watch more television than any viewing group. The average American watches just more than 4 hours daily. Among children 2 to 5 years of age, viewership is 50 percent higher and averages 6 and one half hours.

The Odds: For those who watch during prime time, there is a 100 percent chance that during an average hour they will see 8 acts of violence, according to the National Coalition of Television Violence. Kid shows are especially violent. Saturday morning cartoons, they maintain, have an average of 20 violent acts per hour. The Coalition has cited the following shows as those which tip the acceptability scale for kids:

Teen-age Mutant Ninja Turtles

G.I. Joe

Tiny Toon Adventures

Peter Pan and the Pirates

Dragon Warrior

Toxic Crusades

According to American Academy of Pediatrics there is a high probability that a child watching network television for 3 and one-half hours will see the following:

5 Wine or Beer Commercials

33 Acts of Violence

38 Sexual References or Innuendoes

During an average hour of prime-time programming, the average number of violent acts on certain programs is as follows:

America's Most Wanted	53
Hardball	47
Tour of Duty	45

Young Riders	40
Booker	37
Hunter	33
Mission Impossible	30
Alien Nation	25

Source: Compiled research by editors.

TETANUS

Definition: An infectious disease in which muscle spasms and exaggerated reflexes can cause lockjaw, seizures, respiratory failure and paralysis.

Tetanus, once a scourge of early Americans, has been on the steady decline in the U.S. since the end of World War II, due in most part to widespread immunization and increased physician and patient awareness of the dangers of the affliction.

The Odds: In the U. S. in 1988, the odds of getting tetanus were a slim 5 million to one. Tetanus cases cropped up in 35 states during 1987 and 1988, but no cases occurred in the Rocky Mountains, either in that period or in the several preceding years, so Rocky Mountain folk are relatively safe from the disease. Because of relatively thorough immunization of children since the fifties, tetanus most often strikes older Americans. About 66 percent of all tetanus patients are over fifty years old. The Centers for Disease Control recommend a primary series of three doses of the tetanus vaccine, followed by booster shots every ten years.

The Causes: In most cases, tetanus strikes after an injury of some sort. About 75 percent of all tetanus cases are the result of puncture wounds, cuts and abrasions. The greatest danger is from stepping on sharp objects, such as nails or wood splinters. *One in five* tetanus cases is fatal — but victims can easily prevent the disease by seeing a physician immediately and receiving a tetanus shot. Unfortunately, 58 percent of reported tetanus cases don't seek medical care.

Source: Centers for Disease Control.

TOURISTS, FOREIGN
Where U.S. Visitors Come From

Definition: Men and women who wear "I love New York" T- shirts, have cameras slung around their neck, maps in their hip pocket and overpay for merchandise on Fifth Avenue and Rodeo Drive.

In the heady days when the dollar was booming—just after the two World Wars and in the mid-1980s—Americans flocked to foreign shores to gawk at the treasures, both natural and man-made, of the old world. Contrarily, when the dollar is down, we welcome hordes of camera-toting tourists to our bountiful land. If you become frustrated on the streets of New York in August these days because you're hearing more German, French or Japanese than English, maybe now you'll get some idea why Parisians flood out from the City of Lights every summer to escape the invasion of their city by similar minions from abroad. And if you start to see signs posted in German on the beaches of Miami or in Japanese in Los Angeles, think of the tourist dollars flowing into this country from those wealthy nations.

The Odds: The following list represents countries that send annually the most temporary visitors, either on business or pleasure, to the United States and the odds that an average citizen in that nation will visit the U.S. in one year:

Switzerland	1 in 30
United Kingdom	1 in 41
Sweden	1 in 51
Japan	1 in 59
Australia	1 in 64
West Germany	1 in 67
Netherlands	1 in 85
Mexico	1 in 108
France	1 in 119
Italy	1 in 213

Source: U.S. Immigration and Naturalization Service.

TRANSPLANTS

Definition: The permanent replacement of an unhealthy organ or other body part which usually has its origins from a deceased person or a relative who donates a spare part.

Though transplantation technology is 3 decades old new breakthroughs are making it a more viable option for chronically ill persons. Some of the most bizarre experiments are now taking place.

The Odds: Transplantation success can only be estimated, due to the fact that so many replacement surgery patients have not had their alien parts long enough to determine what rejection rates will ultimately occur. Hair transplants have so far proved to be the most successful. The odds are over 9 in 10 that your scalp will support new hair plugs. The good results stem from the patient using his own tissue, which comes from the back of his head then is implanted forward on the crown and forehead. Rejection of one's own tissue is rare. Cornea transplants are also very successful. Over 9 in 10 of these procedures are successful. Kidney replacements often come from close relatives and the chance that they will be rejected is less than 50 percent. Some patients have almost no symptoms of rejection if the kidney comes from a twin or a sibling with a close genetic match.

Heart and liver replacements are a bit trickier. Because each person has only one of these organs, it is impossible to get replacements from all but the deceased. They are usually in short supply and many who can be saved fail to get a replacement which has a genetic match similar enough to make it be worth the risk. Since the organs are rare, most patients will take what they can get. The body will support the alien tissue for at least a short time. Eventually, even the best matches are rejected by the body and a new one is needed if the patient is to survive. Those in need of heart and liver transplants are frequently told there is a 1 in 2 chance of getting a new organ. If found, it can be estimated as 7 in 10 odds that it will be successful, for at least a while. Given no change in transplant technology, the chances, however are close to 100 percent that hearts and livers will be rejected eventually. The average life of a transplanted heart or liver is about 3 to 5 years.

The following list represents the lifetime odds of undergoing various transplant operations:

Heart Transplant	1 in 3,048
Liver Transplant	1 in 2,293
Kidney Transplant	1 in 365
Cornea Transplant	1 in 95

The Case of Patrick Neary: Perhaps the most unusual surgery ever was performed on an English lad, Patrick Neary, whose right ear was grafted to his thigh after it was bitten off in a fight. Doctors thought it was too mangled to sew back right away. Wanting the ear to live and mend, they hope that 5 months on his leg will be ample time for it to heal and then it will be stitched back on his head.

Source: American Heart Association.

Also See: Organ Donors, Organ Demand.

TRAVEL

Arriving Alive

Definition: Getting to your hotel in good enough condition to tip the bellman.

Your best bet for making it there safely is to stay out of the car. According to William F. Allman, writing in *Science* magazine, automobiles are by far the most dangerous mode of transportation—about ten times as dangerous as flying, judging by the number of deaths per passenger mile. Allman reports that the death rate for automobile and taxi passengers is 10.6 deaths for every billion passenger miles (total number of miles traveled by all passengers). It has been estimated that one's odds in the U.S. of being seriously injured in an auto accident at some point in life are about 1 in 3; about 1 in 140 Americans becomes a traffic fatality.

Overseas, be careful in Canada, Australia or France. According to the International Road Federation, these nations have the highest frequency of traffic fatalities in the developed world—26 per 100,000 inhabitants. The safest foreign country for drivers is Sweden, with just 5.9 accidents per 1,000 cars. That country also has extremely strict drinking and driving laws—a definite correlation.

Scheduled airlines average one death per billion miles and railroads average 0.8 deaths per billion miles. Pilots of small, private planes are most often less-experienced than pilots of big commercial jets and accident rates are higher.

Black Stars: Avoid "Black Star" Airports. The International Federation of Airline Pilots draws up an annual list of airports that pilots consider to be the most dangerous to fly into or out of. American airports consistently on the list include Boston's Logan, Los Angeles International, and Chicago's Midway (deemed "the bull's eye" because of its short runways and its location in the middle of a densely populated neighborhood).

Know Your Carrier; If you're traveling to Jordan, you may want to consider taking a slow boat instead of flying. Over the past 35 years, Royal Jordanian Air has had the highest number of fatalities per billion miles flown. Other airlines ranking high in this category are Turkey's THY and Spain's Aviaco.

The safest mode of transport is buses, which average 0.4 deaths per billion passenger miles, or about 25 times safer than automobiles.

Source: Original research by editors.

Also See: Air Crashes, Automobile Accidents, Automobile Safety, Bus Accidents.

TRUCK TRAFFIC

Definition: Blobs of metal immediately in front of a shower of black exhaust fumes and cigar ashes.

Ever wonder why it's so hard to pass a truck? The nation's interstate highways, which were constructed mainly in the sixties, were designed to accommodate traffic anticipated to be comprised of 6 percent trucks. Naturally, they made the roads too narrow to accommodate today's freight which is shipped 25 percent by trucks, versus 10 percent in 1940.

The Odds: On average, 1 in 6 vehicles on interstate highways is a truck. On some routes leading to large metropolitan areas, as many as 1 in 3 vehicles is a truck. The odds the average piece of merchandise will be shipped by trucks are 1 in 4. Somewhat more than 1 in 3 vehicles sold in the U.S. is a truck or bus.

Source: Department of Transportation, Federal Highway Administration.

TRUST

Professional Credibility

Definition: The feeling that someone will not cheat you or lie to you.

O, Dear Lord, who can we trust in these hazy times? The corner druggist is our best bet. Funeral directors, bankers and journalists also earned high marks for honesty. Clergyman did well, but they were edged out by M.D.'s and dentists.

The Odds: Below are the odds that the following professionals will be held "in high faith" by the average American:

Druggist	1 in 2
College Teacher	3 in 5
Dentist	2 in 5
Medical Doctors	2 in 5
Clergyman	19 in 50
Policeman	37 in 100
Bankers	23 in 100
Funeral Director	1 in 5
Journalist	1 in 5
TV Reporter	19 in 100

Source: The Gallup Report, #279, 1988.

Also See: Distrust.

TUBERCULOSIS

Definition: An infectious disease caused by the microorganism *Mycobacterium tuberculosis* and characterized by lesions, most commonly to the lung.

The Odds: Straight odds against tuberculosis in the average American were about 11,000 to 1 in 1988, the last year for which complete data is available. Total reported TB cases in the U.S. in that year were 22,436. If the incidence of TB had declined at the steady 6.7 percent rate it maintained throughout the early eighties, those odds would have decreased to something in the neighborhood of 11,700 to 1. Unfortunately, the drop from 1987's 22,517 cases to 1988's 22,436 was only 0.4%, although TB is treatable through immunization and drug therapy. This trend reflects the impact of the AIDS epidemic in the U.S. — HIV-infected patients are at a significant risk of developing tuberculosis.

The number of tuberculosis cases increased over the three years from 1985 to 1988 by 981 in those 25 to 44 years old — the category into which the majority of HIV-infected people fall. Numbers also increased for African-Americans and Hispanics, while dropping for Asian-Americans and Native Americans, who are at a lower risk for HIV-infection.

Odds of dying from tuberculosis once you've contracted the disease are about 1 in 9 in the first year.

Source: Centers for Disease Control.

TV FOOTBALL FANS

What's the Big Game?

Definition: Mesmerized males peering at cathode ray tubes while guzzling beer and eating sandwiches and popcorn as Joe Montana lets a long one fly, Al Del Greco kicks a field goal, John Elway . . .

Sponsors know that if they want to get men to buy their cars, razors, beer and you-name-it, TV football programs are the place to advertise. The list below represents the proportions of households which have their television tuned to various sports events:

Super Bowl (Aver.)	1 in 2
ABC's Monday Night Football	1 in 6
NFL Game (Average Sun.)	1 in 7
College Football (Average Sat.)	1 in 14
NBC's NFL Live	1 in 20
CBS's NFL Today	1 in 27
ESPN's NFL Game Day	1 in 35

Source: A.C. Nielsen

TV VIEWING

Worldwide

Definition: A global phenomenon engaged in when people have nothing better to do, or when there are so many things to do, they must invent a favorite program, so they can do them later.

The more myopic among us may believe that television is a Western phenomenon, but in truth it is an absolutely global medium. While the United States finishes a respectable third in overall sets per capita, the real leaders in world video consumption are the tiniest republics of Monaco and Guam. It is some comfort, perhaps, that wherever we venture on the globe we are just a few commercials from home, that in most any of the far-flung reaches of the globe — from

India to Brazil to Mongolia — one can flick on the set and see the reassuring visage of Columbo or J.R. Ewing.

The Odds: In the countries listed below, approximately 9 in 10 homes have TVs. The following list represents the odds each individual in the household has his own set:

Monaco	2 in 3
Guam	3 in 5
United States	3 in 5
Japan	11 in 20
St. Pierre & Miquelon	11 in 20
Virgin Islands	11 in 20
Bermuda	1 in 2
Canada	9 in 20
United Kingdom	2 in 5
Kuwait	2 in 5

Source: Book of World Rankings.

U u

UFO SIGHTINGS

Alien Experiences?

Definition: Lights in the sky ... or skylights in someone's head?

In 1946, a pilot flying in the western U.S. spotted disc-shaped flying objects which he described as saucer-like and almost immediately the term "flying saucers" was introduced to the English language. It was the U.S. Air Force which coined the term UFO, for unidentified flying object. Though the most common speculation is that they may be extraterrestrial spacecraft, the only thing we know for sure is that a lot of people see them. The most frequent sightings are in the U.S., followed—in no particular order—by the U.S.S.R., France and Belgium. In the U.S., Florida traditionally has the most reports of UFOs followed by New York State.

The Odds: Fully 2 in 4 UFO sightings are in the U.S., where 1 in 10 people claims to have seen a UFO. Though the previously suggested places are the most likely places to see UFOs, the odds of seeing them increase during the summer months, most likely because that is when the most people are outdoors in the evening. It could also be speculated that Florida has so many sightings because the year-round warm weather allows people to be outside during most evenings, even in winter. New York, being the second most populous state, has more people to spot them than most places do.

Most sightings which are investigated involve from 2 or 3 people to several thousand.

Hundreds of reports involve dozens or even hundreds of viewers. To cite real odds of seeing a UFO is purely speculation, but some educated guessing can clarify how likely you are to see one. In 1990, there were 4,000 UFO sightings in the U.S. among the 10,000 worldwide. If we can estimate that an average of 5 people are involved in a citing (a conservative estimate), 20,000 Americans among 250 million saw them, hence the odds during that year that an average American would see one are 12,500 to 1. The odds that you will see one on a given night are estimated to be between 2 million and 4 million to 1.

Source: "The UFO Reports", Fox Broadcasting.

Also See: Extraterrestrial Life.

UNCOMFORT-ABLE ENCOUNTERS

Definition: The meeting of disabled people accompanied by the feeling that you are not doing or saying the right thing.

Should you help a stutterer who is trying to get his words out? Should you speak louder to an individual with a hearing aid? Decisions like this make many people uncomfortable when meeting or speaking with those with disabilities.

The Odds: The following list represents the odds that an average individual will suffer some form of uncomfortableness when meeting various types of disabled people:

Mentally Ill	1 in 4
Facially Disfigured	1 in 5
Senile	1 in 6
Mentally Retarded	1 in 6
Deaf	1 in 7
Blind	1 in 10
In a Wheelchair	1 in 16

Acting naturally, and realizing that the disabled individual is not always thinking about his disability – unless he thinks you are – is the best remedy.

Source: Louis Harris poll of 1,257 people for the National Organization on Disability.

UNIONIZATION

Definition: The process of getting workers to join an organized collective to speak in one voice to the management.

The rise of organized labor in the U.S. has proven to be both blessing and curse. Protection for workers (through collective action) is an indisputable good, but the sometimes extortionist tactics of unscrupulous labor representatives often counteracted the benefits of unionization. While heavily industrialized states like Michigan and New York are long-time union strongholds, the more-impoverished states of the South remain primarily unorganized.

The Odds: Unionization is declining considerably as a proportion of the workforce. In 1950, 1 in 4 American workers was a member of Unions. Today, scarcely 1 in 6 is a union member. Workers in manufacturing in the Midwestern "Rust Belt" are between two and three times more likely to join unions than those in the rest of the nation.

The following list represents the ten most unionized states and the proportion of union workers to nonunion ones employed in them:

Michigan	53.6 in 100
New York	48.2 in 100
Hawaii	41.4 in 100
Ohio	40.9 in 100
Pennsylvania	40.7 in 100
Indiana	37.6 in 100
Illinois	33.3 in 100
Missouri	32.4 in 100
Maryland	30.0 in 100
West Virginia	29.8 in 100

Source: Statistical Abstract of the United States.

URBANIZATION

In America

Definition: The process by which the poetic charm of the trees and streams is replaced by light posts and sewer systems.

Although most city dwellers occasionally entertain fantasies of idyllic escapes to pastoral wonderlands, a sizable majority of the American public makes its full-time home in or around cities. The oft-maligned New Jersey is the apotheosis of contemporary urban America, with virtually 100 percent of its people making their homes within 10 miles of a major population center.

The Odds: The following list represents the 10 most urbanized states and the proportion of city dwellers to country bumpkins:

New Jersey	100 in 100
California	95.7 in 100
Maryland	92.9 in 100
Rhode Island	92.6 in 100

Connecticut	92.6 in 100	Nevada	82.6 in 100
New York	91.2 in 100		
Florida	90.8 in 100		
Massachusetts	90.6 in 100		
Pennsylvania	84.8 in 100		

Source: U.S. Bureau of the Census.

Also See: City Slickers, Country Bumpkins, Suburban Flight.

V v

VIDEO VIEWING

Definition: A disastrous spell cast on the television networks, the neighborhood cinema, and television sponsors.

The video cassette recorder has revolutionized our paltry couch-potato lives. There are now more than 60 million VCRs in America. The preponderance of VCRs has triggered the release of an almost unimaginable volume of celluloid fare on cassette, from old movies and television programs to self-help videos and tips on hunting. Not so unexpectedly, the chilled-out citizens of Anchorage are the most avid VCR viewers. One can just imagine those Alaskans hunkered down with industrial-sized canisters of popcorn and a stack of videos as high as a moose's eye, prepared for those endless sub-arctic evenings.

The Odds: No longer do you ask people if they have a VCR; today you ask what make they have.

Better than 2 in 3 households have at least one machine.

The following list represents major metropolitan areas in the U.S. which have the most and least households with VCRs.

MOST HOUSEHOLDS

Anchorage	86 in 100
Las Vegas	84 in 100
Los Angeles	74 in 100
San Francisco	72 in 100
San Diego	72 in 100
Chicago	71 in 100
Reno	70 in 100
Sacramento	70 in 100
New York	70 in 100
Atlanta	69 in 100

FEWEST HOUSEHOLDS

Minneapolis	62 in 100
St Louis	61 in 100
Oklahoma City	61 in 100
Kansas City	61 in 100
Jacksonville	61 in 100
Cincinnati	60 in 100
Cleveland	60 in 100
Albuquerque	60 in 100

Tulsa	59 in 100
San Antonio	58 in 100

Source: Nielsen Media Research.

VIOLENCE
American Cities

Definition: A confrontation between two citizens in which one of them will get his butt kicked but good!

How likely is it that you will be the victim of a violent crime at home or when traveling? America's largest cities are the most likely spots that a violent act will be perpetrated on an innocent victim. The odds, however, are in your favor that you will visit the city unscathed if you stay out of the wrong neighborhoods.

The Odds: The following lists represents the odds that an average citizen will be the victim of a violent crime in the nation's largest cities in one year.

New York	1 in 54
Chicago	1 in 51
Los Angeles	1 in 63
Detroit	1 in 39
Houston	1 in 103
Philadelphia	1 in 102
Baltimore	1 in 48
Dallas	1 in 69
Boston	1 in 49
Atlanta	1 in 36

Source: F.B.I.

VIRGINITY

Definition: The state in which a man or woman has never practiced birth control, child birth, sex acts or fun.

The Odds: If you are an adolescent under the age of 18, the odds are a little better than 9 in 20 that you will lose your virginity between May and August. About 3 in 10 will have their first sexual encounter after the end of classes in late June or July.

Whites and blacks show similar patterns of sexual activity. For Hispanics, the odds of sexual ac-

277

tivity increase in May and June and increase again during the Christmas season. For virgins older than 18, the odds of losing their virginity increase and decrease in patterns similar to their younger counterparts. However, seasonal differences are not as pronounced.

Contraception: The odds are 13 in 20 that teen-age girls will use contraception in their first sexual encounter. Unfortunately 7 in 20 will risk pregnancy and disease while loosing their virginity. Then what? The odds are better than even (53 in 100) that teen-age girls will be sexually active by the time they are 19. In all socio-economic and ethnic groups the odds of sexual activity continue to increase even as governments and social service agencies step up educational efforts.

Source: Compiled research by editors.

W w

WALKING

Definition: A common form of human locomotion in which the traveler simply puts one foot in front of the other.

The Odds: Almost 1 in 125 Americans cannot walk because they are too young. An almost equal proportion cannot walk or need help walking because they are too old. It is estimated some 1 million Americans are confined to wheel chairs or are bed-ridden. Of the 98 in 100 Americans who can walk, 5 in 10 walk for pleasure; 1 in 16 walk to work. A substantial though unknown number of individuals walk simply because they are asked to leave.

Source: U.S. Census Bureau.

WALK, INTENTIONAL

Definition: Allowing a batter in a baseball game a free pass to first base, by purposely pitching four "balls" (pitches outside of the strike zone).

In one extra-inning baseball game in 1989, Chicago Cubs hitting star Andre Dawson was intentionally walked by opposing pitchers five times. The Cubs, however, still won the game. In general, managers use the strategy of the intentional walk to set up the possibility of a double play, or to bypass a good hitter for a worse one.

The Odds: Statistics show that the probability of the opposing team scoring at least one run with one out and a man on second is .390, or about 390 in 1,000. After an intentional walk, however, the probability of the opponent scoring *increases* to .429, or 429 in 1,000. In addition, the average number of runs scored in such situations rises from 671 per 1,000 innings to 971 per 1,000 — setting up the much greater possibility that the enemy will strike for a game-breaking big inning. Thus, unless the next batter is an extremely weak hitter, the manager is much better advised to let the pitcher take his chances with the batter in question, rather than allowing a freebie.

Source: "Statistics, Sports and Some Other Things," Robert Hooke, in *Statistics: A Guide to the Unknown*, Holden-Day, Inc., San Francisco.

WHITE COLLAR CRIME

Definition: A criminal offense committed by someone who has the good intelligence to know how easy the courts can be on well-groomed, educated law-breakers who don't kill anyone, but will steal you blind.

Most white collar crimes are never detected. The odds an executive will get nailed are an astonishing 1 in 7. If caught, the odds are 3 in 4 you will go to the slammer. The slammers at which many white collar criminals are sent are frequently run more like camps or schools. Prison cells are called "dormitories." "Uniforms" can be white shirts and slacks.

Source: The United Way.

WHITE BOYS
Whitebread America

Definition: Men (and women) of America who belong to the Caucasian race.

Integration is imperfect, but ongoing nonetheless. Interestingly, it is the cities with the lowest minority populations that are the most integrated. In these tightly held, brightly lit, ivoried citadels, face of blacks and Asians are few and far between, but at least what small populations there are do not suffer the debilitations of segregation found in the major cities.

The Odds: Just more than 3 in 4 Americans are white. Whites will have the lowest increase in population, 3.2 percent during the decade. This contrasts with a projected increase of 14.6 percent for blacks and 38.6 percent for Hispanics. By the year 2000, only 7 in 10 Americans will be white, a 5 percent decrease.

The following list represents the proportions of blacks to whites and, to a very small extent, Hispanics and Asians, in the "whitest" major American cities:

Salt Lake City, UT	1 in 125
Anaheim-	
Santa Ana, CA	1 in 77
Minneapolis-	
St. Paul, MN	1 in 40
Portland, OR	1 in 34
Phoenix, AZ	1 in 31

San Jose, CA	1 in 27
Seattle, WA	1 in 26
Denver, CO	1 in 19
Riverside-San Bernadino, CA	1 in 18
Boston-Brockton-Lowell, MA	1 in 18

Source: Sales and Marketing Magazine, Survey of Buying Power.

Also See: Honkies, Integration, Segregation, White Racism.

WHITE RACISM

American Biases

Definition: The proclivity of some whites to think that all blacks can dance their socks off.

The civil rights activism of the sixties did much to bring the races together, but there is still a large division. This gap is not found so much in opportunities available to non-whites, but in the beliefs held by many whites who may remain silent about their racial prejudices.

The Odds: The list below represents the proportion of whites who attribute various traits to blacks:

Better at Athletics	1 in 6
Higher Crime	1 in 3
Poverty	1 in 3
Violent Behavior	1 in 3
Dangerous	1 in 3
Lazy	1 in 4
Vulgar	1 in 5
Dirty	1 in 7

Racism is a highly regional phenomenon. Though it is highest in the South, the gap between some other parts of the nation is not great. The list below represents the proportions of "hard-core racists" in various parts of the country

"Old" South	1 in 7
Rust Belt	1 in 7
Mid Atlantic	1 in 8
"New" South	1 in 8
Mountain States	1 in 12
Plain States	1 in 16
Southwest	1 in 25
New England	1 in 33
Northwest	1 in 100

Source: The Day America Told the Truth, James Patterson, Peter Kim.

Also See: Honkies, Integration, Segregation, White Boys.

WOMEN AT WORK

Definition: Female over the age of 16 who labor for financial gain in the U.S. work force; house-wifery, or professions without monetary rewards, are not included in statistics on the U.S. labor force.

The Odds: Gone are the days of the first baby boom just after World War II, when wives of the returned servicemen considered it their duty to stay home, raise children, and care of them until their teens. Then came the late sixties and early seventies, when that baby boom generation had grown up, gone to college, and now considered home just a place to come to from work or play, and a family something that could wait until they had won some self-esteem in the business world, if then.

Amazingly, after 1970, the wave of women workers had swelled to the point where now, with 56 million working women, they comprise 45 percent of the U.S. labor force, a gain of 17 percent since 1950, and still rising. Concurrently, the national birth rate has dropped from a high of 25.3 percent in 1954 to 16.2 percent today, thanks largely to the pill, the feminist movement, later marriages, and the desire of women to find self-worth outside the home.

The Odds: At present, 1 in 4 women can expect to join the top-paying managerial and professional ranks during their careers; 1 in 2 will become involved in technical, sales and administrative support jobs; 1 in 6 will work in service occupations; 1 in 10 in farming, forestry or fishing; and 1 in 10 will find jobs as operators of heavy machinery or as laborers.

But no matter what work they find to do, women can be certain of one thing: As far as financial rewards go, it still is a man's world. Female managers and professionals, as well as those in service careers, earn only 75 percent of their male counterparts; those in technical and sales jobs rake in only two-thirds of an average man's salary.

Source: Bureau of Labor Statistics, U.S. Department of Labor; *The Jobs Rated Almanac.*

WOMEN

In Agriculture

Definition: The process by which women lend a feminine touch to the plowing, cattle driving and hay bailing in the world.

Bella Abzug is mad as hell (so what else is new?). She may have a legitimate complaint however. So she says, "women produce 80 percent of the agriculture in Africa, 60 percent in Asia and 40 percent in Latin America. Yet they don't own land, don't have a credit card, aren't consulted on how best to preserve the Earth."

The Odds: In the U.S. women are "better" represented in agriculture. That is, there are fewer farm labors than elsewhere and a larger proportion have the better agricultural jobs. The list below represents the ratios of females to males in the largest U.S. agricultural occupations:

Farm Operators & Managers	1 in 7
Commodity Sales	1 in 6
Farm Labors	1 in 4

Kathryn Fuller, president of the World Wildlife Fund, griped at a recent convention "Women do two-thirds of the work [in agriculture] but make just 10 percent of the income and own only 1% of the land." Not in America.

Source: The Jobs Rated Almanac.

Also See: Breaking the Glass Ceiling, Women at Work, Women Executives, Women in Uniform.

WOMEN'S EARNINGS

Definition: A female person's wages or compensation.

The Odds: The odds are better than even that by the year 2000, working women as a class will increase their relative pay to 74% of what working men are making.

The Wife as Breadwinner: The odds are now 1 in 5 that the female in a two income household will make more money than her partner. Of the others, almost 1 in 10 will make between 80 and 100 percent of her husband's income. Most men seem fairly comfortable with the idea that their wives might make more money than they do. The odds are 3 to 1 in favor of them accepting the idea. Surprisingly, women are slightly more conservative in this matter. The odds are only 2.13 to 1 in favor of them being comfortable with making more money than their spouses. Statistically, women's pay will likely be behind men's due to the fact that some women will leave the workforce for long durations after becoming pregnant.

Source: Russel, Cheryl *100 Predictions For The Baby Boom*, Plenum Press, New York.

Also See: Women at Work, Women in Agriculture, Women

in Business, Women in Uniform, Women Mayors.

WOMEN EXECUTIVES
The Top Ladies

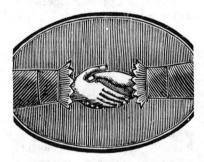

Definition: Women who can boss men around, get paid for it, get away with it . . . and get rich doing it.

Despite a new public consciousness about the wastefulness of not using the resources of women to "man" the captain's chair, there is still a void at the very top. The few areas in which women have had their share of top jobs are in publishing and government service. In the latter of these two fields, women are in high elective offices and appointive positions in the Cabinet and the U.S. Judicial System, including the Supreme Court.

Says Eleanor Smeal, former President of NOW (the National Organization of Women): "At the current rate of increase in executive women [in business], it will take until the year 2466 — or over 450 years — to reach equality with executive men." Statistics support her claim.

The Odds: As far back as in 1976, the odds of a women having a middle level executive, management or administrative position were 1 in 4. Today they have risen to 2 in 5. At the pinnacle, however, the odds are far different. At the very top jobs in the business world, CEOs and presidents of Fortune 500 corporations, there are only 13 women, or 1 in 38.

Corporate Officers: Other top positions, corporate officers and board directors, have considerable authority and there is a case to be built that those who occupy these spots have as much influence as some CEOs and presidents. Among 6,502 corporate officers at the largest corporations, 1 in 37 is a woman, which translates to the same percentage (2.6) of women CEOs and presidents.

The Board Room: Women are faring better at getting on corporate boards than at getting hands-on executive positions. In fact, the odds are 75 percent better that a women can get on a board of directors than into a key top executive position. In 1990, more than 1 in 21 directorships of Fortune 500 corporations were held by women, 254 of 5,384.

Source: Feminist Majority Foundation.

Also See: Women at Work, Women in Agriculture, Women in

Business, Women in Uniform, Women Mayors.

WOMEN IN UNIFORM

Definition: Soldiers, sailors and other military personnel who don't wear government issue boxer shorts under their pants.

When America went to war in the Persian Gulf, much attention was focused on the fact that minorities were disproportionately in the armed forces. So too, it was noted by many that women were playing a role far outweighing their roles in previous conflicts, in which most women in the Armed Forces were nurses.

Today's military forces do not discriminate against women who volunteer for duty; however women are not required to register with the Selective Service like men. The first time women were used in combat roles in the U.S. military was when the U.S. invaded Panama in 1989 and captured General Manuel Noriega.

The Odds: There are 230,000 women in uniform among the U.S. military, which represents slightly more than 1 in 10 individuals in its forces. Just over 1 in 8 women is an officers.

The following list represents the ratios of men to women in the various branches of the U.S. Armed Forces at the time the U.S. committed military forces to fight the War in the Persian Gulf:

OFFICERS

Army	1 in 10
Navy	1 in 10
Marines	1 in 30
Air Force	1 in 8

ENLISTED RANKS

Army	1 in 9
Navy	1 in 11
Marines	1 in 20
Air Force	1 in 8

Source: U.S. Department of Defense.

Also See: Women at Work, Women in Agriculture, Women in Business, Women in Uniform, Women Mayors.

Also See: Military Enlistments.

WOMEN MAYORS

Definition: Women drivers in city halls.

The office of mayor has proven to be the first breakthrough point for minorities in high political offices. Blacks were the initial wave and now, women. Washington, D.C. recently elected its first female mayor, Sharon Pratt Dixon, replacing the embattled Marion Barry. Across the country, more and more women are making inroads into the once all-male dominion of mayoral office.

The Odds: The following list represents the top ten states for the proportions of female mayors of cities with populations of 10,000 or more:

Colorado	28 in 100
Connecticut	27 in 100
Washington	25 in 100
New Hampshire	25 in 100
Oregon	24 in 100
Michigan	22 in 100
Montana	22 in 100
California	21 in 100
Missouri	21 in 100

Source: National League of Cities.

WORK TO DEATH

Job-Related Fatalities

Definition: Death on the job.

For those stuck in a hum-drum office job, the 9-to-5 regimen may be a deadly bore. But for many, work is just plain deadly. Automobile accidents account for the highest percentage of deaths among the workforce.

The Odds: Just over 1 in 4 fatalities (27 percent), which involve work, is auto-related. The second-leading on-the-job killer is heart attacks, dropping from its top ranking in overall causes of death. Those who work outdoors, with heavy machinery and with dangerous equipment are at a much greater risk of dying on the job than the average office drone.

The following list represents the most common causes of death on the job and the proportions of those deaths:

Highway Vehicles	1 in 4
Heart Attacks	1 in 9
Industrial Vehicles or Equipment	1 in 9
Falls	1 in 9
Electrocutions	1 in 10
Assaults	1 in 25
Struck by Objects	1 in 25
Smashed by Objects	1 in 25
Explosions	1 in 25
Aircraft Crashes	1 in 33
Gas Inhalation	1 in 33
Plant Machinery Operations	1 in 50
Fires	1 in 100

Source: U.S. Dept. of Labor.

Also See: Accidents.

WORRIES

Definition: The demons in the mind that will not go to sleep and won't let you either.

Anyone who is looking for something to worry about will not be disappointed. There is unquestionably plenty of choices. Opinion polls will vary enormously as world and national conditions change.

The Odds: Much of the data shown on the list below is from either a Gallup poll in the later half of 1990 or from various news surveys a year later. The following list represents the proportions of Americans who worry about various issues:

Japanese Economic Power	3 in 5
Nuclear War	1 in 13
Arms Reduction	2 in 5
Russian Leadership	1 in 2
AIDS	1 in 2
German Reunification	3 in 4
Tax Increases	2 in 5
Job Loss	1 in 7
Higher Interest Rates	1 in 9
No Worries	1 in 20

So what then should we worry about? Maybe about the guy with no worries. He is likely to be the first to get AIDS, lose his job and start a nuclear war.

Source: Compiled research by editors.

Also See: The rest of the book.

Y y

YOUTHFUL BELIEFS

Around the World

Definition: The notions that the young and inexperienced fancy.

It is commonly believed that the young are more liberal than older adults. A recent opinion poll demonstrated that the individual beliefs of the young may follow more closely than expected with the national conscience. Their views are not too dissimilar from those of their national leaders of a generation ago.

The Odds: Based on an opinion poll of people ages 14 to 34 in Australia, Brazil, Germany, Japan, the United Kingdom and the U.S., the following is held to be true:

WAR SOMETIMES JUSTIFIED

U.S.	3 in 4
Japan	1 in 6
Germany	1 in 3

BELIEVE IN:

God (U.S.)	9 in 10
God (U.K.)	1 in 3
Hell (U.S.)	3 in 4
Hell (Germany)	1 in 6

RESPECT RELIGIOUS LEADERS

U.S.	2 in 5
U.K., Germany & Japan	1 in 6

If the previous list is examined carefully, the actions of their national leaders more or less reflect the beliefs of the young. Considering the behavior of their parents and grandparents when viewed in the light national policies during World War II, the results are not so surprising.

Source: Poll by MTV and Yankelovich Clancy Sculman.

Z z

ZERO-SUM GAME

Nuclear War Survival

Definition: The last chance of noncombatants to bend over and kiss their derriere good-by before meeting their maker.

A conflict involving the use of nuclear weapons — also called armageddon, and the final reckoning — is no longer a concern of just the superpowers with so many third-world countries on the brink of developing nuclear weapons.

To everyone's relief (except, perhaps, those in the military-industrial complex), the relaxation of tensions between East and West following the events in Eastern Europe in 1989 has greatly diminished the chances of a nuclear war breaking out between superpowers. Recent turmoil in the Middle East has shifted the danger elsewhere. Particularly relieved at the decreased possibility should be the residents of Washington, D.C., the nation's capital, and Omaha, Nebraska, headquarters of the Strategic Air Command – two of the highest-priority targets for an enemy in a nuclear exchange. After military targets, major communications and industrial centers would be hit. Experts have estimated the devastation caused by a 1-megaton attack on a number of cities. Such a strike on New York or Los Angeles would kill about 1 in 5 citizens –several million people each. And these figures don't take into account the probable or possible nuclear war after-effects: fallout, disease, mutation, nuclear winter. The popular poster that mocked civil defense instructions in the fifties was no doubt correct in its instructions: "In the event of a nuclear war, bend over, place your head firmly between your legs, and kiss your derriere good-bye."

The Odds: The following list represents the proportions of citizens who would be killed if a nuclear attack took place in various cities:

Los Angeles	1 in 5
New York	1 in 5
Boston	1 in 3
Chicago	1 in 3
St. Louis	3 in 8

Denver	1 in 2
Baltimore	2 in 3
Honolulu	3 in 4
Las Vegas	4 in 5
Lincoln, Neb.	49 in 50

Source: The Almanac of City Rankings.

THE GOOD BETS

What can you count on besides death and taxes? Not much, but there are some things that are likely to happen. Below is a selection of some of the most likely things that will occur. The following events and odds represent those with a greater than 50 percent chance of happening to the average American or those specified below:

You will regain your weight loss after a diet	90 in 100
You will have intercourse this year	90 in 100
A condom will prevent pregnancy	88 in 100
Your flight will arrive on time	85 in 100
Nebraska will win a football game	81 in 100
You will parent a child	80 in 100
You will qualify for a mortgage	80 in 100
A criminal will return to jail	80 in 100
You will live past age 65	80 in 100
You will fly in late at Kennedy Airport	77 in 100
You will masturbate	75 in 100
An executive will lose his job at least once	75 in 100
A youth will graduate high school	75 in 100
You will be married	75 in 100
A smoker will try to quit	71 in 100
The company you own will go bankrupt	70 in 100
An undocumented foreign worker is an illegal alien	70 in 100
A wife will outlive her husband	70 in 100
You will survive your first heart attack	67 in 100
A previously childless female will give birth	67 in 100
You will read this sunday's paper	67 in 100
Your stolen car will be recovered	67 in 100
You will survive a stroke	67 in 100
The U.S. world market share will decline	65 in 100
A mob boss will be imprisoned or killed	60 in 100
You will avoid imprisonment, if convicted	60 in 100
You will buckle your seat belt	60 in 100
An average English couple will make love in the bathroom	58 in 100
You will say a prayer today	57 in 100
A high school student will try marijuana	50 in 100
A homeless person is mentally ill	50 in 100
A college freshman will graduate	50 in 100
A child will live past age 75	50 in 100
A girl will lose her virginity between ages 15-19	50 in 100

THE LONGEST SHOTS OF ALL

Some things, like those on the previous page, might be worth worrying about. The ones below, however, aren't very likely to happen. The following events represent those which have odds of 1 in 100 or greater for happening to the average American or those specified below:

You will undergo an IRS audit this year	1 in 100
The pilot of your air flight will be drunk	1 in 117
You will die this year	1 in 119
You will die in a car crash	1 in 125
You will suffer from schizophrenia	1 in 167
You will be incarcerated	1 in 200
Your child will be a genius	1 in 250
Your child will run away and be a prostitute	1 in 467
You will have a Down's syndrome child	1 in 600
A random stranger you meet is a murderer	1 in 1,000
You will be raped this year	1 in 1,500
You will be a victim of violence in the suburbs	1 in 2,000
A high school football player will play in a future Super Bowl	1 in 2,351
A policeman will be killed in an assault this year	1 in 2,533
You will be arrested for prostitution this year	1 in 3,550
You will be bumped off an air flight	1 in 4,000
You will catch malaria in the tropics	1 in 5,800
Your child will suffer a highchair injury this year	1 in 6,000
You will commit suicide this year	1 in 7,874
The Earth will be devastated by a meteorite in your lifetime	1 in 9,000
You will be struck by lightning	1 in 9,100
You will suffer from tuberculous	1 in 11,000
You will be murdered this year	1 in 12,000
A professional golfer will get a hole-in-one	1 in 15,000
You will be killed on your next bus ride	1 in 24,000
You will be injured at work today	1 in 24,000
You will develop a brain tumor	1 in 25,000
A child pedestrian will be hit by a car	1 in 25,000
You will die in a fire this year	1 in 40,000
You will be hit by a baseball at a major league game	1 in 300,000
You will be dealt a royal flush (on the opening hand)	1 in 649,739
You will drown in the tub this year	1 in 685,000
You will see a UFO today	1 in 3,000,000
You will be killed in your next car ride	1 in 4,000,000
You will win a state lottery jackpot	1 in 4,000,000
You will be killed in an air crash	1 in 4,600,000
You will be killed on your next bus ride	1 in 500,000,000

293

294